Jerus

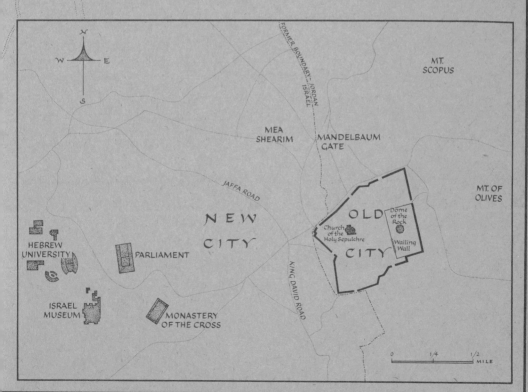

MT. OF OLIVES

Tomb
of the Virgin

Site of the
Ascension

Gethsemane

N

W   E

S

0   1/8   1/4   1/2
MILES

- - - - VIA DOLOROSA

CITY WALLS IN TIME OF CHRIST

N

W   E

S

MT.
SCOPUS

FORMER BOUNDARY — JORDAN — ISRAEL

MEA
SHEARIM

MANDELBAUM
GATE

JAFFA ROAD

NEW

CITY

MT. OF
OLIVES

HEBREW
UNIVERSITY

PARLIAMENT

OLD

Church
of the
Holy Sepulchre

Dome
of the
Rock

Wailing
Wall

CITY

KING DAVID ROAD

ISRAEL
MUSEUM

MONASTERY
OF THE CROSS

0   1/4   1/2
MILE

The Earthly Jerusalem

THE EARTHLY JERUSALEM

Norman Kotker

CHARLES SCRIBNER'S SONS · NEW YORK

PRINTED IN THE UNITED STATES OF AMERICA
Library of Congress Catalog Card Number 69-17037

To My Wife

Acknowledgments

I WOULD LIKE to acknowledge with gratitude the many people who have assisted me during the writing of this book. The government of Israel generously aided me with a travel grant that made it possible for me to see once again a city that had been divided during my previous visits. In Jerusalem I was courteously welcomed by Jacob Yehoshua and Israel Sipper of the Ministry of Religious Affairs; through their efforts, and the efforts of Ram Chaviv of the Israeli Consulate in New York, I was enabled to gain access to a great many sites of interest that are normally closed to visitors. In Jerusalem I also enjoyed the hospitality of the Armenian Patriarchate, of Yoel Yoseph Rivlin, and of Eliezer Frenkel, who is involved in the reconstruction of the Jewish Quarter of the Old City. Abdel Rauf of the Islamic Center in New York was extremely helpful in translating from Arabic and in providing information on Muslem traditions about Jerusalem. Judith Herschlag and Jaleh Bakhshayesh of New York also gave considerably of their time and knowledge. I am also grateful to Richard Oestermann of the Hebrew University and Milton Selden of the American Friends of the Hebrew University in New York for their kind assistance. To the staff of the library of the General Theological Seminary in New York, and in particular to the late Barbara Brown, I owe a special debt of gratitude for the generosity with which the Seminary allowed me access to library facilities.

This book, which covers some five thousand years of history, could not have been written, of course, without considerable reliance on the work of other authors. The accounts of travelers to the city have been especially useful, and I have drawn upon them heavily. A great many of them appear in the numerous, meticulously edited volumes published by the Palestine Pilgrims' Text Society of London. Many others are surveyed in Guy Le Strange's *Palestine under the Moslems*, in Kurt Wilhelm's *Roads to Zion*, and in *Jewish Travellers*, by Elkan Adler. Another valued source of information has been Louis Ginzberg's *Legends of the Bible*, which contains a great many folk traditions about Jerusalem. The chapter on the Crusades derived much material from Stephen Runciman's monumental work on the subject, and from Zoe Oldenbourg's more popular account. For the Mamluk and Ottoman periods, I have drawn on A. K. Sanjian's *The Armenian Communities in Syria under Ottoman Domination*, on Ira M. Lapidus' *Muslim Cities in the Later Middle Ages*, and on the works of the Greek scholar, Nikephoros Moschopoulos. The news columns and archaeological reports of "The Jerusalem Post" have also provided much valuable information. Most important have been the biblical scholars and archaeologists whose studies approach the heart of Jerusalem: the Dominican fathers Hugues Vincent and F. M. Abel, whose work on Jerusalem is a classic; John Gray who has written on the Canaanites; the recent historians of Israel, John Bright and Martin Noth; Kathleen Kenyon, who has excavated the ancient city; and William F. Albright, James B. Pritchard and G. Ernest Wright.

Portions of this manuscript appeared first in *Horizon* and *The Reporter* magazines. All photographs are by Norman and Zane Kotker, except where indicated. For permission to quote excerpts from the Amarna letters on pages 21–22, I am grateful to the Princeton University Press, publishers of *Ancient Near Eastern Texts Relating to the Old Testament*, edited by James B. Pritchard. The letters themselves are translated by W. F. Albright in collaboration with George E. Mendenhall. Portions of Pope Urban's speech inaugurating the Crusades are reprinted on page 169 by permission of the American Book Company, publishers of *A Source Book of Medieval History*, by Frederick Ogg. The Crusader description of the conquest of Jerusalem on pages 175–76 is reprinted, through the courtesy of G. P. Putnam's Sons, from *Putnam's Dark and Middle Ages Reader*, translated and edited by Harry E. Wedeck.

ACKNOWLEDGMENTS

Finally I would like to acknowledge the part played in the writing of the book by my wife, Zane, who has provided, along with great support and encouragement, an astute observation of events and places, keen editorial judgment, and a very rare and very balanced religious sensibility.

NEW YORK, *February 6, 1969*

Contents

1. THE CENTER OF THE UNIVERSE   *3*

2. A CITY IN CANAAN   *14*

3. ARIEL   *36*

4. THE MIRROR OF HEAVEN   *60*

5. DEATH'S DOMINION   *90*

6. AELIA CAPITOLINA   *119*

7. THE DOME OF THE ROCK   *144*

8. "GOD WANTS IT"   *169*

9. VIA DOLOROSA   *195*

10. A NEW JERUSALEM   *232*

11. THE VERONICA PHOTOGRAPHY SHOP   *268*

INDEX   *297*

The Earthly Jerusalem

CHAPTER 1

The Center of the Universe

ORIGINALLY every city was holy. Just as primitive farmers had once sanctified the entire earth which, for all its perils, gave them sustenance and had given them life, their successors, the first inhabitants of cities, came to revere the sheltering place in which they lived. To them it was sacred, like a vast church that protected them from the threatening and untamable universe. In it, they believed, day and night a sacred drama was being enacted between themselves and their god, who watched over them and guarded them from harm in exchange for sacrifice and the punctilious observance of certain religious laws. In Sumer and later Babylon, every city was considered the dwelling place of a particular god; within its walls it contained a ziggurat, a temple shaped like a mountain, where the god ate, slept, and made love, and down which he could walk to make contact with his subjects. The city of Rome was itself a goddess and was worshipped as such by its citizens, and in Etruria towns were considered images of the heavens above; each was divided into quarters and each quarter was placed under the protection or influence of a god. As the world grew less terrifying and more controllable, cities, like their inhabitants, became more secular. But certain ones never lost their sacred character, and some—like Mecca, Rome, Peking, or Moscow—even survived the extinction or eclipse of their original cult to remain sacred, rededicated to the new religion that captured them. Of these, the foremost is Jerusalem.

That city is sacred not to one faith but to three. It is revered by Christians as the site of Jesus' crucifixion and resurrection; by Muslims as the home of the prophets and of the Night Journey, when Mohammed was carried up to heaven to behold celestial glories; and by Jews as their home, the site of their ancient temple and the capital of their nation. Adherents of all three faiths have struggled, and are still struggling, to control the city and to establish there their version of heaven on earth. With Jerusalem's sanctification has come bloodshed—the sacrifice of animals at the temple, the sacrifice of Christ, the endless sacrifice of its citizens striving to defend the holy city against the attacks of enemies. For Jerusalem has been besieged and taken and sacked countless times by countless kings, whose antagonism has usually been inspired by the religion of its inhabitants. That religion may have changed numerous times, but the fanaticism with which it has been held has remained constant, and the price fanaticism exacts has remained large. A list of the kings who have conquered it, ruled it, or affected its destiny reads like a Who's Who of history—Akhnaten and Tutankhamen, David and Solomon, Nebuchadnezzar and Alexander and Constantine the Great, Harun al-Rashid and Saladin and Frederick Barbarossa, whose descendants, the Habsburgs of Austria, still claimed the title of King of Jerusalem down to our own century. Except for the pagans among them all these monarchs, no matter how powerful, have humbled themselves before another and even more magnificent king of Jerusalem, Yahweh, Allah, God the Father.

It is He, they say, far more than the earthly kings, who has made Jerusalem's history. At Jerusalem, He first divided the primeval chaos, separating the waters above from the waters beneath, and establishing the earth. "God started the earth from Zion," the rabbis wrote, " . . . the citadel and central point of the

4

universe, from which it began to be fashioned and from which the whole world is nourished." Below the city He placed the source of all the sweet waters of the earth, the fount from which the four rivers of paradise run. Therefore the water in Jerusalem is sweeter and purer than anywhere else, and the dew, which comes to the city direct from paradise, is of great medicinal value. From the dust of Jerusalem, God formed the first man. Some skeptics say the dust was taken from all over the earth, adducing as proof the fact that men are of different colors. But in Jerusalem they know differently, for some of the dust from which Adam was made remained in the city and was kept for centuries on public display at the Church of the Holy Sepulcher. At Jerusalem God received his first sacrifice, which was slaughtered by Adam when he came on pilgrimage to the holy spot. He was the first man to come for that purpose, but not the first soul for he was preceded by the angels. And at Jerusalem Adam was buried; his tomb is shown today in the Church of the Holy Sepulcher. By providential design, the grave was located directly beneath Golgotha so that at the crucifixion the redeeming blood of Christ could fall upon the skull of the world's first sinner to wash away every man's sins. Cain and Abel also sacrificed to God at Jerusalem; Noah sacrificed there; Abraham sacrificed there, the victim to be his own son Isaac, until God saved the boy by sending a ram as a substitute. And then, it is said, God Himself performed a sacrifice at Jerusalem, to Himself, of Himself, the victim, His own son Jesus.

But the history of Jerusalem has not been one only of bloodshed and sacrifice, for God made His holy city beautiful and pleasant and gave it magical powers. Of the ten measures of beauty given to the world, God gave Jerusalem nine, the rabbis have said. In Jerusalem the men have been handsomer than elsewhere, the women more beautiful. No scorpion or serpent ever stung there, no woman ever miscarried, no man was ever accidentally injured, or tripped or stumbled. No mortgage was ever foreclosed, no house ever caught fire. Every pleasant wind imaginable comes to cool Jerusalem, flying to the holy mountain to make obeisance to its Creator before going off to its appointed place on earth. Whoever prays in Jerusalem, the Muslims believe, will be sure of having a line of descendants to pray there too, and each of their prayers will outweigh in merit a thousand prayers uttered elsewhere. Wherever these worshippers bow their heads to touch them to the ground—as Muslims customarily do in their praying—they will be in contact with a spot where at one time an angel or a prophet has prayed. Whoever dies in Jerusalem is assured of ascending to heaven. Whoever fasts in Jerusalem is assured of escaping hell. For the merit of pilgrims to Jerusalem, seventy thousand angels pray nightly, as Allah looks down upon the pilgrims through a door open in the heavens. Every morning, Muslims say, God, the merciful and compassionate, thinks about mercy for Jerusalem, and only then about mercy for the rest of the world. Every midnight, Jews believe, God reminds Himself of the holy sufferings of Jerusalem and reflects upon them; and it is at that hour that the most pious have been accustomed to go to the Wailing Wall to pray for the city's restoration. One rabbi is even said to have flown there each midnight through the sky from the town of Safed, seventy-five miles to the north.

Jerusalem's holiest spot is a rock: to Christians the rock of Golgotha, to Jews and Muslims, another rock half a mile southeast, that today is sheltered within a Muslim shrine known as the Dome of the Rock. The Jewish and Muslim rock stood in the precinct of Solomon's temple, perhaps beneath the Holy of Holies, God's earthly dwelling place, and from it in later years Mohammed is said to have ascended to heaven. This rock the ancient Jews considered to be the center of the earth, the axis of the universe, joining heaven to earth and earth to the primeval chaos beneath. It was the root of heaven, the lid of hell, the place through which souls spring up when ascending from hell to heaven. As the center of the universe the rock was especially holy; but it was not unique. For all faiths have their own center of the universe, as they have their own universe. So Christians transferred some of the rock's traditions to the rock of Golgotha, Muslims to the sacred rock of the Kaaba in Mecca. Other religions name a particular palace or a sacred house as the center of the universe, and in the most primitive and perhaps most valid religion of all, the animistic, it is sometimes the worshipper himself. "I am the center of the universe," says the Kwakiutl Indian as he is initiated into the mysteries of his faith; and he is probably right. But to Christians, Jews and many Muslims, the center was Jerusalem, and they proved it by the fact that at the summer solstice, Jerusalem's sacred rock cast no shadow. On medieval Christian maps the city is shown at the center of the world, with the three known continents, Europe, Asia and Africa, surrounding it like a halo, or opening from it as petals open from the center of a flower.

"The Muslims say that the dead will be quickened and assembled in Jerusalem and a tradition to this effect is attributed to the prophet," a medieval Muslim scholar wrote. "Many Jews share the same belief. . . ." But, he added, "I have heard someone say . . . that Allah would resurrect the dead wherever it pleased him." Despite his skepticism, most Muslims and Jews, and Christians too, agreed that Jerusalem was to be the site of the last judgment. According to Muslim tradition the entire earth was stretched forth from the city, and one day it will be rolled up toward the city again, like a scroll. On that day, Jews say, Jerusalem will expand miraculously, to reach from the summit of the Mount of Olives to Mount Tabor in Galilee, from Mount Carmel by the Mediterranean to Mount Sinai, where Moses received the law. It will have to expand considerably to contain the souls of all mankind, who will assemble on the Mount of Olives, on the one spot in Jerusalem where there has never been any bloodshed. (Because of this belief, pious men of all faiths have over the centuries been entombed on the Mount of Olives just outside the city, to be assured of rising first on the day of judgment, and earth from Jerusalem has been placed in coffins and in graveyards throughout Christendom, for it was believed to speed the corpse's decomposition as well as its eventual revival.)

With the gathering of all human souls at Jerusalem, Jesus will come—according to Christians—to battle and slay the Antichrist. The Muslims believe this too. On judgment day, they say he will judge all men and then, though this might be disputed by the Christians, break all the crosses in the world. The Jews, however, ignore Jesus in their picture of Jerusalem's last day. According to them, the great final battle will take place not between Christ and Antichrist, but between the forces of good and the forces of evil, represented by all the kings who, throughout history, have made war on Jerusalem—Sennacherib, Nebuchadnezzar, Titus and presumably Gamal Abdel Nasser—who will be revivified to march against the city again, and then be punished by God.

Once the final battle has been fought, the souls of the wicked will descend to pay for their sins in hell (which lies, as one might guess, directly beneath Jerusalem, its entrance variously reported as being under the sacred rock or in one of the valleys east, south or west of the town). Their more fortunate brethren, the good, will rise up, along with the earthly Jerusalem itself, to come to rest in the heavenly Jerusalem. It has always been there waiting for them, hovering above the earthly city. For throughout its history, Jerusalem—even at its most glorious—has been merely an imperfect copy of its heavenly counterpart. For thousands of years now, the temple of Solomon has been gone; but above it there has always remained another and even more beautiful temple invisible to man, where God is enthroned in heaven as he was once enthroned in Jerusalem on earth. This temple lies at the center of a city whose streets are paved with gold, a city with twelve gates, one for each of the tribes of Israel, with twelve angels at each gate. The walls are of jasper, the gates pearly, the foundations adorned with precious jewels. There, in the "happie harbour of the saints" on "sweet and pleasant soyle," David, a former inhabitant of the earthly Jerusalem, leads the heavenly choir, and the Virgin Mary again intones the Magnificat which she had first sung in a suburb of the town beneath.

This beautiful city awaits the faithful, who can see it prefigured in their churches, which, particularly in Orthodox Christendom, are designed to resemble the heavenly Jerusalem. These shimmer with gold and gold mosaic; in their bejeweled icons, haloed saints and angels hover over the heads of earthly worshippers as they will some day hover over those same worshippers in heaven. The New Jerusalem can be seen again in paintings or mosaics within the churches, or in illuminations of sacred books, where it appears as a Gothic fantasy town, all tracery towers and palaces like a medieval World's Fair vision of the future, or as the earthly Jerusalem actually was in the Middle Ages, with shining domed buildings, that are here made even more shining by art. In their midst—as the Book of Revelation promises—is the Lamb of God, standing on Mount Zion where Solomon's temple once stood, surrounded by the redeemed citizens of the town: "harpers harping with their harps," virgins, men without guile, walking by sweet waters, plucking fruit from the trees, their faces shining in the holy light reflected from the walls and buildings of the city. It is lovely. It is Eden, a California, an island of the blest. Naturally, one wanted to go there.

"Jerusalem, my happy home, when shall I come to thee?", Christians have sung in the words of an ancient hymn. In preparation for the day when they get an answer, they—like Muslims and Jews—have come as pilgrims to the earthly city to absorb some of its holiness and get a foretaste of paradise. Almost invariably they are disappointed in the Jerusalem that they see. The city seems surprisingly inconsequential to provide a fair picture of what heaven will be like. All the religions of Jerusalem preach that holiness is humble, but somehow one expects God's city to be a bit less humble than this. One might expect New York to be holy, a city that is an island, on a great river that flows beneath cliffs into an unknown continent; or Athens, built on a commanding escarpment that rises suddenly from a broad plain to hover in midair over the distant sea, like a child's imaginary castle. But Jerusalem is undramatic—outwardly at least. It merges, like the stones out of which it is made, into the hills on which it is set. Little differentiates Zion and the other Jerusalem hills from the hundreds of featureless hills that surround them. And these monotonous and barren hills are a far cry from what we imagine paradise to be. In antiquity, the rabbis say, Jerusalem was surrounded by a garden that reached from the Mediterranean coast to the Jordan and stretched south to the Red Sea. Whatever truth there was to the story has been lost, as war and misgovernment have ruined the countryside, stripping it of trees and leaving only stones. Someday, we are told, God will replant them, but until then, looking about Jerusalem, it is easier to visualize the hell that lies beneath the city than the paradise above.

And throughout history, Jerusalem has resembled hell—or at least modern man's idea of hell—much more than it has resembled heaven. Out of every building anger has hissed; blood has been shed on every stone; and bizarre and tortured fancies, such as we attribute to madmen, have seethed in the heads of its inhabitants. Not all the curious fancies are entertained by the entire populace, but most are shared by a good many. Perhaps they are all true, although it hardly seems likely. True or not, they are the material out of which nightmares are made. In them men and woman fly up to heaven. Stones weep. Slaughter atones for sin. The dead will rise from their graves, wearing flesh again. Indeed one of them already has. Beneath the earth there are djinns. Above the earth there is an all-powerful God, a unique God who is indivisible or a unique God who is divisible into three parts, although he is actually indivisible. A virgin can give birth. Certain quite tasty and nourishing foods poison the soul. Certain stones are holy. It is dangerous to wear a garment of wool mixed with linen or cotton. One day a week it is wrong to carry anything. One must touch one's nose and forehead to the ground seventeen times a day if one is a man. If one is a woman, one must not. Once a winged horse with a peacock's tail and a woman's face flew into the city from Arabia, with a prophet on its back.

These fantasies are permissible in Jerusalem. They have been hallowed by history which surrounds them with persuasive recorded facts making them acceptable: nails pierced Jesus on a Friday afternoon in the spring in the year A.D. 30; on the western road outside the city, David the king danced during a religious procession; at 0945 on 6/7/67 Israeli soldiers penetrated the gates of the Old City. Other fantasies are not acceptable in the city, although they might be as valid. There may for instance also be a heavenly Singapore or a heavenly Denver, or even hundreds of heavenly Jerusalems shimmering in the sky, one, let's say, for every galaxy or for every Christ or Yahweh. Perhaps the stones of the city have their own god, their own history. Perhaps it has all been a mockery and the Canaanites, the original inhabitants of the town, were right: there are a thousand gods. Perhaps the pious will get to their heavenly Jerusalem and find there that the quarrels are even more bitter, the victories even more hollow.

Perhaps the history of this city can be written as accurately in progressions of images as it can be in progressions of facts—in images of stone: letters on stone, altar stone, stone in sling, stone in ballista, tombstone, stone church, parliament of stone. Or, in ascensions: Ascension of Christ, Ascension of Mary, Ascension of Mohammed atop his winged horse. Jews never "go" to Jerusalem; the word they use is "ascend," for it is a city set high among hills; and on judgment day it will rise even higher to ascend to the heavens. Or perhaps, as the prophets said, in progressions of deeds —of good and evil: through the iniquities of the Jews their temple is in ruins and their sins prolong the period of its desolation. A man speaks harshly in New York, and in Jerusalem, in the night, a stone crumbles. A Jewish boy scout helps an old lady across the street, and President Nasser moves toward peace. A woman gives to charity, and in heaven God mourns the suffering of the broken city. Or perhaps there are no progressions at all: Jerusalem is inhabited by the fat, the thin, the childish, the angry, the placid; scholars, the greedy, shoemakers, the pious, and that race apart, the beautiful. It has been exactly this way ever since Canaanite times. Therefore, Jerusalem has no history.

But we religiously hold on to the historic, the real Jerusalem at 31 degrees 47 minutes north latitude, 35 degrees 14 minutes east of Greenwich. That Jerusalem and maybe one or two others. There are, after all, so many to choose from—the Jerusalem of Jesus in the Bible, seen in thousands of steel engravings—on the Via Dolorosa, the bearded savior, thorn-crowned, bowed down under the weight of his cross; the Jerusalem of Mohammed, light and airy, a Persian painting, stars in the sky above and on earth the winged horse and the prophet surrounded by pearly angels; and beneath them, the ancient city of dancing King David, harp, purple Ark curtains, bronze temple pillars, priests with jeweled breastplates.

Then there is the Jerusalem of the movies—wine jars, leather sandals, long-robed, long-haired maidens, about to be stricken with leprosy or religion, clanking Roman soldiers hurrying ominously through the town—and the dervish's Jerusalem, the anchorite's Jerusalem, the missionary's Jerusalem, chaste as heaven. The Jerusalem of the Russian pilgrims (thousands came each year carrying the shrouds in which they would be buried, bowing down hundreds of times before the icons and the sacred stones). The archeologist's dusty Jerusalem; the Jerusalem of the popes and patriarchs (One finds it difficult, wrote Mark Twain when he visited the city, to realize "that Christ was not crucified in a Catholic church."); the Jerusalem of the statesmen, a commodity to be traded for votes or oil; the Jerusalem of the crusader; the Jerusalem of the medieval pilgrim; the Jerusalem imagined on snowy Sabbaths in Lithuania; the Jerusalem of the Jew in China; the Jerusalem of the Jew in Berlin; the city of exiles, Christian, Muslim and Jew.

All of them are possible, all have been historic, and each one, perhaps, is as valid as the next. And so the judicious reader will approach the history of the city with a mind open to the possibility that God may actually exist, that the religion of the Jews is true, and that all other religions and viewpoints false. And equally open to the possibility that the religion of the Jews is false, and only Christianity is true, all Christianity or only one version of it. And to the possibility that Islam is, as it claims to be, the true faith, the fulfillment of monotheism, of which Christianity and Judaism are perversions. And to the possibility that it has all been in vain, that there is no God, or at least that there was none, until here in Jerusalem He emerged from the dust and began to evolve long after man had been created.

CHAPTER 2

A City in Canaan

THE hills of Jerusalem are high. Now they are barren, treeless, hostile; but once they were covered with forests of oak, cypress and myrtle, and everywhere the Jerusalem pine, from which the cherubim that stood guard in the Holy of Holies of Solomon's temple were to be carved. Shrubs grew underfoot, among them the thorny bushes from which one day Christ's crown of thorns would be made. Here and there among the hills are springs and water holes, and occasionally a brook that courses through a valley to the Mediterranean coast or loses itself in the desert hills that lead down to the Jordan or the Dead Sea. A band of these hills, some twenty miles wide, runs the length of the narrow land of Canaan. To their west lies the flat Mediterranean plain along which the armies of Egypt, Assyria, Rome and the crusaders easily marched. To their east is the hot and dry Jordan Valley, the lowest land on earth, and one of the longest occupied by civilized man, its metropolis Jericho having been built and strongly fortified around 7000 B.C., at a time when man first learned to farm. And almost at their crest stands Jerusalem, about twenty miles from the Jordan and forty from the sea, on arable land but very close to the desert. An hour's walk from the city walls are the salty and terrifying hills that overlook the Dead Sea.

Man lived at the site around two hundred thousand years ago. Early Stone Age tools, manufactured by these primitive settlers, have been found in the city a few hundred yards from that characteristic center of machine-age civilization, the railroad station. But Jerusalem was not actually founded until about 2900 B.C., some centuries after a new people first came to the land that was to be called Canaan. They were a Semitic people, related to the Jews, and they had long been living a seminomadic life at the edge of sown land, along the border of the Fertile Crescent that arches westward from Mesopotamia and then south to the Palestinian coast. Eventually these people moved into the entire Fertile Crescent, into Mesopotamia where they mingled with the earlier inhabitants, the Sumerians, and established towns and kingdoms of their own; to the coast of Lebanon where they made contact with the Egyptians and the people of Crete, the nations from beyond the sea; and into Palestine, where they conquered the local inhabitants, whom they vaguely remembered in later centuries as "The Howlers," "The Giants," or "The Ghosts," with that curious mixture of terror and contempt we give to our victims, human and animal. They took over the natives' cities and established new ones of their own, and they were joined in the country by other migrants, people from Anatolia in the north, who founded their own settlements. Many of the important biblical towns were established at this time. One was Jerusalem.

The settlement grew on a rocky hillside overlooking a brook, called the spring Gihon. One of the attractions that encouraged colonization at the site may have been a natural forest of wild olive trees—a tree indigenous to the region; or perhaps an olive grove that had been cultivated by a native farmer, for east of Jerusalem rises a hill, one of Canaan's highest, that is known as the Mount of Olives. From earliest times its slopes were covered with olive groves. On the other side of the town there was a plain, a broad one for that hilly land, where the settlers planted wheat and barley.

The grain they grew was threshed on a large rock directly north of the city. It was a high place where the threshers, throwing grain into the air so the heavier seed could fall away from the lighter chaff, would be aided by the prevailing winds which would carry the chaff away.

Because it was on a high place and very large, the rock probably became a sanctuary, although there was also an official temple within the town. Semitic people often focused their religion on great stones, around which they marched in procession during sacred ceremonies. Like the temple in town, the rock was probably dedicated especially to the god Shalem, a minor deity for whom Jerusalem is probably named. *Warawa Shalem*, Shalem has founded, was the city's original name. He was the god of the evening star, the planet Venus. His name appears again in the name of one of Jerusalem's greatest kings, Solomon, but almost nowhere else.

Jerusalem remained a village of farmers for centuries. At first the inhabitants lived in round huts; later they built square houses not much different from those Arab peasants live in today. They tended their olive groves and vineyards and fields of grain and lentils, and probably exchanged their grain and olives for meat and milk, obtained from their kinsmen who maintained a seminomadic life in the region with flocks of asses and sheep.

Throughout the third millennium Canaan continued to receive new settlers—Semites and a rather mysterious group called the Hurrians. Some time toward the end of this period Jerusalem may have become the possession of two groups of people, perhaps two clans of invading Semites, or of one Semitic clan and a group of other migrants; or perhaps it became the joint property of the old Canaanite inhabitants and new settlers who lived together in an uneasy peace as later communities of Jerusalem have rarely been able to do. (One of the Semite clans may have been the Jebusites after whom Jerusalem came to be known sometimes as Jebus.) At any rate, by 1800 B.C. Jerusalem had developed from a farming village into a real town and had entered recorded history. Around that time it was ruled by two chieftains, which is why we suspect that there were two groups in the town. We have the names of a pair of them: Yaqar'ammu and Setj-'anu, found inscribed on a broken piece of pottery discovered in Egypt. The piece came from an "execration bowl," a bowl on which the Egyptians customarily wrote, along with a curse, the names of Pharaoh's enemies; then, the bowl was smashed to pieces as—it was hoped—Pharaoh's enemies would be smashed to pieces too.

This particular curse, directed not only against the rulers of Jerusalem but against "their strong men, their swift runners, their allies, their associates . . . who may rebel, who may plot, who may talk of fighting or who may talk of rebelling," may have been effective; but a lot of similar curses were not. For Egyptian power was disintegrating at the time. Within a few years, Egypt, which had flourished for centuries in isolated splendor far more powerful and civilized than its neighbors, would be overrun by a group of foreigners called the Hyksos, a mixture of Semitic and Indo-Aryan people based in Canaan and Syria. Jerusalem may have been a Hyksos stronghold. For more than two centuries the city would remain under Hyksos rule.

At almost the same time as the Hyksos were overrunning Egypt, new Semitic migrants came into Canaan, attracted by the rich land which was relatively depopulated, despite—or perhaps because of—the frequent invasions of newcomers. They wandered around the countryside, and gradually set down roots, acquiring land here and there, or grazing rights, or wells or burial places. One such migrant was the patriarch Abraham, who is recorded as having come from Haran along the northern reaches of the Euphrates to Hebron south of Jerusalem where he purchased land, including a cave he could use for a sepulcher. These settlers maintained ties with their kinfolk who had moved into Mesopotamia and Egypt; some of their kin may have entered Egypt with the Hyksos, only to be enslaved there when the Hyksos were overthrown.

In the sixteenth century, Egypt revived, expelled the foreign invaders, and conquered Canaan for itself. Under Egyptian rule, Canaan flourished, developing a prosperous and unified culture along the entire east coast of the Mediterranean. The earliest known alphabet, a Canaanite invention, dates from this time. Jerusalem was a provincial outpost of this civilization, far less sophisticated than the Canaanite cities on the Mediterranean coast. Like them it was an Egyptian vassal, a little city-state, ruling a realm a few miles broad, much of which could probably be seen from the city wall. Under its control were a few nearby villages, incuding at times the town of Bethlehem, five miles to the south. Agriculture was the mainstay of its economy, but Jerusalem profited from trade too. The city stood near the crossing of two minor trade routes. One went up over the hills from east to west, and over it the dates of the Jericho region and bitumen from the Dead Sea could be transported to the seacoast; the other went from north to south, along the crest of the hills, serving the hill towns—in the north Shechem and Gibeon, in the south Bethlehem and the fairly new town of Hebron about twenty miles away.

At this time the town covered a few acres on the southern slope of the hill that was in Biblical times called Zion. At the northern and highest end of town was the temple, and just south of it was the palace where the city's ruler lived. Much of the population lived outside the city gates in houses huddled close to the city walls. In case of danger they could flee within for protection. Within the walls Jerusalem consisted of a few narrow twisting streets with stone-built houses, no wider than the length of the logs of Jerusalem pine that supported their roofs. Each house contained one or two rooms, and storage pits for keeping grain. The rooftops themselves were covered with plaster, and during the rainy season —from December to February—the householder was kept busy rolling the roof to keep the plaster from disintegrating. Occasionally a very prosperous citizen had a house two stories high; certainly the ruler's palace was this high. But Jerusalem had few prosperous citizens; and besides, there was some feeling against building one's house higher than that of a neighbor, for the householder standing on his rooftop could then see his neighbor's women sleeping or passing the time of day on their rooftop—as people sometimes still do in Jerusalem; and women were supposed to be privately kept.

Most of the women that is, for some were publicly kept. These were the sacred prostitutes who plied their trade at the temple, where they labored industriously and conscientiously on behalf of the local religion, the fertility cult. This was the chief religion of Jerusalem, as of the rest of Canaan, with its fertility goddesses and its god of male potency, Baal, who is often represented wearing on his head a hat with a very tall and narrow crown, resembling nothing so much as an erect penis (curiously similar, by the way, to the hats Jews wore in many parts of medieval Europe where they were associated, as wicked foreigners often are, with sex as well as with the devil). The Canaanite temple, like the temple of Solomon which one day would be constructed near its site, was divided into three chambers. Within its precinct there must have been rooms where the ritual prostitutes entertained their clients, and a sacrificial hearth, and picnic places close to the hearth where families could gather to consume the edible portions of the animals sacrificed to the gods. The inedible parts were given to the gods, for Jerusalem has always had a very practical streak about its religion. Under the threshold of the temple, a newborn child was probably buried, as under the threshold of every house newly built in the town. The infant's death was in the way of a bribe; he was sacrificed in the hope of satisfying Death, which then might allow the rest of the family or the town to live.

Although a good percentage of Jerusalem's population was probably literate, as citizens of the nation that invented the alphabet well might be, scribes probably took up stations at one of the city gates to write letters for the public on papyrus or pieces of broken pottery. Here, too, public business was transacted as the king, along with the city elders, administered justice, deciding cases brought to the king by the inhabitants, for according to ancient Canaanite tradition, the king was supposed to "judge the case of the widow . . . decide the suit of the oppressed," sitting "at the entrance of the gate, in the place of the notables. . . ." The Bible records the names of two Canaanite kings of Jerusalem, Adonizedek and Melchizedek. One name means "My Lord is righteousness," and the other "The king is righteousness." *Zedek* may merely be an epithet meaning righteousness or it may be the name of a god who symbolized the concept of righteousness; whichever it is, righteousness was evidently a prime concern in the city of Jerusalem a thousand years before the age of the great Hebrew prophets who made themselves its spokesmen.

Some time after the fifteenth century, the completion of a remarkable engineering feat assured Jerusalem's security in time of war. A long tunnel was constructed beneath the city wall, so that even during a siege the women could carry water into the city from the spring of Gihon outside the walls. Around the same time, as a result of another ambitious engineering project, the area of the town was expanded from the original eight or so acres, not by extending the walls to cover more territory, but by filling in land. Like so many settlements in Mediterranean lands, Jerusalem was built along a narrow ridge. Instead of spreading down into the valley, and thus weakening the defensive position of the town, the inhabitants enlarged Jerusalem by increasing the size of the hilltop, building a platform sixty feet wide.

In the fifteenth century life in Canaan was stable, for Egypt was powerful. Pharaoh, or his representative the provincial governor stationed at Gaza, kept the peace, and Canaanite kings, including, no doubt, the king of Jerusalem, bowed down before them to "beg breath for their nostrils"—as an Egyptian inscription boasts. But in the fourteenth century Egyptian power waned again, and the Canaanite towns began asserting independence, warring with each other or confederating against a common enemy.

The common enemy was a new group of Semitic invaders who had entered the country as Egyptian power diminished. They were known as Khapiru or Habiru, a name that has tantalized scholars, for it is so close to the word that has come down to us as Hebrew. Originally it meant "those that cross over," foreigners, migrants; but it also may have been almost a generic term for soldiers, and indeed many of the Khapiru did sign on as mercenaries in the pay of Egypt or the Canaanite towns, or of other powers in Syria, Mesopotamia or Asia Minor. Some time around 1370 the Khapiru threatened to attack Jerusalem. At that time the city, under the rule of a Canaanite king called Abdu-Heba, was a fairly powerful city-state, expanding southward into the lands of the rival principality of Hebron, but still remitting tribute regularly to Egypt. We have a record of one caravan that set out from Jerusalem for Egypt at this time bearing tribute of maidens, captive slaves and five thousand silver shields. It never arrived, having been attacked by brigands even before it reached the Mediterranean coast. When other Canaanite princes were threatened by the Khapiru, among them the prince of the town of Acre, Jerusalem sent out warriors and a large force of chariots to aid them. But soon the Khapiru dominated almost the entire land of Canaan.

Gaza, the seat of Egyptian power, remained loyal to Pharaoh, but the Khapiru took over the important town of Shechem in the northern hills. Southwest of Jerusalem, the slaves in the town of Lachish rebelled and went over to the Khapiru. The ruler of Jerusalem sent letter after letter to Egypt, to Pharaoh's capital at Amarna, begging for aid.

> O king, my lord, there are no garrison troops. . . . Let the king take care of his land! The lands of the king have all rebelled. . . . Lost are the lands of the king. . . . All the governors are lost; the king my lord does not have a single governor left. Let the king turn his attention to the archers and let the king my lord send out troops of archers for the king has no lands left. The Khapiru plunder all the lands of the king. If there are archers here

in this year, the lands of the king my lord will remain intact; but if there are no archers here, the lands of the king my lord will be lost.

There was an Egyptian garrison in Jerusalem, black troops from Nubia, either slaves or mercenaries, but they were little help; indeed they were often as unruly as the Khapiru. One day they attempted a coup, attacked Abdu-Heba's palace and tried to kill him and loot it. They were expelled from the city, or recalled to Egypt, but no new company of troops came to replace them. "Behold," wrote Abdu-Heba plaintively, "the king has set his name in the land of Jerusalem forever; so he cannot abandon the lands of Jerusalem."

Evidently Pharaoh thought otherwise, for Abdu-Heba was forced to send more letters pleading for aid. "At the two feet of the king my lord, seven times and seven times I fall. . . . I delivered ten slaves . . . twenty-one maidens and eighty captives I delivered into the hand of Shuta [an emissary] as a gift for the king my lord. Let my king take thought for his land. The land of the king is lost in its entirety; it is taken from me; there is war against me. . . . I have become like a ship in the midst of the sea. . . ." And again, "Let the king send fifty men as a garrison to guard the land. The entire land of the king has revolted." Abdu-Heba threatened to go over to the side of the Khapiru himself. "Shall we do like Lab'ayu who gave the land of Shechem to the Khapiru?" He complained that "a town of the land of Jerusalem, Bethlehem by name, a town belonging to the king" had defected to the enemy, or to the enemies, for rival Canaanite towns were also besetting Jerusalem.

During these years many of the major Canaanite cities were destroyed, while the Egyptians, ostensibly their protectors, ignored pleas for help. The ruler of Egypt was Akhnaten, who was devoting his attention to a religious reformation he was initiating at home, an attempt to wrench Egypt away from the numberless gods it had worshipped for numberless years and emphasize the supremacy of one god, the Aten, the creator of the world, the all-powerful, life-giving fiery circle of the sun. This reformation was lost upon Egypt. When Akhnaten died in 1361, it died too. But it may have had a profound effect on a few tribes of slaves who were laboring in Egypt at the time, and whose native thunder god, Yahweh, may have heard from them words such as those with which Akhnaten saluted his own god: "Thou . . . who givest breath to sustain all that he has made, O sole god like whom there is no other. Thou didst create the world according to thy desire."

Centuries after Akhnaten's time, an omnipotent God something like his was to come to Jerusalem, brought by descendants of some of the Khapiru who had overrun Canaan and of their kinsmen who were enslaved in Egypt. Some of these worshippers of Yahweh may have been known to others as a group of the Khapiru, but among themselves, they were known by other names, mostly those of families or clans. Some called themselves Reubenites, others after the name of Judah, others said they were descendants of Levi, and among these there were some who joined together in a clan claiming descent from Aaron. Almost all the Khapiru clan groups who worshipped Yahweh also claimed descent from the Patriarch Abraham and his grandson Jacob, or Israel. And so they called themselves B'nai Israel, the Children of Israel. Israelites, Hebrews or whatever they are called, they were the ancestors of the Jews of today (whose name is derived from that of one of the clan groups, Judah). Among the many misfortunes of the Jews, one has been this change of name which cuts them off in the popular mind from their ancestors, the Hebrews. The Hebrews, God's favored people, gave the world the prophets and the holy Bible. The Jews, on the other hand, killed Christ, fought Mohammed and cheat at the corner store. This split has had a considerable effect on the history of Jerusalem, for it has encouraged Muslims and Christians to think of the Jews as intruders in the city, even though they are fully aware of its ancient role as the holy city of the Hebrews. And so, from the start, let us distort history somewhat and call the earliest Jews Jews, even though they themselves did not do so.

For centuries the people of Jerusalem watched as the Jews established settlements in the hills around the city, mostly in empty, abandoned or uncultivated places as the Jews' descendants were to do again in the twentieth century. Occasionally the Jews captured a Canaanite city and its surrounding fields, or squeezed it into subjection. The Jews generally dwelt outside the city walls, and slowly assimilated their rather uncivilized ways to the advanced culture of Canaan. Their language, a Northwest-Semitic tongue closely akin to Canaanite to begin with, was gradually modified until they came to be speaking a dialect almost identical with that of their neighbors. They adopted the Canaanite alphabet and learned to write. The process of assimilation was slow; for centuries the Jews' artifacts remained more primitive than those of their Canaanite neighbors. But the Jews did learn Canaanite agricultural practices, more sophisticated than those of the steppe-land to which they were accustomed, and more efficient. And they began to celebrate the Canaanite agricultural festivals which were to play a large role in the development of Jewish religious customs. In these festivals they placated heaven through songs and prayers, shouts of "Hosanna" and acts of magic—offering up flour, waving branches in the air. Still they refused to adopt the characteristic and dramatic fertility rite at the center of Canaanite religion —ritual sexual intercourse, which, through sympathetic magic, was supposed to increase the fertility of the fields and flocks. Officially at least they refused to adopt it; but naturally the people found the rite too attractive to ignore entirely, too attractive and, they suspected, too effective. Child sacrifice was another Canaanite custom they refused, officially, to learn, although they themselves had traditionally sacrificed the first born of their flocks to their God, and made an offering to Him in lieu of sacrificing their first-born sons.

One Canaanite custom the Jews did readily acquire was that of making and drinking wine. The hills around Jerusalem and Hebron were famous for their vineyards. Another was the practice of worshipping and sacrificing at local sanctuaries. In the hill country where the Jews tended to settle, Shiloh and Bethel were the most famous of these sanctuaries; in the plain beside the Jordan, Gilgal was the major shrine. Jerusalem was not among them, for it remained a Canaanite stronghold long after most of the other Canaanite hill towns had been taken over by the Jews.

But one of the Jewish clans, Benjamin, settled directly north of the city, its border reaching to the valley of Hinnom just below Jerusalem's walls. To the south was the land of the collection of clans that eventually coalesced and took the name of Judah. They established their center at Bethlehem. The tribe of Dan settled first in the region that lies east of the modern town of Tel Aviv, but was unable to gain a firm foothold there; it sent out scouts, found an isolated Canaanite city in the far north, attacked it and took over, renaming it Dan. There the tribesmen thrived, partly from profits derived from attacks on caravans that were traveling to and from the nearby city of Damascus. Another group of Jews moved from across the Jordan into northern Palestine some time around 1330, selling themselves as bonded farm laborers to the country's Egyptian overlords who were attempting to restore order and resettle the land after the troubled times in which Abdu-Heba had been caught. These families, four clans in all, eventually took or were given the tribal name of Issachar, which means hired laborer. By the year 1240, which is the most acceptable guess for the date of the exodus from Egypt of the Hebrew slaves who made up another branch of the children of Israel, there was already a considerable Jewish population in Canaan.

The exodus from Egypt was to weld the Jews into one people although only a small minority of them took part. Their slavery, their deliverance from it and from Pharaoh's pursuing army, their seemingly random wanderings in the desert, their survival in the bleak wastes of Sinai, their visions—pillars of cloud and pillars of fire, a mountain burning, water rising from dry rock—the sounds they heard of thunder, of heavenly trumpets, of a voice commanding commandments, all these were to transform them and all the Jews. For the descendants of the former slaves and desert wanderers scattered among their fellow Jews, and imposed their voices and their visions upon them, making them the first of countless nations on whom these voices and visions were to be imposed.

From Sinai the escaped slaves, fighting almost every mile of the way, moved in slow stages across the desert and around the Dead Sea into the land east of the Jordan to join kinsmen who were already settled there. And then around 1200 the conquest of Canaan began, as a second wave of Jews moved across the Jordan and into the promised land. The conquest took centuries. As the Jews have learned several times, the promised land was not to be had easily. "I will not drive them out from before thee in one year," they were informed in the name of the benevolent, but sometimes unpredictable God who had promised them Canaan, "lest the land become desolate and the beasts of the field multiply against thee. By little and little will I drive them out from before thee, until thou be increased and inherit the land."

Many towns, such as Gibeon six miles north of Jerusalem, remained completely Canaanite in population, although the Gibeonites probably had to pay some form of tribute to the invaders. Other places, like the sanctuary town of Bethel, changed hands several times, with the Jews eventually gaining the upper hand. Some towns were captured and burned and slowly rebuilt by the Jews. Archaeologists can tell when the Jews arrived by the marks of burning and by the fact that the material objects found in the rebuilt town—pottery, tools, houses—are much more primitive than those the town possessed while the Canaanites were living there. In the first stages of the conquest, the king of Jerusalem led a coalition of five Canaanite cities against the invader. But, it is reported, "The Lord discomfited them before Israel and slew them with a great slaughter at Gibeon." Some time thereafter Jerusalem was captured and set afire by Jews of the tribe of Judah, but they were unable to hold onto the city.

Meanwhile other people were also interested in living in, or off, the promised land. Desert tribesmen, among them the Midianites, swept through the lands north and south of Jerusalem and even reached the sea. They were a barbarous sight, with their golden earrings dangling and their camels adorned with shining necklaces. They came at harvest time to steal the crops of Jew and Canaanite, and Jerusalem farmers were wise to bring their crops into the house as soon as they were gathered, even if it meant the messy job of threshing wheat indoors. For a time the Moabites, Ammonites and Amalekites from across the Jordan held the region northeast of Jerusalem and exacted tribute from it until they were expelled. The Ammonites were especially persistent coming over the Jordan in force to attack the territory around Jerusalem which the Jews had invaded themselves. Around 1200 a powerful prince from the upper reaches of the Euphrates marched through Canaan en route to conquer Egypt. Soon thereafter on his way back he marched through again, unsuccessful. He could make no headway in Egypt, but in Canaan he could plunder the land and Jews and Canaanites both felt the burden. As if conflicts with foreigners were not enough there was a ferocious civil war between Benjamin and the other tribes of Israel. In it the Benjaminites were almost annihilated. The war culminated in a mighty battle that could have been seen from the hills of Jerusalem; the Bible claims that twenty and five thousand and a hundred men of Benjamin were slain. The Benjaminite stronghold of Gibeah was burned to the ground as the Canaanites of Jerusalem watched, rejoicing no doubt at the strife among their enemies.

Around the same time, the entire East was shaken by the incursion of a people who are called "the Sea People" in Egyptian records. They overwhelmed the once mighty Hittite empire in Asia Minor; they marched down the coast of Canaan and attacked Egypt by land and sea. Held back by the Egyptians, one branch of them settled on the coastal plain west of Jerusalem and became known to history as the Philistines. It was they as much as the Jews who killed Canaanite civilization. In every part of their country the Canaanites were pushed back, by Philistines and Jews in the land that came to be called Palestine, and by another Semitic people, the Aramaeans, in Syria. They were left with only the coast of Phoenicia, today the country of Lebanon, where a few city-states managed to hold on to their independence, and with one important inland town—Jerusalem.

For around a century after the Philistine invasion, Jews and Philistines lived in relative harmony. But some time around the year 1075, a confederation of five Philistine city-states attempted to take over all Palestine. They established a garrison at Gibeah, three miles north of Jerusalem, effectively cutting off the Jewish tribes in the north from their kindred in the south. In northern Palestine, they moved along the plain of Jezreel to the fortress of Bethshean, thus separating the Jews of the central highlands from those of Galilee. They attacked and destroyed the town of Shiloh, by then the Jews' major shrine, carrying off the Jews' most sacred possession, the Ark of the Covenant, a wooden chest which contained stone tablets inscribed with the Ten Commandments, and which the Jews believed was pervaded by Yahweh's presence. The priests of Shiloh fled and resettled outside Jerusalem, probably on Mount Scopus overlooking the town. Why they picked that site no one knows.

Jerusalem, with a powerful Philistine garrison nearby, probably favored the Philistine cause rather than that of the Jews. Although the Philistines were a far more aggressive breed than Canaan was accustomed to, they were by then practically Canaanites themselves, having thoroughly assimilated local culture. The Jews may have adopted some Canaanite customs, but for the most part they remained different; they scorned the local gods and maintained their own peculiar social structure. Jerusalem and the Philistine towns were ruled by princes as was traditional in Canaan. The Jews, on the other hand, mistrusted central authority, although they had gone so far as to group themselves into a tribal confederation centered around the shrine at Shiloh. They were country people not townsmen, and they were ruled by tribal elders rather than princes, by tribal elders and by custom. At times more than one tribe followed the leadership of a particularly effective elder or soldier; at times prophets or seers swayed their fellow tribesmen. The Canaanites of Jerusalem had prophets too, who delivered oracular pronouncements from the gods; but they were far less likely to meddle in political affairs than the Jews' prophets were. The Canaanite towns still maintained a tight tax structure, a tight control over the populace, inherited from the days when the Egyptian administration was squeezing tribute from the country. Canaanite princes owned large estates, demanded and got contributions of labor from their subjects and were surrounded by a court of aristocrats. The Jews had rich and poor too, with marked distinctions among them, but their society was, and remained, unusually egalitarian for antiquity.

To free themselves from Philistine domination, the Jewish tribes abandoned their traditional mode of government and subjected themselves to a central authority by choosing a king. The man they chose, under the supervision of Yahweh in heaven and his representative, the seer Samuel on earth, was a warrior named Saul. He was taller in stature than any of the other Jews, but as he said, "a Benjaminite of the smallest of the tribes of Israel and my family the least of all the families of the tribe of Benjamin," which may have been why he was chosen. He was the son of a farmer at Gibeah, three miles north of Jerusalem, the town where the Philistines maintained a fort and a garrison. That garrison he expelled after defeating the enemy at a battle nearby.

At Gibeah Saul built the Jews' first royal palace, a square citadel of golden Jerusalem stone, with double walls and corners that were fortified again with towers. From the palace Saul continued the rebellion against the Philistines. Soon his authority extended throughout the Jewish lands, from Dan in the north to the desert south of Judah; but it was effective only in the hills and even there it was challenged by the tribes' traditional autonomy as well as by the enemy. The Philistines were now confined to the coastal plain and the valley of Jezreel, but they refused to accept defeat and maintained constant pressure on the Jews so that Saul's entire reign from 1020 to 1000 was devoted to war. Outside the territory surrounding his capital the king did little to enforce his rule. But he did establish a shrine at Gibeah, and to increase its influence destroyed the priestly settlement near Jerusalem that had been founded by refugee priests from Shiloh. Along with the settlement the priests were destroyed; evidently they had begun to rival the king in importance.

In his palace Saul surrounded himself with soldiers. One of them was "ruddy and withal of a beautiful countenance and goodly to look to . . . a cunning player on the harp . . . and a mighty valiant man and a man of war, and prudent in matters and a comely person," a son of Jesse the Bethlehemite, the eighth and youngest son David. Through military prowess and political skill he rose in royal favor to become Saul's singer, Saul's armorbearer, the friend of Saul's son Jonathan, Saul's son-in-law, and eventually Saul's rival and successor. Saul was in a precarious position. He was the first to be king of Israel; he shared power with the elders of each tribe; his position was threatened by the formidable Philistines and by unfriendly desert tribes; he had antagonized the prophet Samuel who had chosen him to be king and the religious establishment of the Jews; his position depended on military prowess—that was why he had been chosen king to begin with—but his military accomplishments were receding into memory as David's were gaining renown. "Saul has slain his thousands," his subjects sang, "and David his ten thousands." The king began feverishly imagining that everyone was turning against him. It is not difficult to see why he was paranoid; indeed it is difficult to see why all other rulers have not been.

One day in the great stone hall of the citadel at Gibeah Saul sat listening to David play on his harp. It is difficult to write the sentence without discomfort. The scene, like so many others in Jerusalem's history, is pre-written and has acquired its own reality, traveling from the Bible through the Sunday School tale through the historical novel and into the movie epic. All the props are there; the costumes are familiar—the kilt, the leather breastplate—and the great flickering Cecil B. De Mille torches. The king, grey-bearded, pensive, leans his brow on his fist, listening to the rippling harp music. A maidservant rustles by in a long and clinging gown, pours wine for the king (no doubt it comes from the local vineyards), bows low and then moves respectfully away. David watches, but cunning player that he is, does not miss a beat; the harp music and the song ripple on. But somewhere off on another sound stage music gets louder and increasingly dissonant. Heaven is directing the scene. The king's insane ruminations reach their crescendo. He reaches for his javelin that is leaning against the wall and hurls it wildly at his young rival. David, hardly surprised, leaps agilely out of its way. But his leap is merely *pro forma*. Everyone knows the javelin will miss, for the spirit of the Lord is upon David.

The spirit of the Lord tends to foster ambition. With each success David appeared more threatening to Saul. The breach became wider and David eventually fled the court and made his way southward to the borderlands between the country of the Philistines and the territory of his own tribe of Judah. He gathered a troop of outlaws, "everyone that was in distress and everyone that was in debt and everyone that was discontented," and made himself their commander. As a mercenary he hired himself out to the Philistine king of the town of Gath, but he managed to keep from making war on the Jews. In an attempt to track him down Saul chased him into the Negev, the southern desert of Judah, but was unable to capture him. Through protecting the farmers of Judah against marauding desert tribes and against his nominal overlords, the Philistines, he attracted a great following. In return for his protection he demanded and received money from the wealthy farmers and herdsmen who lived along the southern reaches of Judah, and if his clients failed to pay, he would attack them. The elders of the tribe of Judah came to treat with David as an equal. Like the condottieri of Renaissance Italy who acquired principalities through military prowess, he made himself the greatest power in the region. When news came of the death of Saul and his son Jonathan in a battle against the Philistines, David proclaimed himself king of Judah in the town of Hebron. There was no opposition.

For two years Saul's son Ishbosheth ruled the northern tribes in his father's place while David ruled Judah. David was a skillful diplomat and he knew how to capitalize on the mistakes made by his rival; soon Ishbosheth was overthrown and David proclaimed king of all Israel. He made his capital at Hebron and there it remained for more than seven years. Then he determined to capture Jerusalem.

When he marched against the city, the Canaanite inhabitants scoffed at his pretensions. Blind men and cripples, they told him, would be enough to hold off his army. The site was strongly fortified; it had to be to have held out so long against the Jews. A frontal assault would have been almost useless, and so David worked his way into the city another way. According to one interpretation of the ambiguous Bible texts describing the conquest, his men sneaked into Jerusalem through the water shaft which had providentially been left unguarded, travelling along the tunnel that had been built centuries earlier to ensure the city's water supply during a siege. A more dramatic and less reliable tradition has it that one of David's men flew over the wall, having first stood on the king's head to reach a cypress tree that could catapult him in. Legend reports that David himself did not have to catapult over the wall or sneak in through a water conduit. For him a miracle occurred: the city wall bowed down before him and he walked over it without hindrance. Because he was so noble, it is said, he purchased the city he had just conquered, paying the inhabitants 600 shekels, fifty for each of the tribes of Israel.

In an effort to unify the tribes of the south and the north, David made Jerusalem his capital. He had been selected as king by the men of Judah and then once again as king by the men of the northern tribes. His subjects had chosen him "with a perfect heart," and celebrated their choice with a three-day feast with "meat, meal, cakes of figs and bunches of raisins and wine and oil and oxen and sheep abundantly; for there was joy." But they could revoke their choice; kingship was not that strongly established among the Jews, either in the north or the south. David had conquered Jerusalem himself however, and he was king of the city in his own right, ruling it as a Canaanite warrior prince might rule his domain. As was customary, Jerusalem took the name of its conqueror as an epithet. Thenceforth it was to be known also as the city of David.

The Philistines, who may still have considered David their vassal, became uneasy at his increasing power. They marched up to Jerusalem and encamped on the plain of Rephaim, southwest of the city walls. If they could capture Jerusalem they could cut David's kingdom in two. They were driven away and defeated in battle; but they returned, only to be defeated again, by divine intervention according to the biblical report. God's presence rustled through the top of the trees and went ahead of the Jewish army to attack the enemy. All David and his men had to do was finish the job. After their defeat the Philistines were made David's vassals, although they were allowed to retain some autonomy. Less fortunate were the Moabites and Ammonites east of the Jordan. The Ammonites were subjected and cut up "with saws and with harrows of iron and with axes." The Moabites were dealt with more gently, for David was related to them; his greatgrandmother Ruth had been one. They were merely smitten. They "became David's servants and brought gifts." The Syrians also became David's servants and brought gifts. The king garrisoned Damascus; he conquered Edom in what is now southern Jordan, thus assuring command of the trade routes leading from Damascus to the Red Sea. He controlled most of Syria up to the Euphrates River and dominated the land routes from Mesopotamia and Asia Minor to Egypt.

In the capital of this considerable empire David sat enthroned, wearing a bejeweled crown of gold that he had taken from the king of the conquered Ammonites. He allowed the Canaanite natives of the town to remain in Jerusalem, but he brought in his own followers to dwell there too, men who had remained with him when he was a refugee from Saul, and representatives from all twelve tribes of Israel, thus assuring him of the loyalty of all the Jews. His own bodyguard was not made up of Jews however, but of Philistines and mercenaries from the island of Crete, who probably spoke an early form of Greek. Vast stores of booty were gathered into the storerooms of the cedarwood palace the king built at the northern edge of the city—vessels of gold and silver, ingots of bronze, and golden shields taken from Syria. With all this was kept the tribute sent by the Jews and by the subject realms of David's empire.

With the conquest of Jerusalem David had subjugated one of the last of the independent Canaanite cities. But his victory marked Canaan's conquest of the Jews as well. Now, like her neighbors, Israel was to have a powerful king and her God was to have a special shrine, a royal sanctuary, as was the custom in the ancient Near East. Both changes were adjustments to the world of Canaan. Both excited and continued to excite fierce opposition among the Jews. Saul had recaptured the Ark of the Covenant from the Philistines, but he never dared, or perhaps even thought, to bring it to his capital. His relations with the religious establishment of Israel were equivocal or openly hostile. Saul was a madman, but David was sane and he made certain to link his power firmly with that of Yahweh. He brought the Ark of the Covenant to Jerusalem and danced before it in prayer and celebration, and placed it in a tent beside the spring of Gihon just outside the city. In doing this he was performing a political as much as a religious act, although the biblical chronicler who records the story, reflecting and perhaps encouraging the importance that the Jerusalem temple later obtained, invested the move with the most profound religious significance. Of course there is no reason to doubt that David also invested it with deep religious feeling. "Sing unto Him, sing psalms unto Him, talk ye of all his wondrous works," sang the king after he had slaughtered bullocks and rams as a sacrifice to Yahweh, ". . . for all the gods of the people are idols; but the Lord made the heavens."

To house the Ark properly David had to build a temple. No other royal capital was without one. "See now, I dwell in a house of cedar," he said, "but the ark of God dwelleth within curtains." To provide an appropriate site for the temple, he eventually purchased, for fifty shekels, the field surrounding the sacred rock of Jerusalem, and there he performed a sacrifice to Yahweh. But David never got to build the sanctuary because, the Book of Chronicles explains, he was a warrior and had shed blood in abundance. Bloodshed would have ample place in the temple but the blood shed by David was human blood not animal blood and evidently it was not considered suitable. Yahweh washed his hands of it and forbade the king to build the shrine. And so David had to content himself, if the Bible is to be believed, with amassing supplies that his son and successor Solomon would later use for the work.

"Iron in abundance," was collected, ". . . and brass in abundance without weight and cedar trees in abundance . . . and a hundred thousand talents of gold and a thousand thousand talents of silver." The gold was to be used "for things to be made of gold, and the silver for things of silver, and the brass for things of brass, the iron for things of iron and wood for things of wood . . ." Beside these there were "onyx stones and stones to be set, glistery stones and of divers colors, and all manner of precious stones." And if all that were not enough, there were "marble stones in abundance." Jerusalem had never seen such a treasure.

Ariel

Sometime around the year 960 B.C., all the suns of heaven, the stars, the angels, the seraphim and cherubim ran to the celestial gates to greet King David who had just died on earth. They escorted him to the throne room of God in the heavenly Jerusalem, and seated him on a throne made of fire; there he sat entertaining God with his psalms as he had entertained King Saul. Beneath him, his son Solomon ruled in his place. During David's lifetime, Solomon had secured the succession to his father's kingdom after a prolonged palace intrigue. He had ridden his father's royal mule down from David's palace to the spring of Gihon outside the city wall to be crowned before the tent containing the Ark of the Covenant. Saul's royal diadem and the royal bracelet were placed upon him, and the priest Zadok and the prophet Nathan had anointed his head with oil taken from the Ark. A trumpet was sounded by a royal herald and Solomon was acclaimed king by tribesmen invited from the countryside and by the Jewish population of Jerusalem, which was itself composed of representatives of all twelve tribes.

The kingdom Solomon inherited controlled the trade routes between Egypt and Asia, and Solomon was able to take full advantage of that fact. At that time international trade was usually a royal monopoly; its exploitation was to make Solomon—and Jerusalem—rich. The king imported linen from Egypt and sold it to the countries of the north. He also imported chariots from Egypt, and horses from the pasturelands of Asia Minor, trading the horses to the Egyptians, the chariots to Asia Minor, and both to the Syrians. The horses cost him 150 silver shekels each, the chariots four times as much. Profits from the operation enabled him to acquire 1400 chariots for his own army. Controlling the Negev and the route over which the caravans traveled to and from Arabia, he could tax spice merchants and trade in spices himself.

During his reign, one of his royal colleagues, the Queen of Sheba, a trader herself, came to Jerusalem with wares from her southern kingdom, "with camels that bare spices and very much gold and precious stones." The Bible records her trading expedition—as ancient annals often did—as if it were the bringing of tribute rather than trading goods, "a hundred and twenty talents of gold, and of spices a great store and precious stones" brought to Solomon as a gift. What the queen got in exchange for these gifts the Bible does not say. Fortunately ancient lore and modern learning fill in some of the gaps in the record. According to Abyssinian tradition she left Jerusalem bearing Solomon's child, from whom the emperor of Abyssinia, Haile Selassie, the Lion of Judah, claims descent. Jewish tradition credits her with turning her passions more to God than to man and with being inspired by Solomon's piety as well as his body. Along with a child in her womb and a new faith in her heart, she also doubtless carried home Egyptian linen and Jerusalem oil, and perhaps horses and chariots as well, and the promise of receiving a supply of the chief export that the Jewish kingdom produced, the copper of King Solomon's mines.

This was mined in the Negev by Edomite slaves in mines so rich that they have recently been reactivated by the Israelis. The copper was smelted at Ezion Geber, beside the Gulf of Aqaba, in a complex refinery, the largest ancient refinery excavated so far, and it was shipped over the Red Sea to the mysterious gold-producing land of

Ophir, probably present-day Somaliland. Perhaps some even reached India. Ships for carrying the copper were constructed at Ezion Geber and manned by Solomon's allies, the Canaanites of the rich trading city of Tyre on the Phoenician coast. Solomon probably shared the expenses and profits of some Tyrian expeditions to the west, and the Tyrians, in turn, probably profited from the Jews' ventures to the south for gold and spices.

Solomon was shrewd as well as wise. He made, his chroniclers tell us, "silver and gold at Jerusalem as plenteous as stones," the stones that are so abundant in the city. With the wealth gained from trade and from the tribute of his subjects, he constructed fortresses and administrative centers throughout his empire, "cities of store" for receiving and storing tribute and taxes in kind, and "cities for his horsemen" and "cities for his chariots." They were built with the aid of war captives and the descendants of war captives who had been taken by David—bondsmen as the children of Israel had been in Egypt—and by Canaanite forced laborers. For the Canaanites this was nothing new. Canaan's feudal system had traditionally required the lower classes to contribute labor to their rulers. The king's most spectacular buildings were reserved for Jerusalem; by the time he had finished them, he had doubled the area enclosed by the city. One was a great palace complex that suitably reflected Solomon's glory. The other was the temple built to reflect the glory of his God, a temple that was to transform the narrow Canaanite fortress into Jerusalem the holy, and bring with it centuries of warfare and slaughter, starvation and sacrifice.

The palace complex was built on the high ground north of the Canaanite city. For its construction and that of the temple, slave labor was not enough; Solomon imported workmen from his ally Hiram of Tyre, paying for them with shipments of corn and oil and wine, and probably copper too. "Send me now therefore," Solomon wrote, "a man cunning to work in gold and in silver and in brass, and in iron, and in purple, and crimson, and blue, and that can skill to grave . . . any manner of graving." (A thousand years after the correspondence took place, copies of Solomon's letter reportedly still existed not only in the Jewish Scriptures but in the municipal records of Tyre.) The Phoenicians sent their stonemasons, woodcutters and woodcarvers, sculptors and brassworkers. They also felled cedars on the hills of Lebanon, dragged the logs down to the Mediterranean and floated them along the coast to Jaffa, from where they were dragged uphill again to Jerusalem.

The palace complex was more splendid than Jerusalem, and perhaps all Canaan, had ever seen. One of its buildings, "the house of the forest of Lebanon," which was probably used as an assembly chamber and treasure house, had rows of square cedar pillars, three stories of windows, and on the walls hundreds of plaques, shields of beaten gold, each one of which reportedly contained three pounds of gold. Cedar lined the interior walls of Solomon's own residence; and on the outside, the stone was smoothed on all its surfaces, not just where it abutted other stones, although dressing it in this way was an expensive and time-consuming process. Within the throne room was an ivory throne, covered with gold and raised on six steps, each of which was guarded by two winged lions or cherubim, like the thrones of the kings of Canaan and indeed like that of Yahweh himself. The king of the Jews was guarded by Yahweh of course, but the lions were there anyway, just in case. Solomon's subjects were impressed. It was so much more rich, so much more beautiful than the palace of David, the conqueror of Jerusalem. It was also so much more spacious. It had to be to accommodate Solomon's three-score queens, four-score concubines and his virgins without number, or even one-tenth as many as the Bible attributes to him.

One of the ladies of the royal harem had a dwelling of her own, "the house of Pharaoh's daughter," built for the Egyptian princess who had come from her homeland as a wife for Solomon. Although Egypt was relatively weak at this time, Pharaohs usually considered themselves too godlike to give their daughters to foreign princes. It was a mark of the power of the Jewish kingdom that Solomon was offered one as his wife, and it was a mark of Egypt's distinction that she received a palace of her own. In Jerusalem Solomon's subjects greeted her arrival with mixed feelings. On the one hand they were properly impressed; the last Jew who had anything to do with Pharaoh's daughter had been Moses himself. But mostly they remembered Egypt with hatred and contempt, and they scorned the princess and the thousand musical instruments rumor claimed she had brought along with her to Jerusalem, each of which was to be played before one of her thousand idols.

"In the four hundred and eightieth year after the children of Israel were come out of the land of Egypt, in the fourth year of Solomon's reign, in the . . . second month" Solomon ". . . began to build the house of the Lord." In building God's house he was also helping, he hoped, to establish his own. For the temple was to be a royal sanctuary, attached to the palace, and its priests were to be servants of Solomon as well as of Yahweh. There had been and there were to be numerous places of sacrifice used by the Jews, some like Shechem and Beersheba tracing their sanctity back to the time of the patriarchs. But under the influence of the dynasty of David and Solomon, Jerusalem slowly eclipsed all rival cult centers. The king and his capital captured the religious structure of the nation as they had captured the civil structure. Actually the word capture is an unfair one; for they were giving something as well as taking. Just as kingship helped create the Jewish nation, so the establishment of the temple and its sacrificial cult at Jerusalem would help create the Jewish religion.

The temple was built north of Solomon's palace, beside or perhaps around Jerusalem's sacred rock. No one knows exactly how it was sited in relation to the rock; the rock may have been used as an altar or it may have been in the most sacred part of the temple building. No one knows what the temple really looked like either, although the Bible does provide a sketchy description of it. For centuries scholars and artists have exercised their ingenuity and their fancy trying to reconstruct it. It has been shown as a Romanesque chuch or a flamboyant Gothic cathedral adorned with statues of the saints. It has been depicted in Renaissance style, or as Neo-classical, with a neat row of columns and a chaste pediment as though it had been designed by Palladio or even Thomas Jefferson. Its representations through the centuries provide a history of architectural taste. By the seventeenth century artists began basing their representations more closely on the biblical description of the temple; and these views began giving some idea of the ponderous and rather tasteless style in which the shrine actually was constructed.

To our eyes the temple building, set in the midst of a broad courtyard, would appear ill-proportioned; according to the Bible, it was higher than it was wide and its height was increased by a parapet which the Jewish law required for safety on all flat-roofed buildings. The architecture was Canaanite, a bastard provincial style, imitative of the Egyptian but without its elegance. The building, made of gleaming white limestone quarried near Jerusalem, was about fifty feet high and only thirty wide, with its width increased somewhat by side-chambers, set back a bit from the main façade. Before the entrance were two tall pillars, cast in bronze by Tyrian artisans and topped with capitals depicting pomegranates, the symbol of fruitfulness. These phallic objects may have been placed there to represent the power and permanence of David's dynasty.

The exterior was simple, but beyond the two cedar doors that gave access to the interior, elaborate decoration caught the eye. The floors were of cypress, the walls of cedar inlaid in gold with designs of palm trees, flowers and gourds. According to the Bible the very nails that held the boards together were of gold. Within the building were three rooms, an arrangement that followed exactly the standard temple plan of the Canaanites and the Egyptians. First was an entrance chamber or portico, then a great chamber, called in Hebrew the *hechal*, and furthest within the Holy of Holies, as long as it was high as it was wide, ornamented like the rest of the temple interior with gold-inlaid carvings, and containing the Ark of the Covenant, sheltered under the wings of immense carved wooden cherubim "of image work." No light entered here. No one entered either, except once a year on the Day of Atonement when a priest solemnly walked in to sprinkle the walls, the floor and the Ark with the blood of a sacrificed bullock. Most of Solomon's subjects probably came to believe that this room was the actual earthly dwelling place of Yahweh, their God.

Only the God to whom it was dedicated distinguished this temple from the others of the ancient East. Like them this temple, and the ritual objects surrounding it, were carefully designed to reflect the cosmos. The great altar on which the priests offered sacrifices was built in stages, like a Sumerian or Babylonian ziggurat whose structure was supposed to reflect that of the universe. Indeed one of the altar's names, *har-el*, the mountain of God, is comparable to the Babylonian word ziggurat which means mountain peak. There were cherubim on the Ark and on the walls of the temple; they were winged beasts, like those on Yahweh's and on Solomon's throne, and they were analogous to the heavenly beast on which the thunder god of the Syrians was supposed to ride through the skies. In the temple courtyard was a great vessel of bronze, containing water and called the brazen sea; perhaps it was a symbol of the waters beneath the earth, the primeval chaos of the Babylonian and Hebrew creation myths. As in Egypt and much of the Levant, the temple building faced east; thus like the world itself, it could welcome the sunrise and the morning. The temple's three rooms were explained, a millennium after Solomon's death, as representing the three elements that compose the universe: water, earth and sky.

At the ceremony for the dedication of the sanctuary, a two-week festival that took place during the harvest season, Jews came from all over Canaan to see the rich new building. Solomon's other subjects came too, to worship the god who had proved stronger than their own. In a great procession, the Ark of the Covenant, containing the tablets of the law, was carried uphill from its temporary home near the spring of Gihon to rest in the Holy of Holies. After it had been solemnly deposited in the chamber, the cult officials and a chorus dressed in white linen robes and accompanied by an orchestra of trumpets and harps, cymbals and lyres— sang out "Hallelujah; praise the Lord." From heaven, according to the report of the scene, an answer came back to them; a thick cloud issued out of the Holy of Holies, a cloud like that which had signaled God's presence leading the children of Israel as they wandered in the desert after fleeing Egypt.

Solomon mounted a podium of bronze above the heads of the assembled people to address them and God. He prayed for the establishment of his dynasty, and he welcomed all gentiles, including those outside the boundaries of his realm, to visit his capital and convert to the worship of Yahweh. Most important, he declared that the new temple was now the appropriate place for God to listen to prayers for rain, for victory, or for remission of sin or guilt for a minor trespass against the law. "If there be dearth in the land, if there be pestilence, if there be blasting or mildew, locusts or caterpillars; if their enemies besiege them in the cities of their land; whatsoever sore, or whatsoever sickness there be . . . what prayer or what supplication soever shall be made of any man . . . [that] shall spread forth his hands in this house: then hear Thou from heaven Thy dwelling place . . ." Heaven was still God's dwelling place; but the temple in Jerusalem was man's approach to it.

Yet Jerusalem had not completely taken over the religion of the Jews. For there was another tradition among them, one that was present long before the temple was built, long before the chroniclers wrote down Solomon's prayer of dedication: "The heaven, even the heaven of the heavens can not contain Thee; how much less this house that I have built." This tradition was unversal whereas the temple cult was parochial, and it stressed morality while the other stressed ritual, particularly the ritual of sacrifice. One tradition was of the prophets and the people; the other was of the priests and the royal city of Jerusalem. Jerusalem and its temple may have provided man's route to God, but there was another and more direct route, and it was within each man. "Hear Thou from heaven Thy dwelling place," Solomon's prayer continued, "and forgive and render unto every man according unto all his ways, whose heart Thou knowest; for Thou only knowest the hearts of the children of men."

The children of Israel completed their ceremony with slaughter, with the sacrifice of "sheep and oxen that could not be told nor numbered for multitude." Each head of a household, from Jerusalem or the countryside, probably performed his sacrifice himself, bringing God a gift, an offering to be consumed by fire on the hearth atop the great horned altar in the temple courtyard, the hearth that came to be called Ariel, the hearth of God.

Like the altar hearth, Jerusalem itself became known as Ariel, the place where sacrifice was burned. Each day as the sacrificial cult became more central to the Jews' religion, hundreds of animals were dispatched. Through destruction and rebuildings of the temple, through the rise and fall of Jewish kingdoms, and through profound changes in the Jewish religion, the sacrifical cult survived in Jerusalem with scarcely an interruption for a thousand years. Over this millennium it developed many different rituals and was given different interpretations, becoming for some believers romanticized as the bringing to Yahweh of a free-will gift, rather than a propitiatory offering, or as a mysterious but bloody burden that had been placed on mankind by a wise and even merciful Deity. But throughout the millennium the heart of the cult remained the same. Always there was the slaughter of living beings. The knife for slaughter, the fire for burning, hands bloodied, the smell of freshly killed meat, the ashes out of which life had been burned to disappear into the air back to the God who had created it—these were the trappings of Yahweh's cult in Jerusalem. Death for cattle, death for sheep and turtledoves in exchange for life for the children of Israel. For life was the Jews' obsession. Even today, when Jews raise their glasses to drink, their toast is "To life." For them eighteen is a lucky number, for in Hebrew letters and numbers are interchangeable, and the letters for eighteen spell "life." "Remember us unto life," they pray, "O Thou that delightest in life, for the sake of life, Thou living God."

The Hebrew word for altar, *mazbeach*, means the place of slaughter. At the place of slaughter the priests poured out the blood and burned the carcasses of sacrificial victims on a fire that was always kept alive. Twice each day, morning and evening, as the sound of silver trumpets rang out over the city of Jerusalem, priests offered to God two yearling lambs, unblemished males, as a sacrifice for the people of Israel, along with wine and flour soaked in oil. The victims' throats were slit; they were skinned and cut into quarters, salted and hung so that their blood would run out into golden basins that had been set beneath to receive it. After the blood had been collected, the animals' four quarters were set aside; but the head, hooves and innards were washed in vessels of shining bronze. Then they were placed on the altar fire by the priests to be consumed completely. The victims' blood was also taken aside by the priests and sprinkled over the altar; it represented the life which belonged to God. "God neither eats nor drinks what is offered to Him," explained one rabbi many centuries later. But the Jews of Solomon's era and for many centuries thereafter were certain that He enjoyed the sweet savor of the burning meat, as well as the spices, wine and other offerings that were made to Him.

The public offerings of animals burned for the well-being of Israel made up only a small part of the sacrifices at the Jerusalem temple. Each day there were also offerings by individuals, most of them sinners sacrificing to propitiate God's anger at their having wittingly or unwittingly trespassed one of his regulations; or by unclean persons who had been cured of leprosy or venereal disease, or been polluted, as the Jews believed, by giving birth to a child. Sacrifices were made to fulfill vows, to gain divine favor, and often to show gratitude. Sometimes family groups would go up to Jerusalem from the countryside to make a sacrifice together, utilizing it as an occasion to visit the big city. And of course the three great pilgrimage feasts in the spring and autumn, which brought enormous crowds to Jerusalem and became increasingly important as the centuries passed, were great occasions for sacrifice.

All sorts of animals were sacrificed, and for all sorts of reasons, and with the incredible complexity of primitive logic, in all sorts of combinations. Rams, bullocks, heifers, male lambs and female lambs and suckling lambs of either sex, kids, and pigeons and turtledoves —these last the common sacrifice of the poor who couldn't afford anything better—were slaughtered and offered to heaven. Jerusalem became a great stockyard. Sheep and cattle were driven up to the city from pasturelands east of the Jordan, great numbers of them arriving just before the festivals. As a result of the temple cult the hills around Jerusalem came to support small flocks of sheep, too, and the city developed an export trade in wool. Much of the traffic in these animals was in the hands of the priests, who imported them, and peddled them to pilgrims coming to the city to sacrifice, and then had the satisfaction of feasting on choice portions of the slaughtered animals that were their due according to the laws of the cult.

When sheep or cattle were sacrificed, sometimes the entire animal was burned, and sometimes only the inedible parts, with the remainder consumed by the person offering the sacrifice, except for a portion that was reserved for the priests. Sometimes the priests received only a leg, sometimes a leg and shoulder along with the jowls and maw, sometimes all that plus the skin. It all depended on what the reason for the sacrifice had been. Usually the worshipper himself slit the animal's throat, after—if it was a sin offering— placing his hand on the victim's head to transfer his guilt. Then the priest took over the task of butchering. But the poor could not participate even that much in their sacrifices for turtledoves and pigeons had to be slaughtered by the priest himself directly over the altar. Usually the sacrificial animal was unblemished, but for certain offerings imperfect animals could be used. It was rare that an aged animal was offered; they were generally no more than three years old. And it was forbidden to kill a beast before it was eight days old, the same age at which the Jews' sons were called upon to sacrifice their foreskins.

The chief sacrifice was living flesh, or rather blood which was equated with life. Both blood and life were holy and belonged to Yahweh; and they were more effective than anything else for expiating sin. It is a concept that has long survived the destruction of the temple. "Apart from shedding of blood there is no remission of sin," wrote Saint Paul to be echoed by generations of Christian preachers explaining the crucifixion. But blood was not the only offering made to Yahweh at Jerusalem. There were offerings of grain and of fruits and each day the burning of incense, which was a mixture of galbanum and frankincense, stacte, onycha (from a Red Sea shellfish), salt, oil of myrrh, cinnamon, cassia and other spices, with the exact formula known only to the temple priests. With a shovel a burning coal was taken from the main altar and carried inside the temple building to the altar of incense before the door of the Holy of Holies. There the incense was placed on the hot coal, and the sweet savor ascended toward heaven for Yahweh's delectation. Once a week on the Sabbath, a dozen loaves of bread were placed upon a golden table especially designed for their reception. They were set outside the door of the Holy of Holies in two rows of six along with frankincense in a golden cup. At the end of the week they were consumed, not by fire but by priests, who ate them within the sanctuary. Although a week old they were probably in good condition, since it is likely that unleavened bread was used. Occasonally the table on which they were displayed was replaced too, for there were ten golden tables made for the purpose, the extra ones reposing in one of the numerous storerooms that stood along the side of the temple building.

Centuries after the time of Solomon a Greek visitor wrote a description of the temple priests and Levites performing the various sacrifices.

> "Each man does his own appointed share of the work, and they work without ceasing, some bringing the wood, others the oil, others the fine wheaten flour, others the incense, while some sacrificed the burnt offerings in doing which they showed great strength for they take calves' legs weighing rather more than a talent apiece in each hand, fling them a good way up in the air with either the right hand or the left and never miss catching them again; and so they do with the legs of sheep and of goats some of which are wonderfully heavy and fat. . . . So great is the silence everywhere that one would suppose that there was no one in the place although the priests number seven hundred and they who bring the victims to the temple are many; but everything is done with awe and reverence for its great sanctity."

The job of cleaning up after the sacrifice belonged, in time, to the Levites and their assistants, called the *nethinim*, who were descendants of Canaanite prisoners and did the dirtiest work, sweeping and washing the temple pavement of the filth that resulted from the butchering; eventually a special water line was installed in the temple precinct for this purpose. The Levites, who, like the priests were members of a special caste, passed their office on from father to son. They lived all over the land of Israel; from the age of twenty-five or thirty until they reached fifty, they were liable to come to Jerusalem to serve in the temple for stated periods. It was they who assisted the priests in butchering the animals, carried wood for the altar fire, scrubbed the golden basins clean of blood, polished the sacred utensils, baked bread for the sacrifice and sang the psalms for the temple services. They, or the young priests, swept away the ashes of burned animals and carried them out to be dumped on a great ash heap that stood outside the temple walls, a grisly testimonial to the city's faith in Yahweh. For their services the Levites collected a tithe from their fellow citizens. In turn they, like everyone else, had to give a tithe of their income to the priests.

The priests were in charge of this immense and complex operation. From the time of Solomon they formed—as priests still do—a sizable portion of Jerusalem's population. Eventually they came to be led by one of their number who bore the title of High Priest; only he was allowed to enter the Holy of Holies of the temple. Over the white gown worn by all priests, he wore the robes of his office; a blue tunic, and over that an apron of cloth of gold and other colors; and over that a breastplate of precious stones each inscribed with the name of a tribe of Israel so that their names would appear before God. On his brow was a plaque of gold with the words "sacred to Yahweh" written upon it. As he stood before the people in the temple courtyard, his hands raised high in blessing and his fingers opened wide so that the spirit of God could come through, the breeze on the temple terrace jangled the little golden bells that were sewn onto the hem of his tunic and the golden pomegranates that were sewn among them. The sound recalled other and more primitive forces than Yahweh, forces before which the Jews were also in awe—the demons who were to be frightened away by the sound of the bells and the powers of fertility which were to be summoned by the magic of the pomegranate, that fruit bursting with hundreds of seeds.

These mysterious and terrifying forces had, like Yahweh, their own sacred hill in Jerusalem, a hill that was higher than Yahweh's hill and more wild, the Mount of Offense, southeast of the town and opposite the temple mount. This was the hill the citizens of Jerusalem faced when they looked outside the city walls. Yahweh's hill, Mount Moriah or Zion, was behind them, invisible from within the town itself, up past twisting narrow streets and hidden behind the compound of the royal palace. Perhaps they might catch a glimpse of the temple roof, but most likely looking up from any place in the city, one could see only the houses directly above and nothing beyond. To most people in the city however, the Mount of Offense was quite visible, like the foreign gods who were worshipped there.

On this hill Solomon, in the later years of his reign, erected a shrine for the devotions of his wife, Pharaoh's daughter, and shrines for the idols adored by his other foreign wives. To these sanctuaries, the people of Jerusalem—both the original Canaanite inhabitants and curious, eclectic or defiant Jews—could repair to worship other gods. When Solomon, in his old age, drove southward in his chariot, as he enjoyed doing, to visit the royal garden resort in the town of Etham, he could look back at his monuments on two hills, the hill of the idols and the Mountain of Yahweh, which some day would be give over to foreign gods.

With Solomon's death around 920 B.C., his empire was divided. The ten northern tribes seceded from the confederation and formed a kingdom of their own known as Israel, leaving only Judah and its satellite tribe of Simeon loyal to the dynasty of David. To keep northerners from resorting to the Jerusalem temple where they would come under the influence of David's dynasty, the Kingdom of Israel built new temples for them within its own territory. This immediately diminished the revenues of the Jerusalem temple and of Jerusalem. Once more it was a small and relatively insignificant town, cut off from the tribute lands north of the Sea of Galilee, and from the Phoenician ports that had sent it so much wealth.

The territory directly north of Jerusalem became a battleground, as Judah fought to conquer Israel, and failing that to establish its border a few miles north of Jerusalem rather than at the city's gates. After a series of border wars, in one of which the king of Judah dipped into the temple treasury to bribe the Syrians to attack Israel from the rear, Judah succeeded in fixing the frontier along a line some distance north of the capital. During the centuries that followed Solomon's death, the annals of the two Jewish kingdoms of Israel and Judah are filled with battles that took place between them, and between them and their enemies, Damascus and Edom, Ammon, the Philistines, and the ominous Assyrians in the north. King followed king; the chroniclers judge their effectiveness by the loyalty they rendered to Yahweh and find most of them wanting. When it became evident that Judah could never impose its will on the more powerful land of Israel and that the kings of Israel could not oust David's dynasty from Jerusalem, a symbiotic peace was arranged. Judah retained its independence, more or less as a satellite of Israel, maintaining relations with the Phoenicians through Israel, and enlisting the help of Israel in controlling the Edomites and the trade routes to the Red Sea.

Jerusalem was less prosperous now than it had been, but it remained a center of trade. Wheat was exported to the Phoenician coast and oil and wine may have been sent abroad too. Woolen goods were woven for export. Craftsmen had been imported by David and Solomon, Tyrian artisans who worked in precious metals and stone. Some of them must have stayed in Jerusalem to set up shop in the bazaar and sell their goods to the citizens and to the peasants of the surrounding territory. Much of their trade was in jewelry; the daughters of Jerusalem wore, among their more common adornments, headbands of gold or silver, armlets, nose rings and anklets that tinkled as they walked. But some of their business must have been in graven images: small and rather coarse figures of the thunder god Baal riding on a bull, or the Canaanite war god Resheph armed with sword and club, or Anath, a goddess of fertility, shown proudly holding her breasts, or her male counterparts, the Moabite Chemosh or the Egyptian god Min who were depicted with erect phalluses. These were probably traded to the south and east; other, more sophisticated markets were controlled by the Egyptians or by the Canaanite cities on the coast, with their long tradition of skilled crafts.

Jerusalem's existence was a precarious one. Judah was almost always threatened by powerful neighbors. A few years after Solomon's death, the Pharaoh of Egypt invaded Palestine with 1200 chariots, attempting to restore the power his predecessors had enjoyed in the land. He was unsuccessful in that, but he did manage to seize the golden treasure in Solomon's temple and take it home as booty. Jerusalem surrendered without a fight. The people of the city consoled themselves with a comfortable fiction: the gold had been Egyptian to begin with, having been stolen by the Jews centuries earlier when they had fled the land of Egypt. Now it was going back from the house of God to the house of bondage. According to one report, the Egyptian king left behind in its place pillars engraved with "the secret parts of women," as he was accustomed to do as an insult to cities that refused to fight him but surrendered instead. Perhaps the pillars were much less lurid than that and were merely obelisks engraved with hieroglyphics.

For much of the ninth century, the Aramaeans of Syria dominated the region. By 800 however, another power had appeared on the horizon, a power that was to have a profound influence on the history of Jerusalem—the Assyrians. They were quite amiable at first; they just destroyed the Aramaean kingdom of Damascus, exacted tribute from both Jewish kingdoms, and then departed, leaving Israel and Judah prosperous for decades. But by the second half of the eighth century Assyria began to expand and destroy the small independent states of the Levant one by one. In 743 and again in 738 the Assyrians marched along the Mediterranean coast, terrorizing their enemies into submission, tearing out the tongues of the living, cutting up the corpses of the dead. Both Israel and Judah surrendered to them, but then Israel had the temerity to rebel, and in 721 it was destroyed and its population was carried off to captivity. Foreigners were settled on its territory. They adopted Judaism of a sort and became known as Samaritans. For a hundred and thirty-four years thereafter the kingdom of Judah survived, while the ten exiled tribes of Israel were losing their identity among the peoples of the Assyrian empire. For most of that time Judah balanced uneasily as an Assyrian vassal state, until it, too, was conquered and Jerusalem was destroyed in 586 B.C., not by the Assyrians but by the Babylonians, another Assyrian subject people that had rebelled successfully and taken over its master's realm.

Throughout these centuries, Jerusalem's priests and prophets struggled tenaciously to rid the city of the relics of Canaanite religion and to establish the temple as the center of Jewish life. Despite the best efforts of the Jerusalem hierarchy, rival sanctuaries maintained their influence. The books of Kings and Chronicles contain a record of their stubborn survival. "The high places were not taken away," it is reported of reign after reign, and, "They left the house of the Lord God of their fathers and served groves and idols."

Under Solomon's son and grandson, Jerusalem was a hotbed of paganism. A fertility cult was centered on the Mount of Offense in a sanctuary that had been constructed by Solomon to the Moabite deity Chemosh. It featured sacrifice, including perhaps the sacrifice of children, and ritual sexual intercourse with temple prostitutes—male and female—within the holy precincts or sacred grove. During the reign of Asa, Solomon's great-grandson, Jerusalem was purged. Asa cut down the sacred groves, destroyed the pagan shrines, and carried the idol of Chemosh down the hill to the brook of Kidron and burned it on the banks of the stream beneath the city walls. But the pagan cults were not fully extirpated.

Their survival depended on the character of the kings who ruled in Jerusalem. Some were pious; others were paragons of vice. The sinful ones whored after foreign women and foreign gods, patronized the high places, placed sacred prostitutes of either sex in the temple, and persecuted the prophets—men who lived in communal settlements throughout Israel and Judah and who traveled through the countryside and into Jerusalem preaching against idolatry, and warning of impending doom. King Uzziah supposedly killed the prophet Amos with a redhot iron. He was following in the footsteps of his grandfather Joash, who, it is reported, killed the prophet Zechariah after that worthy had berated him for setting up an idol in the temple. King Manasseh condemned the prophet Isaiah to death, and committed incest with his sister. He was also guilty of erecting a five-faced idol in the temple; no matter which direction the pious approached the temple from, they were forced to confront it, and even God, looking down from His heavenly dwelling place to His earthly one, could see it insolently looking back up at Him. And King Jehoiakim—O abomination!—tattooed the ineffable name of God on his penis. No wonder Jerusalem was destroyed, exclaimed the Jews of later times who related these stories to each other with shivers of pious horror.

Righteous monarchs were fewer. There was, of course, Asa, who destroyed the idol in the brook Kidron (supposedly the water of the brook turned to fire to consume the horrid thing), and Joash, who became pious only after he had killed Zechariah. He expelled the idols from the temple and collected money for repairing the building. Most notably, there were Hezekiah and Josiah, both of whom made profound efforts to return their countrymen to the pure worship of Yahweh. They were hampered in their attempts by political pressures. For when Judah surrendered to an Assyrian army, purchasing peace in exchange for tribute, the Assyrians imposed on Jerusalem the worship of their god Ashur, who was after all more powerful than Yahweh since his wards were conquerors. Whenever Assyria was dormant, the cult of Ashur was expelled from the Jerusalem temple; but whenever the Assyrians came back, woe to the rebels! Some time at the end of the eighth century, king Hezekiah decided nevertheless to expel the priests of Ashur and the other pagan gods from the temple and reconsecrate the building to the sole worship of Yahweh.

It was unwise however to rely solely on Yahweh for aid against the inevitable Assyrian reprisal. Hezekiah coerced the Philistine cities on the coast to join his rebellion and sent emissaries to Egypt to seek help against the Assyrians. (The prophet Isaiah warned against it; "Egypt is a broken reed," he told the king.) To make sure that Jerusalem would have an ample water supply in case of an Assyrian siege, a water conduit, six feet high and 1700 feet long, was dug. One of the oldest Hebrew inscriptions in existence describes its construction: "While there were still three cubits to cut through [there was heard] the voice of a man calling to his fellow, for there was an overlap in the rock. . . . And when the tunnel was driven through, the quarrymen hewed, each man toward his fellows, axe against axe, and water flowed from the spring . . ." With a plentiful supply of water flowing into Jerusalem, Hezekiah could afford to rebel, or thought he could afford to; and in the year 701 he withheld tribute from the Assyrians.

It was a mistake. The armies of the Assyrian king Sennacherib marched into Palestine; "all the kings of the west . . . brought sumptuous gifts. . . . and kissed my feet," Sennacherib's chronicler wrote of the campaign. "As to Hezekiah the Jew, he did not submit to my yoke. I laid siege to 46 of his strong cities, walled forts, and to the countless small villages of the vicinity . . . himself I made prisoner in Jerusalem, his royal residence, like a bird in a cage. I surrounded him with earthwork in order to molest those who were leaving his city's gate . . ." Outside the walls of the city Assyrian emissaries shouted up to the defenders on the wall, explaining to them in Hebrew the futility of resistance. The Assyrians customarily maintained scouts who spoke foreign languages so that they could remind enemy populations, over the heads of their rulers, of the horrifying bloodshed that would follow if Assyria were defied. Within the walls, the prophet Isaiah also reminded the king how foolish it was to resist. Hezekiah stripped gold leaf off the pillars and doors of the temple to pay off the invaders in the hope they would leave him in peace, and not uproot the Jews of Judah as they so recently had uprooted the Jews of Israel. The Bible reports that the Jerusalem treasury provided thirty talents of gold and ten times that amount of silver for tribute. Assyrian annals agree on the figure for gold; but they say that Hezekiah gave 800 talents of silver along with other gifts—precious stones, antimony used for eye paint, couches inlaid with ivory, ebony and boxwood, elephant hides, male and female musicians, and several of the king's daughters to be Sennacherib's concubines.

As soon as Sennacherib faced difficulties in other parts of his empire, Hezekiah rebelled again. Sometime around the year 688 Sennacherib came back and invested Jerusalem preparing for a siege. But this time there was no victory. The army encamped north of the city, and the night before it was to attack "it came to pass that night that the angel of the Lord went out and smote in the camp of the Assyrians a hundred fourscore and five thousand; and when they arose early in the morning, behold, they were all dead corpses." Modern scholars attribute the collapse of the Assyrian army to a sudden epidemic. Ancient authorities claimed that a plague of rats came and devoured the leather of the Assyrians' harnesses; their chariots could not be driven and their bows could not be shot. Lord Byron, who wrote a famous poem about the episode, attributed it to a miracle, and the Jews do too. They claim that the Assyrians were killed by a sharp noise, the sound made by the Angel Gabriel clapping his wings to accompany the sound of Levites singing praise to God in the temple courtyard. To make the miracle even more miraculous, God arranged for it to occur on the anniversary of the destruction of Sodom and Gomorrah and of the fall of Jericho. Whatever the cause, Sennacherib broke camp and left, and didn't return—not because he feared the Jews and their angels, but because Hezekiah died soon thereafter, and his successor hastened to mollify the Assyrians with the payment of tribute again.

The Jews continued to pay until the Assyrian empire could no longer impose its will on them or on almost anyone else. Sometime around 630, Judah was effectively independent again. At that time the king of the country was the pious Josiah, who seized the opportunity offered by the decline of Assyria to reassert Jerusalem's control over the Assyrian province of Samaria, the territory that had once been the Jewish kingdom of Israel. He too expelled the priests of Ashur from the temple, along with the image of their god. Ordering the priests of Yahweh to cleanse the temple of all relics of other pagan cults, he had the vessels used in their rites transported out of the temple and brought to the brook Kidron to be burned. Their ashes were carried far from Jerusalem so they would not defile the holy city. There was a house of sacred prostitution next to the temple, that had been set up again since the attempted reforms of Hezekiah decades earlier. Josiah destroyed the building and its inhabitants. Thenceforth the citizens of Jerusalem would have to remain faithful to their wives as well as to Yahweh. All high places in the vicinity of Jerusalem where foreign gods were worshipped were closed down. Among them was the place of sacrifice called Tophet southeast of Jerusalem, in the valley of Hinnom on a slope facing the city. Here citizens had been accustomed to sacrifice their sons to Moloch or Baal in full view of the hill where God had held back Abraham from sacrificing his son. Josiah's grandfather King Manassah had here sacrificed one of his own sons, and his great-grandfather King Ahaz had done the same. "Cut off thine hair O Jerusalem and cast it away," cried the prophet Jeremiah, "and take up a lamentation . . . for the children of Judah have done evil . . . and they have built the high places of Tophet which is in the valley of the son of Hinnom to burn their sons and their daughters in the fire." The altar of Hinnom was defiled, the priests of the sanctuary executed.

Out of the entranceway to the temple went the images of horses that the predecessors of Josiah had dedicated there in honor of the god of the sun. Chariots dedicated to the sun had also stood in the temple; both horses and chariots symbolized the journey the sun made across the sky each day, and both were burned. Now it was forbidden to bow down at the temple gate each morning to greet the rising sun, an embarrassing pagan custom which unfortunately resulted in its devotees presenting their posteriors to the shrine of Yahweh as they bowed to venerate his rival. Now no one sacrificed horses to the sun god either; according to report, such sacrifices had been celebrated even at the temple altar in the time of Josiah's father, although the horse is an unclean beast, unfit to approach the sanctuary of Yahweh.

The temple of Jerusalem, newly purified, now stood alone. Throughout the country all other shrines were closed. Those of pagan gods were destroyed or ritually polluted, probably by burning corpses upon them or long-dead bones, instead of the living flesh required as a sacrifice by other gods as well as by Yahweh. Other sanctuaries dedicated to Yahweh were also closed down. These were spread throughout the territory of Judah and Israel. There was even one in the public square by one of the gates of Jerusalem. All of them conflicted with the primacy of the temple cult, and all of them had to go. Their priests were invited to Jerusalem to serve in the great temple, but on a level inferior to that of the house of Zadok, the clan that traditionally controlled its services. They grumbled and attempted, often without success, to integrate themselves into Jerusalem's sacred community.

But the most important result of Josiah's reform was the publication of the book of the law which the temple priests, cleaning the building, had supposedly discovered hidden under a threshold, where it had been placed for safety some years earlier during one of Jerusalem's periodic orgies of paganism. This was the Book of Deuteronomy, or at least one version of it, and when it was brought to Josiah he received it with wonder, rending his clothes in mourning when he read it and realized just how distant from its fulfillment his subjects had strayed. He ordered assembled in the temple courtyard "all the men of Judah and all the inhabitants of Jerusalem . . . and the priests and the prophets and all the people both small and great." Standing on a platform before them, he read them the law, and together, king and people, they made a covenant to uphold it, "to walk after the Lord and to keep his commandments and his testimonies and his statutes." The ceremony had such profound effect on their minds that they began to date historical events from that moment. It was the third time that the Jews had assembled to swear to that covenant. The first time was at Sinai, under the leadership of Moses, when the law was given. The second time was at Shechem, under Joshua, when the land of Canaan had been taken. The third time was at Jerusalem, in that land.

"Hear ye the words of this covenant," the prophet Jeremiah would soon shout in the streets of the city. " . . . cursed be the man that obeyeth not the words of this covenant." His auditors ignored him, having fallen away from the religious reformation as soon as Josiah had died. The result of their defection would be, they were told, the destruction of Jerusalem, their temple and their pride. "They have turned back to the iniquities of their forefathers . . ." Jeremiah complained. "According to the number of thy cities were thy gods, O Judah; and according to the number of streets of Jerusalem have ye set up altars . . . to burn incense unto Baal . . ." "Shall I not visit them for these things? saith the Lord; shall not my soul be avenged on such a nation as this? . . . I will make Jerusalem heaps and a den of dragons; and I will make the cities of Judah desolate, without an inhabitant."

CHAPTER 4

The Mirror of Heaven

THE making of the covenant between the Jews and their God was celebrated at Passover some time around the year 622 with the most impressive animal sacrifice Jerusalem had ever seen. According to the report, King Josiah had provided 30,000 kids and lambs and 3000 oxen for the slaughter. The chief priest supplemented his offering with 2600 lambs, and the chief of the Levites with 5000 lambs and 500 oxen. The killings were enough to gladden the heart of the most enthusiastic and most pious temple priests, and the king who was so zealous in following the newly discovered law of his God. But they were not enough, it turned out, to gladden Yahweh for whose pleasure 40,000 throats had been slashed by the temple knives.

"I hate, I despise your feast days and . . . solemn assemblies," one of the city's prophets had cried in a voice he said was sent from heaven. "Though ye offer me burnt offerings and your meat offerings I will not accept them. . . . Take thou away from me the noise of thy songs, for I will not hear the melody of thy viols. But let judgment run down as waters and righteousness as a mighty stream." "Woe to Ariel, to Ariel, the city where David dwelt . . ." another prophet shouted. "Let them kill sacrifices. Yet I will distress Ariel and there shall be heaviness and sorrow: and it shall be unto me as Ariel."

Jerusalem *was* to be like a sacrificial hearth in the years that followed the covenant of Josiah. Like a proper sacrificial victim, the city had grown fat. By the time of Josiah it had spread from the hilltop that had comprised the city of David, expanding westward into a narrow valley and up the side of the next hill. Now the temple and the royal palace were not its only showplaces. There were also the great houses of the rich, some of them painted red for show, where officials and prosperous landowners of Judah lived— men "full of violence," one of the prophets called them, men with "wicked balances" and "deceitful weights." In the valley between the two hills was the street of the Tyrian traders, who made part of their livelihood by lending out money at interest, a practice that was forbidden to Jews by law, because it was considered immoral. Canaanites they were and Canaanites they were called, a term that was to become synonymous in Hebrew for the word merchant. Much of the city's wealth ended up in the temple, into which were deposited not only the tithes given to the religious establishment, but also the proceeds of state-controlled mercantile ventures.

Through the seventh century Jerusalem had increased in population. When the country was prosperous and the king strong, the city naturally attracted numerous immigrants from the countryside. When conditions in the countryside were unstable and the king weak, people sought the security of the capital. The centralization of worship in the city had attracted many priests. Individual prophets and entire schools of them tended to settle in the city too. By the time the Babylonians destroyed it in 586 B.C., Jerusalem had grown so that it was in essence a city-state, surrounded by its hinterland, Judah, which was about the same size as the contemporary state of Attica in Greece and equally dominated by its capital.

Ample warning of Jerusalem's destruction was given to its population by the prophets, in Hebrew and in seventy other languages, legend reports, just in case the message should happen to escape anyone. All classes of the sinful populace were warned and cursed: avaricious merchants, princes and judges—those "roaring lions" and "evening wolves," Jerusalem's freethinkers, "that say in their heart, the Lord will not do good, neither will he do evil"; priests who polluted the sanctuary with their sins and lived off the money of the poor; the poor themselves—men who worshipped Baal on the city's rooftops in privacy; women who baked little cakes to offer to the fertility goddess, the queen of heaven; children who gathered brushwood on the hills outside the city to feed the sacrificial fires of the pagan gods. Even prophets would suffer, prophets who prophesied falsely, for not all prophets saw eye to eye. All other living things would suffer too: "Behold mine anger and my fury shall be poured out upon this place, upon man and upon beast and upon the trees of the field and upon the fruit of the ground, and it shall burn."

The instrument of divine wrath was Babylon. At first it was Jerusalem's ally rather than its enemy. In 609 a Jewish army marched out of Jerusalem to aid Babylon against Assyria and Assyria's ally Egypt. The Jews had had their sad experiences with Egypt and with Assyria; Babylon was a new power, the enemy of their enemies and so deserving of their help. The Jews' intervention in the affairs of larger and more powerful states was worse than futile; it backfired. There was a battle at Megiddo with the Egyptians and the Jews lost. Jerusalem was forced to pay tribute to Egypt, but only for a few years. For Babylon, their hope, their help against Assyria and Egypt, came invading to collect tribute and enlist unwilling vassals. Around 600, Josiah's son Jehoiakim refused to send his tribute to them. The Babylonians first sent the armies of their satellites against Judah—Syrians, Moabites, and Ammonites— and then they came themselves. In December, 598, a Babylonian army encamped on the plain outside Jerusalem. That same month, within the city, the king died, perhaps assassinated, and was succeeded by his eighteen-year-old son with the similar name of

Jehoiachin. In March the city surrendered. The young king, his wives and his mother, "his officers and the mighty of the land . . . and craftsmen and smiths a thousand" were carried away into exile in Babylon.

With the king and the leaders of the city gone, and the temple treasures carried off, the structure of society all but disintegrated and Jerusalem's economic life was brought to a virtual standstill. But the city still had a decade more to live. It was a turbulent decade. Some of Jerusalem's prophets promised that Yahweh would restore the king in two years. But at least one prophet, Jeremiah, spoke otherwise. The city and kingdom of Judah were getting their just deserts. The days of the dynasty of David and Solomon were all but over.

This was a dangerous message to preach. Under Jehoiakim, Jeremiah had already been arrested once for his preachings, displayed for public ridicule in the stocks that stood in one of the temple gates, and then upon his release, forbidden to enter the temple precinct. One of his colleagues, also preaching doom, had been sentenced to death; although he fled to Egypt to escape sentence, he had been extradited and executed. The last representative of David's dynasty, the new king Zedekiah, listened sometimes to Jeremiah and sometimes, hopefully, to opposing prophets, sometimes to the hawks who urged war against Babylon (thus neatly serving the interests of Egypt) and sometimes to the doves, who served the interests of Babylon. All, of course, claimed that God was on their side and that they were serving as instruments of His will.

Naturally the war party was more popular, because it was considered more patriotic, and naturally its counsels prevailed. The Jews joined a coalition of vassal states rebelling against Babylon. Under the leadership of their king, Nebuchadnezzar, the Babylonians marched in to besiege Jerusalem. An Egyptian relief expedition lifted the siege for a time, but their relief did not last long, and the Babylonians soon returned.

During the siege, Jeremiah, who had been warning the king of the inevitable defeat, attempted to leave the city, presumably to pass out through enemy lines to his native town of Anatoth, a few miles northeast of Jerusalem. At one of the northern gates of the city—the Benjamin gate—he was apprehended, accused of treason and placed in prison. The king soon released him, but kept him under guard. He was, after all, a prominent man with a considerable following, and his imprisonment might be expected to demoralize Jerusalem's already frightened defenders.

Within a short time the king himself was in prison, captured while attempting to flee toward the desert hills as the king of Babylon entered Jerusalem. It was the ninth day of the Hebrew month of Ab, 586, in the full heat of summer. Nebuchadnezzar "burned the house of the Lord and the king's house and all the houses of Jerusalem, and every great man's house burned he with fire. And all the army of the Chaldees . . . brake down the walls of Jerusalem round about."

The Bible and the history books say that the house of the Lord was burned by the Babylonian army, but pious Jews prefer to believe that it was the angels of God who performed that awesome holocaust. At the four corners of the building, they say, four angels with four torches set four fires, as another angel stood on the city walls calling out to the Babylonians, "Come and enter the house for the Master of the house is no longer therein." The chief priest heard his call and saw the temple burning. In horror, he threw the keys to the temple up to heaven, and there they remain in obedience to the law of God and in defiance of the law of gravity. Into the flames rushed priests, Levites and holy virgins, who had devoted themselves to temple service. They knew what bestial sins the Babylonians were capable of, and they preferred death to dishonor. According to rabbinic tradition, of all the temple, only one part was left, the *shethiyah*, or foundation stone, probably the great sacred rock around which the Muslim shrine of the Dome of the Rock is built today.

Jerusalem was in ruins, Judah all but destroyed. The level of population decreased radically and was not to be restored for three centuries. Town after town was ruined by the Babylonians; most of them were abandoned for a time and a good many abandoned forever. No town excavated so far, within the borders of Judah, seems to have escaped the general doom. Some Jews fled to Egypt, others across the Jordan to the land of Ammon, others perhaps as far as Arabia. Many were taken captive to the city of Babylon, marching north to the Euphrates valley in Syria and then down along the Euphrates to the capital of their victorious enemy. There they were allowed to dwell in peace, in their own towns and on their own farmlands. Abraham, the ancestor of the Jews, had come from Babylon, from a land of idols; and now his progeny were forced to return there.

To gain his victory at Jerusalem Nebuchadnezzar had traversed, one of his chronicles reports, "steep paths, blockaded roads, where the step was impeded, where there was no footing, difficult roads, desert paths . . ." His prisoners, "the disobedient . . . the enemies . . . the bad and evil," were conducted back to Babylon along a road even more difficult, the road of captivity, a road, they later told their children, that was flowing with the blood of the slain and lined with their corpses. The Jews, Jeremiah had reminded them, had once traveled out of Egypt "through the wilderness, through a land of deserts and of pits, through a land of drought and of the shadow of death, through a land that no man passed through, and where no man dwelt," to rest briefly in the rich land of Canaan. Now they were uprooted again. Now, not for forty years or for centuries, but for millenniums, this wilderness, this exile, was to be their path once more, even though many of them were to return to Jerusalem again.

Until its destruction by the Babylonians, Jerusalem had been officially holy, politically important, dynastically valuable. But now, empty and with its inhabitants in exile, it was to achieve an authentic holiness, to become in the imagination of its exiles the seat of all virtues and a mirror of heaven. This sanctification could hardly have occurred earlier; absence, as they say, makes the heart grow fonder. The exiles in Babylon were overwhelmed with longing for the city. "If I forget thee, O Jerusalem," they sang, "let my right hand forget her cunning; let my tongue cleave to the roof of my mouth; if I set not Jerusalem above my chiefest joy." They built their vision of their homeland around the city, and their prophets ecstatically described its restoration, not just as the Jerusalem of Judah, but as a new Jerusalem, an ideal city of justice and beauty. Jerusalem came to symbolize their dreams of what the world *should* be like, and it symbolized their faith in Yahweh. Their elegies of mourning for Zion provided a pattern for the mourning of the Jews in exile throughout the centuries, and not only for the Jews but for all exiles. Their songs and oracles of hope, promising a return to a new and holier Jerusalem, sustained the Jews throughout the centuries, and not just the Jews but the troubled everywhere.

But in the meantime, Jerusalem was desolate. Foxes from the Judean hills scampered among its ruins. "Is this the city that men call the perfection of beauty, the joy of the whole earth," wrote one of the mourning exiles in Babylon. "All that pass by clap their hands at thee; they hiss and wag their heads at the daughters of Jerusalem." "Thus saith the Lord," the prophet Ezekiel cried to the Jews in exile, "Behold, I, even I am against thee." His words rang true to them. Their temple, the core of their religion, had fallen; their God had turned on them. They were, Ezekiel bitterly proclaimed, "a waste and a reproach among the nations . . . a reproach and a taunt, an instruction and an astonishment unto the nations."

Yet, their prophets promised them in the name of their absent God "I will turn away your captivity, and I will gather you from all the nations, and from all the places whither I have driven you . . ." to return to the city of Jerusalem. The fulfillment of this prophecy took only a few decades. Babylon fell the way Jerusalem had fallen and the Jews were allowed to return home. In the year 539, Cyrus of Persia conquered Babylon and marched peaceably through the great gate of the city and down its broad processional way. "All the kings . . . from all quarters of the world," an inscription commemorating his conquest proclaims, ". . . All their people I assembled and returned them to their dwellings." Among the people liberated were the Jews.

"Awake, awake," proclaimed the second prophet Isaiah at this time, "stand up, O Jerusalem, which hast drunk at the hand of the Lord the cup of his fury . . . Shake thyself from the dust; arise and sit down, O Jerusalem, . . . sing together, ye waste places of Jerusalem; for the Lord hath . . . redeemed Jerusalem." Two years after the fall of Babylon and exactly half a century after the destruction of the temple, the Jews came back to their city under the leadership of Sheshbazzar, a prince of the Davidic dynasty. The population was meager, Jerusalem was still in ruins, and the return was followed by years of famine and drought. All Judah had only about twenty thousand inhabitants, including the old inhabitants who had not been carried off to exile. In many cases both the old inhabitants and the returning Jews claimed the same property, leading to bitter divisions, divisions exacerbated by the fact that the Babylonian Jews mistrusted the piety of their brethren who had remained at home. Even after the temple's destruction pilgrims had come regularly to sacrifice at a makeshift altar on the site, but not all the sacrifices were offered to Yahweh; the Judeans had allowed pagan cults to return to Jerusalem.

As part of its policy of allowing subject nations as much autonomy as possible, the Persian government appropriated money for the reconstruction of the temple, but the money was insufficient to provide for a sanctuary as fine as the one Solomon had built. The demoralized Jerusalem community lagged in their rebuilding until the year 520, when inspired by the prophet Haggai, they took up the work in earnest. Once again cedars were imported from Lebanon for the building, and five years later in the spring of 515, the shrine was rededicated. Haggai promised the Jews that the glory of this jerry-built temple would surpass that of Solomon's; but at the ceremony of rededication, old men who remembered the splendor of Solomon's temple, wept with chagrin. The loud noise of their lamentations was audible far off, mingled with the sound of songs of rejoicing that were sung at the ceremony.

In the next decades the population of Jerusalem remained small, although groups of Jews returned little by little, from Mesopotamia and Egypt. Not all the Jews of those lands returned home. Some remained in exile in Babylon, solaced by prosperity; some ventured further east into Persia where a few attained positions of prominence; others settled in Asia Minor or were scattered throughout the vast Persian empire as mercenary soldiers of the king. Jerusalem retained a certain amount of local independence. The High Priests—their office a new one evolved in the absence of a king—administered the city and the surrounding region. The temple cult enjoyed official privileges, and its priests and Levites were free of imperial taxes. The Persians paid little attention to the city; in these decades they were occupied with another equally august, Athens, which was leading the Greeks in a war of survival against them.

In the year 444, a Jewish official at the court of the Persian king, the royal cupbearer, Nehemiah, prevailed upon his master to send him to Jerusalem as governor with a commission to rebuild the city. Three days after his arrival, at night, he made a circuit of the walls, "which were broken down, and the gates thereof . . . consumed with fire." He left the city at the Gate of the Valley, at the northwest corner, situated roughly where the city's main gate, the Jaffa Gate, stands now. Turning southward, he rode along the hill that is now called Zion; then at its brow he headed east, descending into the valley between Jerusalem's two hills and then rode uphill again past the sepulcher of King David. At the old Canaanite gate, at the southeast corner of the city, he tried to enter

Jerusalem again, but the way was blocked by rubble. The path along the outside was blocked by rubble too, and so he descended in the Kidron valley and rode along it beneath the temple and then around the northern side of the city to complete his circuit.

Nehemiah was probably a eunuch; as cupbearer to the Persian king, with access to the royal apartments, he had to be one to be considered safe. But he was by no means lacking in force. He had not yet told the priests and officials of Jerusalem about his commission, but as soon as he had completed his circuit and had seen the extent of the destruction, he approached the local officials and explained his presence in the city. "Come," he told them, "and let us build up the wall of Jerusalem that we be no more a reproach."

The work was divided up with the entire community taking part: corporations of tradesmen, groups of Levites and priests, nobles and the peasants who worked their lands, citizens of nearby towns, Jericho, Gibeon, Tekoah, Mizpah. Individual householders repaired the section of the wall behind their houses. Priests, led by the High Priest, rebuilt the Sheep Gate and its doors, which gave access to the temple court from the north. The gate may have acquired its name because sheep for sacrifice were probably brought directly into the temple through it instead of being driven along the narrow streets of the town; the sheep and goat market of Jerusalem is still in the vicinity. Trade corporations of goldsmiths and merchants repaired the wall leading east from the Sheep Gate to the northeast corner of the city, and then a portion beyond that going from north to south. The most prominent and prosperous goldsmith in town, a man named Malchiah, was responsible for one part of their quota. The remainder of the city wall abutting the temple was repaired by individual priests, who dwelt in houses in the temple court that backed against the wall. The temple's east gate was rebuilt by the man with the hereditary post of keeper, who was responsible for barring the gate each night and reopening it at dawn. South of the wall of the temple was the quarter of the city called Ophel; here the population was largely made up of the lowest temple servants, the caste of *nethinim*. They built much of the wall of the quarter, and a fortified tower overlooking the valley of Kidron.

Inhabitants of Jerusalem unaffiliated with a trade group, people who were neither Levites, priests or *nethinim*, rich householders or nobles or clients of nobles, were probably divided into two groups, under the leadership of foremen. Both groups worked on the western wall of the city. (One group was led by a man named Rephaiah Ben Hur, whom the King James Version of the Bible calls "the ruler of the half part of Jerusalem," thus mistranslating his official position. A nineteenth-century novelist casting about for a suitable family name for a Jerusalem aristocrat living at the time of Christ, lighted on this one—Ben Hur, and with some assistance from Hollywood, made it notable.)

The work of rebuilding the walls was probably done by members of every social class, with their own hands. There was constant danger of attack by the Samaritans, who were jealous of the Jewish revival; although Nehemiah had a patent for his work from the king, the king was a thousand miles away. Nehemiah had a troop of Persian cavalry with him, but the Samaritans and their Ammonite allies could still probably destroy the work before the Persians could arrive in force to stop them. And so the work was done under arms. "They which builded on the wall and they that bare burdens, with those that laded, every one with one of his hands wrought in the work, and with the other hand held a weapon. For the builders, every one had his sword girded by his side and so builded." All the men working on the wall slept within the city for safety. "Neither I," Nehemiah wrote in his chronicle of the events, "nor my brethren nor my servants nor the men of the guard which followed me, none of us put off our clothes saving . . . for washing."

The work took less than two months to complete. When it was done Nehemiah brought Levites from the countryside into Jerusalem "to keep the dedication with gladness, both with thanks-

givings and with singing, with cymbals, psalteries, and with harps."
Priests and Levites washed ritually, to cleanse themselves, as it
were, of a time when Yahweh was absent from his people, and then
they similarly purified the people, and blessed them. The throng of
Jews—all those who had worked on the wall—divided into halves.
Each half went up on the wall, one group led by Nehemiah, and
the other, according to the biblical account of the scene by the
prophet Ezra. To the sound of trumpets and the singing of psalms,
each group marched along the wall in a different direction, until
they came together at the temple, where sacrificial animals were
slaughtered and a ceremony of thanksgiving was held. They sang
and shouted so loudly, "that the joy of Jerusalem was heard even
afar off."

The walls were built, but the city was still dangerously underpopulated. In case of attack, Jerusalem was very vulnerable. And
so Nehemiah ordered one man in every ten of the population of
Judah—men chosen by lot—to settle in the city. In the outskirts
new villages were established, and populated by Levites who
worked in the temple and who would defend it if necessary. Soon a
normal commercial life developed in Jerusalem. Around this time
the temple began minting coins, enjoying a prerogative that was
granted to certain sanctuaries throughout the Persian empire. (The
idea of coinage had originated not too long before in the Anatolian
kingdom of Lydia, which was now a Persian province.) Jerusalem's coins displayed the Hebrew letters for YHD on them, for
Yehudah, or Judah, and in a few stylized lines the barely discernible outline of an owl or a face. The face was that of Zeus, the owl
was the owl of the goddess Athena, which appeared on the
"hard" currency of the era, the coins of Athens, the foremost trading power. Other mints imitated it as best they could although the
Jerusalem priests never would have used the motifs if they had
known what the lines symbolized.

The rebuilding of the walls had been only part, and a minor
part, of the restoration of Jerusalem. According to the biblical

Book of Nehemiah the ceremony of their dedication was followed by another more solemn ceremony for which the town's new populace was assembled in a square near the temple to listen to the reading of the law. Standing before them on a wooden pulpit, the prophet Ezra—Ezra the priest, Ezra the scribe, as he is variously described in the Bible—read and explicated the law from morning until midday; and then when he had finished reading, he held up the scroll he had been reading from and displayed it to his audience. After he had finished the people stood, raised their hands and bowed their heads, and answered, "Amen" to his reading. A regular course of instruction in the law was developed, and teachers, called scribes, gathered disciples around them to study it.

The laws were enforced as well as studied. The Sabbath was rigidly maintained. During it no one was permitted to bring merchandise in or out of the city gates, which were shut and guarded all day. All merchants were restrained from transacting business on Sabbath, including gentile merchants and Tyrian fishmongers, whose stalls were located beside the north gate of the city. Those who had the temerity to set up stalls to transact business outside the city walls were chased away. Jewish peasants who had broken the law by gathering grapes or figs on the Sabbath found vigilantes waiting for them in the Jerusalem marketplace on weekdays, urging prospective customers to boycott their now-forbidden fruits. The taking of usury was ended, and taxation of the poor decreased to a reasonable level. And the laws against marriage with gentiles were enforced, so strictly that Nehemiah himself pummeled Jews who had married foreign women.

This religious reformation was to be a more lasting one than the others Jerusalem had witnessed. For the Jews had been forced to redefine themselves while they were in exile in Babylon. Their God had abandoned them, but they refused to abandon Him and His laws. That was all they had remaining. And so Israel now came to mean not merely a people united by blood or by residence in a particular land, but a people that followed one law and worshipped one God. It was the birth of the concept of religion, a remarkably abstract concept for that antique time.

The Jews took this concept of religion back to Jerusalem with them. Under the Persians the city became a sacral principality or province, ruled not by princes but by priests, who came to play an increasingly important political role among Jews. The temple was no longer a royal shrine attached to the king's palace; it now belonged to the populace. A new institution, the synagogue, was born; perhaps it was a native growth; perhaps it originated among the exiles in Babylon. Or it might have originated as an imitation of the philosophical academies of Greece, or of Greek fraternities devoted to religious practices. The temple was a place of acts—killing, burning, eating, and of things—the sacrificial knife, the silver trumpet, the sacred meal; and it was a place of the books of the law, with their hundreds of commandments. The synagogue was a place of words, of sermons, study, prayer, and of the books of the prophets, the wisdom literature, and the instructive histories which at this time came to be canonized in the Old Testament.

The development of the synagogue and the growth of religious fervor gave great impetus to the centuries-old process of selecting and editing sacred writings. The five books of the law took definite form, the books which the Jews call Torah. The word refers first to the teachings in the books and then, by extension, to the books themselves. The psalms were collected, and edifying proverbs were arranged into an anthology which was given cachet by being attributed to Solomon. A chronicler gathered accounts of the history of the kingdoms of Israel and Judah and compiled them in four other books, Kings 1 and 2 and Chronicles 1 and 2. The Jews had long since achieved the intellectual feat of composing a connected narrative of history, the so-called Yahwist narrative enshrined in the Torah, which was written in Jerusalem some time in the tenth century at the court of Solomon or perhaps David. It was composed in the Jerusalem dialect, which it made standard literary Hebrew, as Dante made the dialect of Florence the standard for Italian, and as Chaucer made London's English the ancestor of today's language. This narrative managed to set forth not only a history of the Jews, but a history of the world, and to connect the two. Its authors also invented a theory of history that appears throughout the Bible, particularly in the prophets' books, which were also written down after the Jews returned from Babylon. Nations and cities rise and fall according to their pursuit of justice, and Israel, chosen by Yahweh to demonstrate His ways, rises higher and falls lower than all the rest.

With a canonization of the Bible came a canonization of temple functions. The liturgy recited or sung in the temple court was set; rites and ceremonies were fixed, and although there were occasional accretions, ceremonies remained essentially the same until the final destruction of the temple in 70 A.D. The temple servants were rigidly stratified by family and function. Any who did not pass a strict genealogical scrutiny to ensure that they were of priestly lineage—descended from Aaron as all priests claimed to be—were expelled from office, as were priests who married gentiles or women who were not virgins. The holy days of the Jews were given their classic form, with every male commanded to come to Jerusalem three times a year "to appear before the Lord God." On the three pilgrimage festivals thousands of worshippers came to the city to sacrifice at the temple, not only Jews from the Holy Land, but Jews from throughout the vast reaches of the Persian empire. With their coming, Jerusalem's economy was set on a course from which it has hardly ever deviated since, that of a pilgrims' city living off the rental of housing and the sale of food and ritual objects.

The first of the pilgrimage festivals, Passover, took place early in the spring. It was said to commemorate the exodus of the Israelite tribes from Egypt but actually it was a combination of a Canaanite agricultural ceremony featuring the consumption of unleavened bread and a nomadic shepherds' rite involving the sacrifice of a young lamb in the hope of guaranteeing the fecundity of the rest of the flock. In celebration of Passover, families or groups acting together as families, brought sacrificial lambs to the temple to be slaughtered. If they were too far from Jerusalem to make the transport of a lamb feasible, they would purchase one there. All available priests were enlisted to handle the holiday rush. On the afternoon of the festival, the beginning of the sacrifice was announced by the sound of a trumpet ringing out from the temple hilltop over the city and the surrounding valleys. Before the echo of the first blast died, another was sounded and then another. The first temple official cut the throat of the first lamb, and the blood ran into a basin of silver or gold, while the Levites sang psalms.

For the remainder of the afternoon, lambs were slaughtered. The blood and fat were reserved for the God who had enabled his flock to live through another year, and the carcass was returned to the worshipper who had brought it. He and his family would roast it and feast together, eating it along with unleavened bread—*matzoh*—and other ritual foods. Every member of the group was required by religious law to eat some of the paschal lamb. If the group was very large, composed of many poor people who had chipped in to purchase a lamb, individuals could satisfy Yahweh though not themselves by eating only a tiny portion, so long as it was a least as big as an olive. The people of Jerusalem made money by renting out rooms and utensils for the feast, for each group customarily gathered in a room of its own. Such was the upper room which was rented one Passover by Jesus and his disciples and in which they held the Last Supper, a Passover feast. With the destruction of the temple in 70 A.D., the Passover sacrifice ceased; but Jews still gather annually to celebrate it symbolically. The leader of the family or group traditionally wears a white robe, for white was worn by the temple priests. Psalms are recited that were sung at the temple as the animals were slaughtered, and the shank of a lamb is eaten in commemoration of the paschal sacrifice. At the end of the feast the assembled worshippers cry out together: "Next year in Jerusalem."

Seven weeks after Passover came the second great pilgrimage feast, called Shavuoth, the Feast of Weeks, in celebration of the wheat harvest and the gathering of the earth's first fruits. This was always the least important of the festivals, coming as it did so soon after Passover. It was marked by the sacrifice of lambs and a bullock and the presentation to Yahweh of two loaves of bread made from the new wheat. All through the summer, after the festival, peasants came up from the countryside to Jerusalem bringing sacrifices of wheat to the temple priests in appreciation of heaven's generosity.

The final pilgrimage feast was Sukkoth, the Feast of Booths, in the autumn. As the centuries passed it was celebrated more and more elaborately with bizarre and picturesque rites, many of Canaanite origin, involving processions, circumambulation of the altar and ritual dancing. By the time of Jesus it was considered the holiest of Hebrew holy days, and was called simply "the feast," or *Hag.* (*Hag* was a word that was used for all three pilgrimage festivals; essentially it is the same as the Arab *haj,* which is the word used for pilgrimage to Mecca, a pilgrimage also marked by processions around a sacred rock and the sacrifice of lambs.)

Autumn was the time of the olive harvest, and the feast's booths, or tabernacles, were simply shelters made of branches, under which the olive harvesters used to sleep during harvest week so they could guard their crop from thieves. The feast also celebrated the grape harvest, the ripening of pomegranates and nuts and field crops. Some time during the month a vintage festival was also celebrated in Jerusalem and the nearby wine-producing towns which exported great quantities of wine to the capital for sale to pilgrims. The young girls of Jerusalem went out to the nearby vineyards, gowned in white to display themselves and dance before the town youths. New wine was drunk, often to excess. The girls sang and in answer the boys sang a courting song about that great local ladies' man, Solomon, on one of his numerous wedding days: "Go forth, O ye daughters of Zion and behold king Solomon . . . in the day of the gladness of his heart."

Around the temple courtyard, priests and pilgrims carried

fronds of willow and myrtle twigs bound together with palm leaves, and a citron. Originally all had to be collected in the vicinity of Jerusalem. Naturally the natives cornered the market by gathering the crop themselves before the festival started and selling it to the pilgrims. Daily throughout the festival, priests marched in procession around the altar, waving their fronds toward heaven while the assembled Jews shouted, "Hosannah! Save us Lord!" On the seventh day the priests marched seven times around the altar; but this time instead of waving the fronds toward heaven, they beat them on the earth over and over again. Having already enlisted the aid of heaven for fertility for the next year's harvest, they now had to enlist earth to hasten the growth of seed in the ground. The success of the crops was ensured by pouring out water on the temple court, to encourage the fall of rain from heaven and the rising of the earth's underground waters that were held in place, it was believed, beneath Jerusalem's sacred rock.

Each night the temple enclosure was illuminated by four immense seven-armed candelabra, menorahs that are the symbol of the Israeli state today. By their light, pilgrims and natives of Jerusalem sang and danced almost all night. Storytellers, jugglers, acrobats, performed before the people, and on at least one occasion they were joined by a pious rabbi, who juggled torches to demonstrate his joy, and perhaps his faith and talent too. On each step of the staircase leading up from one temple court to another, the Levites sang a different psalm: "Our feet shall stand within thy gates, O Jerusalem . . . Pray for the peace of Jerusalem . . . Peace be within thy walls and prosperity within thy palaces." Or: "As the mountains are round about Jerusalem, so the Lord is round about his people."

Their Lord must have been pleased with the piety of the Jews, for He rewarded them by allowing them to enjoy more than a century with almost no history. Once the city walls had been rebuilt under Nehemiah, there was, so far as we know, peace within them under the tolerant rule of the Persians. In the middle of the fourth century, there may have been a brief revolt—there is some evidence to suggest it; but if there was it was quickly squelched. Even when the Persian empire collapsed late in the fourth century before the conquering armies of Alexander the Great, Jerusalem's life remained calm. Later, Jews told the tale that Alexander, while en route to Egypt, journeyed inland from the Palestinian coast to subdue Jerusalem. Outside the city he was met by the High Priest, bearing the name of Yahweh on his headdress. At the sight of it, Alexander fell down and worshipped, and then reverently entered the city to offer sacrifice. A pretty tale—delightful to the Jews and useful to convince the often scornful Greeks that Jews and their God deserved respect. But Alexander was too busy to be diverted by trifles such as Jerusalem. He sent one of his generals into the hills to receive Jerusalem's submission, which was peaceably given.

When Alexander died young at the age of 33, sighing that there were no more worlds to conquer, Jerusalem and the rest of the Holy Land fell under the control of the Ptolemies, who ruled it from the newly founded Greek city of Alexandria on the Mediterranean coast of Egypt. In 312 B.C., after Alexander's death, the first of the dynasty, Alexander's general, Ptolemy, had made himself master of Jerusalem. Whatever opposition there was to his takeover was rendered impotent by Ptolemy's cleverness in marching against the city on a Sabbath, when no inhabitant would take up arms against him. Evidently the religious reforms of the past century had borne such fruit that by now the entire population observed the Jewish law with minute attention to its details.

At home the Ptolemies worshipped Egypt's countless gods, but in Jerusalem they diplomatically declared the Torah to be the official law. Under their rule, the city enjoyed royal favor and relative prosperity for another century. It was the priestly caste that enjoyed most of the prosperity, along with members of the landowning class. The High Priest, aided by a council of elders, many of whom were his kinfolk, ruled Judah for Egypt. Education was widespread, not only synagogue learning, but among the rich of Jerusalem, the new and entrancing learning of the Greeks, that alluring people who had conquered the East. The poor remained faithful to the synagogue, and to the endless interpretive discussions of the Torah that took place within its walls. But the rich succumbed to the craze for Greek culture that was sweeping all of the ancient world. They began to study Greek poetry and philosophy, and strove to acquire those athletic skills, physical and mental, that played so large a part in Greek life.

When the Greeks first encountered the Jews, they admired them too, immoderately. The Jews were holy men, they decided, wise as the Brahmins of India, indeed members of a sect of the Brahmin religion that incorporated all occult knowledge. They were a nation of philosophers and their holy city and temple were founts of virtue. But the Greeks' admiration soon turned to contempt, and both Greeks and Greek-speaking Easterners, came to condemn the Jews as extravagantly as they had praised them. They were, it was said, a nation of lepers, beggars and robbers who had not fled Egypt but been expelled from the country as undesirable aliens. They had fought their way to Judah or Judea as it came to be called by the Greeks, stealing whatever they could along the way, making a specialty of temple-robbery, *hierosyla* in Greek. When they got to Judea they founded a city and named it Hierosyla, so proud were they of their thievery. Eventually, in deference to public opinion, they changed its name to Hierosolyma, Jerusalem. According to their story, they worshipped an invisible god within that city. But the Greeks didn't believe that one. They knew that the Jews worshipped an ass, or an ass-headed god, and were ashamed to admit it. (In this report there may be an echo of an ancient ass-cult that existed among the early Semites and that survived into historic times in the tradition that the Messiah would one day enter Jerusalem riding on a white ass.)

Pious Jews ignored these slanders, but their countrymen who longed to assimilate the Hellenistic culture that increasingly dominated the Levant were thrown into a panic. They pointed out that if their ancestors had indeed been so insolent as to name their capital "Temple-robbery," they would have used the Hebrew word for it rather than the Greek one. They invented a fake genealogy relating the Jews to the Spartans, and they studied Greek philosophy all the more intently seeking ways to link it with their ancestral traditions.

Their task of reconciling Hebraism and Hellenism seemed to be made easier after the year 198 B.C. when the Hellenistic king Antiochus III of Syria marched against Jerusalem, his army reinforced by a herd of elephants. The inhabitants, happy to exchange one foreign ruler for another, greeted his army courteously, expelled the Egyptian garrison from the citadel overlooking the temple, and provided food for the men and fodder for the elephants. Jerusalem's new ruler generously rewarded their cooperation. He was willing to reconcile Hebraism and Hellenism. He subsidized certain temple sacrifices, sponsored the redecoration of the sanctuary, reaffirmed the primacy of the Torah in Jerusalem, freed priests, Levites, elders and "scribes of the temple" (evidently the rabbis, the interpreters of the law) from taxation; and as a final boon freed all residents of the city from all taxes for a period of three years, and from one-third of their taxes thereafter. At the urging of the Jerusalem priests, Antiochus went to great lengths to ensure that the city's religious purity remain unsullied, for by now Jerusalem was considered so holy that people swore by it as one might swear by God.

"It shall be lawful for no foreigner," Antiochus decreed, "to come within the limits of the temple round about; which thing is forbidden also to the Jews unless to those who, according to their own custom, have purified themselves. Nor let any flesh of horses or of mules or of asses be brought into the city whether they be wild or tame, nor that of leopards of foxes or hares, and in general that of any animal which is forbidden for the Jews to eat. Nor let their skins be brought into it; nor let any such animal be bred up in the city."

Despite these concessions, it proved impossible to reconcile Greek and Jewish ideals. Soon after Antiochus IV came to the throne of Syria in 175, it became evident to the Jews of Jerusalem that many of the city's aristocrats had reached this conclusion, and had chosen to abandon Judaism and become Greeks.

Some Jerusalem aristocrats were so eager to imitate the Greeks that they underwent operations to repair their circumcisions. Some joined, as absentee citizens, the polis of Antioch, the capital city of Antiochus' empire, thus making themselves equals of the Greeks, but cutting themselves off from the Jews, for it was impossible to subscribe to citizenship in a place without also putting oneself under the protection of its gods. To demonstrate their devotion to Greek ideals, Antioch's new citizens subscribed three hundred silver drachmas as a donation to the celebrations of the rites of the god Hercules. But some loyalty to their ancestral traditions remained; they sent the money, but insisted, rather churlishly, that it be spent for anything but a sacrifice to the god in honor of whom the celebration was held. And so it was used to purchase a ship.

In Jerusalem a group of men attempted to modernize the city and give it a Grecian tone by establishing a gymnasium, probably located in the valley west of the temple mount. To it were allowed to resort only the chosen among the chosen people, for in Greek cities the gymnasium was the focus of civic life and it was customary to limit the number of inhabitants who participated in government. At the gymnasium youths and their elders threw the discus and competed in the other events of the pentathlon—racing, jumping, wrestling and throwing the javelin. They practiced martial exercises, running sometimes in armour and sometimes without it, and punched bags filled with grain, sand or fig-seeds. The youngest among them played at ball. All cultivated the beauty of their bodies. "What a disgrace it is," one of the Greek philosophers had said (reportedly it was Socrates), "for a man to grow old without ever seeing the beauty and strength of which his body is capable." The Jews were not prejudiced against strength. They would match their Samson against Hercules; the two had, after all, been mined out of the same mythological lode. Nor did they object to martial prowess, as they were soon to demonstrate by rebelling successfully against their Greco-Syrian masters. But the beauty of the body, the male body especially, was quite another thing; it was suspect, heathen. Increasingly, the Jews were coming to consider the body as corruptible, sinful, open to innumerable impurities; and they might have continued even further in that direction had not Christianity pre-empted that mode of thinking. Jews saw nothing but trouble in having young men, and graybeards too, running about in the open air stark naked.

The pious of Jerusalem were appalled by the modernization of the city. "Such was the height of Greek fashions and increase of heathenish manners . . . ," the Second Book of Maccabees relates, "that the priests had no courage to serve any more at the altar, but despising the temple and neglecting the sacrifices, hastened to be partakers of the unlawful . . . in the place of exercise after the game of discus called them forth."

Antiochus IV was eager to raise money, and the priests of Jerusalem, by now quite corrupt, were eager to help him, providing they could help themselves in the bargain. Rival claimants for the position of High Priest tried to outbid each other for the profitable office. The first successful bidder was a man named Joshua, who went by the fashionable Greek name of Jason. He held the office for three years, when he was outplayed by a higher bidder, with a name equally Greek, Menelaus, but qualifications that were very questionable since it is doubtful whether he was even of priestly lineage at all. When the populace of Jerusalem discovered that Menelaus was selling the gold and silver vessels that were used in the temple ritual, they rose in rebellion against him. In the year 168 B.C. Antiochus came to his aid, massacred the rebels and helped himself to the temple treasures. The king, the First Book of Maccabees reports, "entered proudly into the sanctuary and took away the golden altar and the candlestick of light, and all the vessels thereof, and the table of the shewbread, and the pouring vessels and the vials and the censers of gold . . ." He also stripped the gold leaf decoration off the temple façade and requisitioned private funds that had been deposited in the temple by the Jews of Judea, who used it as a sort of banking establishment.

Raising money was only part of Antiochus' policy, and the Jerusalem temple was not the only shrine he raided. Another of his programs, equally important, involved the unification of his heterogeneous domain through the promotion, and where necessary, the imposition of Hellenic culture, and the worship by all his subjects of him as a god, the earthly manifestation of Zeus. To this end the king added to his name the title "Epiphanes," which means "God made manifest." If the Jews so desired, Jerusalem could remain their holy city—whatever that meant; but thenceforth it was also to be a Greek city, in which the king and Zeus were to be worshipped.

Many of the faithful fled from Jerusalem to seek refuge in the countryside, or in Alexandria in Egypt where Jews were safe under the tolerant rule of the Ptolemies. But a good many Jews remained. Among them there were some, members of the upper classes, who welcomed the change with pleasure for they were eager to abandon their barbarous native traditions for the clear light of Hellenism. Joined by Syrian colonists sent by the king, they lived under the protection of a Syrian garrison which guarded them from the wrath of their former coreligionists. To the city came a philosopher from Athens, the big-time, to teach the neophyte Greeks how to comport themselves in a proper Greek way —or from another point of view, that of the Second Book of Maccabees, "to compel the Jews to depart from the laws of their fathers and not to live after the laws of God."

The Jews were the only subject nation that opposed the king's

Hellenization campaign. They were also close to, and very susceptible to the blandishments of Antiochus' rival, the king of Egypt.
And so Antiochus resolved to end the danger of Jewish opposition
by eradicating the Jewish religion. The practice of Judaism was
forbidden; circumcision was declared a crime; the burning of the
Torah was ordered. Jews were forced to participate in pagan religious festivals, worshipping Zeus, carrying ivy instead of willow
twigs and singing hymns to Bacchus instead of to Yahweh. Throughout Palestine they were forced, on pain of death, to sacrifice to idols,
killing not a clean beast, but swine; then they had to eat the unclean flesh. Before committing this sin, many Jews preferred to
sacrifice themselves. Women who chose to defy the royal edict by
circumcising their sons were punished by the slaughter of the
offending innocent whose corpse was hung about its mother's
neck. The temple was given over to the worship of Olympian
Zeus, and to the various Eastern gods identified with him. His altar
was erected in the forecourt, and probably his image as well, and
swine were sacrificed in his honor. "It is the abomination of desolation!" cried the Jews as they fled the polluted city.

A rebellion quickly broke out, led by the family of the priest
Mattathias who had fled Jerusalem as a result of the persecutions to
settle in the small Judean town of Mod'in. When the Jews of
Mod'in were summoned to perform a pagan sacrifice, Mattathias
refused to betray his religion, and when another Jew volunteered
to slay an animal for Zeus, Mattathias, outraged, slew him for
Yahweh, along with the government official who was charged with
making sure that the Mod'in Jews obeyed the law. Accompanied
by his five sons, Mattathias fled the town and sought refuge in the
Judean hills. There others joined them. From their strongholds the
rebels sallied forth into the towns of Judah, overturning altars
dedicated to the pagan gods, killing Syrian officials and their Jewish
collaborators, and inspecting whatever baby boys they encountered to make sure they were circumcised. If they were not, the
rebels performed that sacred operation for them.

When a Syrian army was sent against them, the sons of Mattathias, called the Maccabees after one of them, Judah, who was nicknamed Maccabeus or Hammer, defeated it, and then another, and then a third and a fourth; and then they marched on Jerusalem which was defended by a small garrison of Syrian troops. The Syrian garrison, not daring to emerge from the citadel, watched impotently from narrow windows as the Jews marched into the polluted temple, inspected its pagan trappings and rent their clothes in grief. Covering their heads with ashes, the Jews sang songs of lamentation and sounded a ram's horn; and then they groveled on the ground before Yahweh to demonstrate their grief and horror. Only then did they proceed to purify the shrine. Guarded in their work by a contingent of men whom Judah Maccabee had placed opposite the citadel to make sure the Syrians gave no hindrance, the priests who were appointed for the task of purification destroyed the altar that had been used for pagan sacrifice. Its unclean stones were stored somewhere on the temple mount "until there should come a prophet to show what should be done with them."

The sacred grove of trees that had been planted in the temple court to shelter pagan rites was cut down. A new altar was built for Yahweh of freshly gathered unhewn stones. To make fire for it, the priests rubbed two flints together so that even the temple's fire, that most pure element, should be new and pure. The façade of the sanctuary was refaced with gold; the priests' chambers were rebuilt; and new vessels were provided for the business of sacrifice —new knives for slaughtering the animals, new basins for receiving the blood, new tongs for carrying hot coals, new flasks for oil. A feast of rededication and consecration was held on the 25th day of the Hebrew month of Kislev in the year 164, three years after the temple had first been polluted. It was celebrated "with mirth and gladness" for a week, and of course with animal sacrifices. And it was decreed that thenceforth "every year those days should be kept of the whole nation of the Jews," a decree the Jews have obeyed calling their festival Hanukkah, which means "dedication" or "consecration."

The Maccabees concluded a treaty with the Syrians, giving the Jews religious freedom once again and virtual independence, although a Syrian garrison remained in Jerusalem to exert nominal control. A new High Priest was appointed, acceptable to both the Jews and the Syrians. But he proved to be too pro-Syrian, and a struggle lasting two decades ensued between the Maccabees and the Syrians. Four of the sons of Mattathias were killed off one by one, but year by year the Maccabee cause gained more power and the Jews gained more independence. In 161 B.C. Jerusalem sent an emissary to Rome to invite her help against the Syrians. The Romans gave moral but no military support. The Jews had to fight alone. But they were aided by the weakness of the Syrian royal dynasty, and in 142 the foreign garrison was finally expelled from Jerusalem. Two years later the surviving Maccabee brother, Simon, became ethnarch of Judah, entitled to wear royal purple, to serve as High Priest of the temple, to govern the country with decrees issued in his own name, and to pass his position on to his descendants. He was not appointed as a Syrian official but elected by the Jews, by a great assembly of priests and people called the Knesset, which is what the Israelis today call their parliament. For the first time since the Babylonian conquest in 586 B.C. Jerusalem was independent. The second of the three Jewish commonwealths that have arisen in Jerusalem had come into being.

It was to survive little more than two centuries, one of many little Levantine states that arose as the power of Syria decayed, and that decayed themselves as the Roman empire gobbled up the lands of the Eastern Mediterranean. Simon, its first ruler, was called Simon the Just by his subjects and their posterity, although the inhabitants of the town of Jaffa, which he conquered and gave the choice of exile or conversion to Judaism, might question the justice of that appellation. He led the young commonwealth on a path of conquest and the direction he chose was a significant one. His sei-

zure of Jaffa, a port barely forty miles from his capital, gave Jerusalem an outlet to the Mediterranean world whose commercial
prosperity was soon reflected in the city. Under the Hasmoneans,
as the Maccabee dynasty was called, Jerusalem and Judea flourished. Simon's son, John Hyrcanus, resolved to regain for the Jews
the territories they had lost over the centuries. He marched against
the Samaritans in the north, conquered their land and destroyed
their temple which claimed to rival that of Jerusalem. In the south
he moved into the Negev and overwhelmed the Idumeans, giving
them the choice of conversion to Judaism or death. They converted. As a result of the conquests and forcible conversions
effected by John, his father and his son, by 100 B.C. the Jewish
state stretched from Lebanon to the southern deserts and from the
Mediterranean to the Eastern bank of the Jordan. Its foreign inhabitants had been converted, exiled or completely cowed. The
land was Judaized as completely as Antiochus had hoped to Hel-
lenize it. It was not a gentle process.

The Hasmoneans were no less ungentle at home. Their dynastic history after the first few generations is marked by a melancholy
record of fratricide, matricide, tyranny and greed, drunkenness,
and civil strife. The Jews quickly decided that they deserved better
than that, rebelled and sought to end Hasmonean rule. A delegation came to bloody John Hyrcanus requesting him, without success, to resign as High Priest and retain only his position as ethnarch.
When Hyrcanus' son Aristobulus assumed the title of king, although his father and grandfather had been content with that of
ethnarch, the populace of Jerusalem was outraged. Kingship belonged to the dynasty of David, and to the Messiah, who they believed would some day arise from that dynasty and usher in the age
of the heavenly Jerusalem; by right there ought to be no other
king in the city. The next ruler (and king) Alexander Jannaeus,
had to build a special bridge in Jerusalem to provide a sheltered
passageway from his new palace to the temple and protect him
from the reproaches of his subjects. That did not save him from

being pelted with citrons in the temple courtyard one day during the Feast of Booths by an angry mob, which was armed with that fragrant and easily hurled fruit in observance of the religious law. The offending worshippers were slaughtered on the spot. In the future the king protected himself in the temple court behind a barricade which kept his subjects from getting too close to him as he was performing his religious duties.

The rebellions that broke out against John Hyrcanus and against his son Alexander Jannaeus were popular movements led by the Pharisees, a party of the devout who refused to associate themselves with aliens or Jews who adopted alien customs. Their very name may derive from a word meaning "separate." Separate though they imagined themselves, the Pharisees managed to involve themselves deeply in the affairs of the world. Simon the Just had been enlisted to their point of view as had the mass of Jews in Jerusalem who agreed with the Pharisee position that called for adherence to the Torah, but not an adherence so strict as to impose an intolerable burden on people. The opponents of the Pharisees were the Sadducees, the party of the priests, who were by now almost completely estranged from the populace. They were absolutely inflexible in their interpretation of Jewish law and brooked no modifications of it. The conflict between these parties became political, social, economic and philosophical, reflecting an increasing polarization between the rich and the poor. Naturally the Sadducees were on the side of the king.

Jerusalem was the major center of the Pharisee movement, and its citizens constantly made their disapproval of the king evident. They were appalled by the presence of Alexander, a drunkard and a warrior, officiating at the temple. It was to Jerusalem that Alexander carried eight hundred captured Pharisee rebels, whom he crucified before the eyes of the horrified citizens, who had never before seen the barbaric punishment that was to be linked so inextricably to their city's fate. The king himself, the story goes, sat feasting and drinking with his concubines overlooking the execution place. Despite his efforts, or perhaps became of them, Alexander never fully suppressed the rebellion. A group of Pharisees, refusing to dwell in the holy city made so unholy by his presence, left Jerusalem and established a communal settlement at Qumran overlooking the Dead Sea, and there waited for God to send another ruler, a priest-king of righteousness, to replace the criminal.

These refugees formed the nucleus of the group known as the Essenes, one of a number of fanatical groups that sprang up at the time as the Jews attempted to adapt their national and religious life to the complex Hellenistic world. The Essenes adapted by fleeing from that world, by ignoring it and inventing another world to take its place. Instead of its rich colors, they dressed themselves in white. Their answer to the literature of the Greeks was a cryptic literature of fantasy. Abandoning the Jerusalem on earth, with its corruption, its impostor king, its invalid sacrifices performed by spurious priests, they pinned their hopes on a new Jerusalem in heaven. Instead of this distasteful world, they awaited the next, expecting the imminent arrival of the Messiah, who had been promised to them by God's prophets.

Their path—escaping from earth to heaven—was to be followed in one form or other by most of the Jewish nation for the next two centuries. Though many Jews scoffed at the age's Messianic movements, its bitter sectarianism, the suicidal holy rebellions that sought to bring the Kingdom of Heaven alive on earth, the tone of Jewish history in these years was to be set by men who fanatically refused to accept the world the way it was then. Sadly for them, the way it was then was controlled not by their prophets, or their Messiahs, or their rebellious zealots, but by realists, those supreme realists who were now confronting the Jews—the Romans.

CHAPTER 5

Death's Dominion

THE Romans came to Judea in the year 63 B.C., not as enemies but as invited guests, dangerous guests whom it was impolitic
to cross, but guests nevertheless. They had been invited as a result
of a civil war between two princes of the ruling Hasmonean
family, Aristobulus and Hyrcanus, brothers, both of whom claimed
the Judean throne. Each pleaded for aid from the Romans, whose
empire now stretched from Spain to Syria, and their pleas were
countered by those of a delegation of Jerusalem citizens who came
to the Roman general Pompey urging him to listen to neither
claimant, but rather to abolish the monarchy, place Judea under
Roman protection and leave the government of the country in the
hands of the priests. The Romans accepted the bribes they were
offered by both princes, and, naturally, made their decision in
favor of the one they supposed they could control more easily,
Hyrcanus. The loser decided not to lose without a fight; he was, as
the Romans had judged, not very tractable. With a company of his
supporters he seized the temple. But when the Romans, led by
Pompey, came marching up to Jerusalem to enforce their decision,
he thought better of his resistance and offered to buy them off. At
this juncture his supporters refused to support him anymore. They

destroyed the bridges connecting the temple with the rest of the city and prepared to hold it against a siege.

Pompey besieged Jerusalem for three months, catapulting stones into the temple courtyard to the peril of the priests who were offering sacrifices there. Three months at six days a week that is, for on the Sabbath, out of respect to the Jews who would not fight on that day, the Romans gallantly refrained from fighting, even though they did continue to build an earthwork embankment from which they could batter down the temple wall. Finally, when the mound rose high enough, they gained entrance. The priests, who were offering sacrifices in the temple courtyard were themselves sacrificed and sent to heaven along with the incense they were burning. They had just finished splashing the blood of a sacrificed bullock on the altar when their own blood was splattered on the pavement.

Curious about the mysterious religion of the Jews, which was known as peculiar throughout the classical world, Pompey walked into the Holy of Holies, and looked around. To his disappointment, he found nothing inside of interest, no idol, no sign of the ass-headed god which rumor asserted that the Jews worshipped. Disappointed, he left the place, giving orders that nothing was to be disturbed, neither the ample temple treasures, nor the sacrificial system. New priests came in and sacrifice was resumed, without the loss of a day. There was, however, another loss for the Jews.

"Now we lost our liberty, and became subject to the Romans," wrote Josephus, the great Jewish historian of the times, ". . . and the royal authority, which was a dignity formerly bestowed on those that were High Priests by the right of their family, became the property of private men." The losing Hasmonean brother, Aristobulus, was taken to Rome, to be kept a prisoner after being marched in disgrace through the streets of the city in Pompey's triumph. The winning brother, Hyrcanus, also lost. The Romans refused to allow him the dignity of kingship; he had to content himself with the title of High Priest, while real power remained with a proconsul appointed to represent Rome. The Judean realm shrank to include only regions populated primarily by Jews. The Greek cities that had been conquered by the Hasmoneans regained their independence under Roman protection.

During the next two decades the Jews rebelled four times against Rome, always expecting and sometimes receiving aid from the Parthians who were building an empire in the East that rivaled Rome's. During these decades, the Romans looted the temple. Not only did they take the considerable sums of gold placed there for safekeeping by Jews from all over the Mediterranean world (in ancient times temples, safe and holy, often doubled as banks; the Greeks used the shrine at Delphi in this way), they also took away the sacred vessels, and even got hold of secret treasure, a hollow wooden beam with a large ingot of gold hidden within. The beam had been offered to Rome's representative in the East, an inordinately wealthy and even more avaricious consul, Crassus, in exchange for his promise that he would loot no more. Crassus took the bribe and then proceeded to requisition the rest of the temple treasure. He got his comeuppance a short time later when the Parthians captured him and killed him by pouring molten gold down his throat.

The Jewish rebellions were failures. One was so bad that 30,000 Jewish captives were sold into slavery by the Romans. Jerusalem was thoroughly battered and the Jews earned a bad name in Rome. "Even while Jerusalem was standing," Cicero wrote, "and the Jews were at peace with us, the practice of their sacred rites was at variance with the glory of our empire, the dignity of our name, the customs of our ancestors. By now it is even more so, when that nation by its armed resistance has shown what it thinks of our rule."

When Julius Caesar gained control of the Roman empire, there was a brief respite for the Jews. Caesar named one of his local admirers, an Idumean princeling named Antipater, procurator of Judea, and under him Jerusalem enjoyed peace, if not contentment.

Thanks to Caesar, Jews were exempt from military service, which was against their religion for it involved sacrificing to pagan gods, and were taxed at a lower rate than other Roman subjects, throughout the empire as well as in Judea. Upon his assassination, Jews were among Caesar's most fervent mourners. And well they might be, for with his death and the struggle to succeed him, they were caught up in another incredibly complex and costly series of wars.

In Rome one man emerged victorious from the wars, Augustus Caesar, who became Rome's first emperor after destroying Brutus, Cassius and Mark Antony, his rivals. In Judea, which was subjected to bloody power struggles like the empire of which it was now a part, the victor was Herod, Antipater's son, an opportunistic and ruthless prince. The sequence of events that preceded his triumph involved a Parthian invasion, a rebellion, tortures, extortions, assassinations, and the expulsion of the High Priest from office. (This was effected by a rival who bit off a piece of his ear and thus disqualified him, for the High Priest had to be a man "without blemish.") From these horrors, Herod emerged unscathed and made his way from Judea to Rome. Although he had no legitimate claim to the title, he convinced the Romans that he ought to be named king of the Jews. The nomination was proposed before the Roman Senate and there approved, with Herod appointed king and "friend and associate of the Roman people." In celebration of the occasion Herod and his Roman lords marched in sacred procession uphill from the Forum to the temple of Capitoline Jupiter, leading a bull decked with garlands to be sacrificed in gratitude to Jupiter.

To the Jews in Rome and in Jerusalem, it seemed as though Yahweh, or at least Yahweh's faith, his chosen people and his chosen city had been sacrificed, too, in the pagan ceremony. When Herod returned to Judea to assume his diadem and the rule of his new kingdom he was forced to fight his way to Jerusalem mile by mile and month by month with the help of a Roman army. After he finally got to the city he besieged it for five months before he could take it. The siege was so bitter and the defending Jews fought with such determination, that when the Romans finally did breach the walls, they killed and looted even more zealously than conquering armies were accustomed to do. Herod feared being left king of a desert, with his capital depopulated and impoverished. He pleaded with the Roman commander of his army to call off his men and spare Jerusalem. When Herod offered him and them a big enough bribe, the Romans finally listened.

For almost forty years Herod was to rule in Jerusalem, despised by the Jews but appreciated by the Romans. The year he conquered the city he began building, and he was the greatest builder Jerusalem had ever seen. Under his rule, Jerusalem became rich and beautiful, "by far the most famous city of the East" as Pliny called it. Herod strengthened the city walls, constructing defensive towers every 200 feet and a massive fortress at one corner of the temple area, the northwest, which he named Antonia in honor of Mark Antony. For a few years he used the tower as his palace, building a secret passage that gave him safe access to the temple, but then he decided he deserved a grander home. At the western end of the city, about where the Jaffa Gate now stands, he erected another palace, "raising the rooms to a very great height," Josephus reports, "and adorning them with the most costly furniture of gold, and marble seats and beds." The rooms were so large "they could contain very many companies of men." Three towers protected the palace. They were named Phasael, after Herod's brother, Hippicus, after a friend, and Mariamne, after his late wife whom he had recently killed. (Parts of the fortifications still remain incorporated into the foundation of the present-day Citadel of Jerusalem.) Thus protected by the memory of his dear ones, even though he had killed one of them, and by a troop of mercenaries that included a company of Germans, Herod was safe from the animosity of his subjects. In his hundred-room palace and its garden that stretched away to the south, he could study Grecian history with his tutor, play with his pet pigeons (he was a great pigeon fancier), and attend theatrical performances, for the palace contained a theater, smaller and safer than the public theater that the king constructed outside the city.

That theater, a hippodrome which lay almost beneath the temple walls, and an amphitheater on the plain outside the city, were constructed by Herod a decade after he conquered Jerusalem, to bring Greek culture to the city, even though history showed that Greek culture was the last thing its inhabitants wanted. Regular games were established on the model of those at Olympia, with competitions in music and poetry, chariot racing and other athletic events, and with that most un-Greek and un-Jewish of sports, gladiatorial contests. The matches, held every fifth year and attracting famous athletes to Jerusalem to compete for rich prizes offered by the King, were named the Actian games in honor of the battle of Actium at which the power of Herod's friend and one-time protector Mark Antony had been destroyed by Augustus Caesar.

The amphitheater where gladiators were thrown into the arena with beasts was particularly abhorrent to the Jews. To them, Josephus wrote, "It appeared . . . barefaced impiety to throw men to wild beasts for the purpose of affording delight to the spectators." They were also dismayed at the gold and silver trophies displayed around the amphitheater, suits of armor set on poles, each representing a nation conquered by Augustus Caesar. The Jews considered them to be graven images, even after Herod took some of the city's leading rabbis to the amphitheater and stripped the armor down to the bare poles to show how harmless they were.

His impiety did not endear Herod to his subjects. To win their loyalty, the king, in the eighteenth year of his reign, embarked on the great building project of his career, the reconstruction of the Jerusalem temple, transforming it into a much finer, larger, and more splendid shrine, but one on which, some rabbis claimed, the holy spirit of God never really came to rest. "I have advanced the nation of the Jews to a degree of happiness which they never had before," Herod declared to his subjects. Therefore, he would render thanks to God for his kingdom and for his wealth by building the temple anew. When he informed the Jews of his project, they were so wary of him that they suspected a trick and refused to allow him to remove one stone of the old edifice until he had gathered enough material to build the new one. To reassure them, Herod collected a thousand wagons, hired ten thousand workmen, and trained a thousand priests in the arts of stonecutting and woodwork; and he collected sufficient stone, "stones that were white and strong," to construct the building. The priests, wearing sandals, for no shoes were to be worn within the holy place, cut them into massive oblongs, 37 feet long if the figures of Josephus are to be believed—and they are dubious as all ancient numerical records are. Only four of these stones were required to compass the full length of the building. The stones were of marble, so that the shrine gleamed in the sunlight. Its massive doors plated with gold and silver shone, too, and its roof was studded with spikes that dazzled the beholder when they caught the sun's rays. They also served the more prosaic purpose of keeping birds, including Herod's pet pigeons, from resting on the sacred roof and soiling it with their droppings.

The temple was set within a wide courtyard and surrounded by a vast double colonnade of pillars that were Hellenistic in style; each pillar was almost forty feet high and carved from a solid block of pure white marble. The gates of the courtyard were golden, and one was more than a hundred feet high. Above it was a great golden vine from which hung huge clusters of golden grapes. "No stranger may enter within the balustrade round the temple," read an inscription in Greek and Latin at the gates that led from the temple's outer court, the Court of the Gentiles which was open to anybody, to the temple mount proper where only Jews could enter. "Anyone caught doing so will bear the responsibility for his death which will surely follow."

Unlike his predecessors as rulers of the Jews, Herod was not a priest and he could not enter the Court of the Priests that surrounded the temple. Even in the Court of Israel that surrounded the Court of the Priests his presence was suspect for he was barely a Jew. He symbolized his own interests by enlarging the Court of the Gentiles so that its dimensions were much greater than they had been in the temple of Solomon. Thus the Jerusalem shrine came to cover more ground than any other temple in the Roman world. To make this vast court, Herod's engineers bridged over part of the valley that lay west of the temple mount, carrying the broad pavement on arches that can still be seen in Jerusalem under the Haram esh Sharif, the Muslim shrine that now stands on the temple site. The walls of the enclosure, made of massive stones almost as big as those that were used on the temple building, are still visible too. They can be seen in the southeast corner of the temple enclosure, which today forms part of the Jerusalem city wall, and at the Wailing Wall, which the Jews call *Kotel Maaravi*, the Western Wall, because it was the western wall of the temple.

The money for building the temple was provided by Herod. Much of it was derived from the highly rewarding Arabian trade whose caravans passed through the desert city of Petra where Herod's mother had been born, the daughter of a merchant prince. Once the temple was built, money for its upkeep came from the Jews. By this time there were millions of them, almost as many perhaps as there are today. Wherever they were they contributed an annual offering to the Jerusalem temple, a half-shekel which was equal to two Greek drachmas. In every city of the Diaspora there was a bank where this money was collected, and a special dispensation from the Roman government allowed the Jews to export bullion to Jerusalem. The self-imposed temple tax paid for the priest's garments and for the precious incense burned to Yahweh, for the daily sacrifice customarily celebrated on behalf of the Jews, and the one that had been instituted on behalf of Caesar and the Roman people. When pilgrims came from the lands of the Diaspora to sacrifice at the temple during the pilgrimage festivals, they brought their contributions with them. Money-changers set up their tables in the temple's Court of the Gentiles to exchange the pilgrims' coins for temple shekels, which had no graven images on them and were the only coins valid for the temple tax and for the purchase of sacrificial animals.

The broad temple court was the center of Jerusalem life, as busy in its own way as the markets and bazaars to its west and south, with its pigeon salesmen, their coops filled with unblemished pigeons ready for slaughter, its scholars studying the law, its foreign tourists and newly arrived Roman soldiers gawking at the sights as they wandered across the immense space or peered curiously into the inner court where they were forbidden to go. (Sometimes, no doubt, they sneaked in at the risk of their lives and sometimes they entered with the help of Jews; Saint Paul was brought to trial on a charge, probably trumped up, of bringing a gentile into the inner court.) In the temple court food vendors and souvenir salesmen probably hawked their wares. Wandering preachers—Jesus was one—delivered sermons, excoriating the government when they dared. On Mondays and Thursdays the court was especially crowded. These were the days, along with the Sabbath, of course, when the populace of the city made a special point of coming to the temple to pray. At the synagogue in the temple precinct, one of hundreds in the city, rabbis and their disciples studied the Torah and engaged in debate about it, exchanging views by letter with their colleagues in the Diaspora, particularly in that center of Jewish life and learning, Babylon.

To the synagogues and schools of Jerusalem came Jewish youths from abroad eager to learn the Torah, much as their Hellenistic neighbors went to Athens to study philosophy at the famous academy that had been founded by Plato. Saul, later Saint Paul, came to one from Tarsus in Asia Minor; Hillel, who was to become the most influential rabbi of his or any time (Jesus was not, strictly speaking, a rabbi) came from Babylon. The students earned their keep as they learned, Saul, or Paul, as a weaver of some sort in the weavers' quarter at the southern end of town, Hillel as a woodcutter. And when they did not earn enough to pay for their lessons, they eavesdropped on the classes. The rabbis who taught them in Jerusalem's 394 synagogues and 394 academies were usually artisans, too: shoemakers, apothecaries, or even common laborers, woodcutters, or market porters.

At this time, the population of the city was about 100,000, a figure that was doubled or even reached as high as a quarter-million during the pilgrimage feasts. That population lived in the narrow and twisting streets that went up and downhill between the temple at the east side of the city and the palace of Herod at the west. The great mass of the people lived in the lower city, south and west of the temple mount. In the valley west of the temple were the markets and bazaars, as they have been in Jerusalem ever since. Here, too, was the xystus, the colonnaded open space which Herod hoped to make the public meeting place of the town, comparable to the agora or open market of Athens and other Greek cities. The valley was called the Tyropoeon, which means cheesemakers; here evidently cheesemakers plied their trade, along with workers in copper, clothesmakers, and other tradesmen, the more pious among them wearing, in accordance with God's command, headbands and armlets inscribed with portions of His law. Behind the shops, tiny booths as they still are in Jerusalem, most of them no more than six or seven feet square, were the houses in which the lower classes lived. A dark doorway gave entrance into a court-yard; off the courtyard were ten or a dozen rooms, and perhaps an upper story with ten or a dozen more. Each, scarcely larger than one of the shops, sheltered a family, which shared the courtyard with its neighbors.

The courts and the alleys that gave access to them were dirty and malodorous; and their noise and smell was made more offensive by the slaughterhouse sounds and smells coming from the temple above. The worst slums were in the southern part of the city, the old Canaanite town that sloped down beneath the temple walls. Here, between treasure and treasure, between the temple with its vast stores of gold and the tomb of King David where, according to legend, even more gold was buried, lived the poorest of the poor. These were the common laborers and the beggars, many blind or crippled, who loitered about the city gate, at the temple court, or beside the fountains and public baths to beg for alms.

As there was poverty there was hatred—against the king, against the rich who lived in the upper quarter, the fashionable part of town on the west side (it is still the nicer part of town), and against the High Priest and his wealthy colleagues, puppets of Herod and of the Romans, venal men, some so ignorant they did not even know how to write their names. Although the populace stood in awe of the office of High Priest, there was a great gulf between many of the priests and the people. "Woe is me . . . ," wrote one of the rabbis, "they are High Priests, their sons are financiers, their sons-in-law trustees, and their servants beat the people." One High Priest's wife had the streets between her house and the temple covered with silk on the Day of Atonement when the devout were supposed to go unshod, so that she could go to see her husband perform the ritual of his office without setting her bare feet on the dirty streets. Members of the priestly caste lived off rents from their great estates in the countryside, and off tithes and other offerings given by the people. They looked down on the townsfolk and took great delight in tracing their genealogies back to the time of the patriarchs, although many of their poor compatriots could trace their families back as far.

A few of the rich priests and aristocrats did exhibit some social consciousness and some interest in the new religious movements of the time. The historian, Josephus, who was of priestly lineage, went out to live in the desert for a few years to purify his soul. Joseph of Arimathea supported the Galilean prophet Jesus. Jerusalem society ladies formed charitable organizations to help the poor and the suffering; one such group gave narcotics to criminals condemned to die at the hill of Golgotha outside the city, "wine mingled with myrrh," which Jesus refused to take. And a number of aristocrats turned their backs on the party of the Sadducees to which their kinsmen belonged and joined with the Pharisees who were much more concerned with the interests of the poor.

Both Sadducees and Pharisees, both rich and poor shared the prime concern of Jerusalem however, which was the fulfillment of the law (although the Sadducees tended to be even more concerned than their fellow-citizens were.) The rest of the country was much less preoccupied with it. It was physically impossible for the peasant in Galilee to visit the temple for purification each time he defiled himself through contact with a corpse, as at a funeral, or through any one of the other ritual impurities, that according to Jewish law, require a sacrifice before they can be healed. Centuries earlier, before the only authentic temple was at Jerusalem, this was not so much of a problem. Now it was, and so certain aspects of the law fell into disuse outside Jerusalem. But in the city, careful attention was paid to the most minute details of the religious code. As a result, the population of Jerusalem was, as a rule, ritually pure; and other Jews were, as a rule, defiled. And so there was limited contact between citizens and countrymen, and what contact there was was often marked by contempt on the part of the citizen and mistrust on the part of the peasant.

The people of Jerusalem went to great lengths to keep themselves separate from contamination by their less obsessive coreligionists. A description of the city dating from around 250 B.C., reported the existence in the Jerusalem streets of "steps leading to raised pavements, and some walk above and some below—a special precaution to protect those who are purified from contact with anything unclean." But Jerusalem had to make some concessions to the impurity of the countryside; the citizens had to eat. And so it was assumed, sometimes quite arbitrarily, that wine and oil produced in Judea, though not in Galilee, were ritually pure, having been properly tithed and having been produced by men who were not themselves defiled; and that the grain in the grain market had been gathered according to Yahweh's instructions, with one corner of the field left for the gleaners. Anything or anyone coming from within a radius of fifteen miles of the city was acceptable; but the rest of the country was suspect. "Can anything good come out of Galilee?" they asked in Jerusalem when they were confronted with Jesus. And Jesus and his followers in response suspected little good in the priests and Sadducees of Jerusalem.

Jesus was much closer to the city's Pharisees, although the Bible makes it seem otherwise. Like them, he stressed the spirit of the law, rather than its letter, and, like them, he fiercely condemned the excesses of the rich. Like them, he believed in an afterlife, which the Sadducees denied, perhaps because life on earth was so easy for them, although it was so difficult for the poor. But the Pharisees were suspicious of Messianic speculation, of talk about the end of the world although they did say—like Jesus—that much of the Jewish law would be unnecessary when the Messiah did come; men would then know in their hearts the right thing to do, and they would do it. And Jesus believed that the end of the world was at hand, that the Messianic Age had come.

Throughout the century in which he lived, Jewish history was dominated by the curious belief that the time for the end of the world had arrived. Only a part of the people accepted this strange doctrine, but they carried Jerusalem and the rest of the nation along with them. Some believers, like the Essenes, isolated themselves to prepare for the awesome time. Others grouped themselves around wilderness preachers such as John the Baptist, who attracted great crowds with the message, "Repent for the kingdom of God is at hand"; or followed Jesus or one of several other men who were believed to be the Messiah. John and the Messiahs were killed by the authorities, in part because any agitation about the end of the world implied that people were free to disregard the power of the Roman government. And that is what happened a few decades after Jesus' death, when the sporadic rebellions that had been seething for years broke out into a full-scale religious revolt against Rome. The Essenes, the rebels, John who was decapitated, Jesus who was nailed to a cross, the other men who were considered to be the Messiah, all believed that the world was dying, and with its end they believed that death would die too. All believed that they were immortal. The promise of life was the theme of all their preaching.

It has been the theme of Jerusalem's entire history, of the Jews' religion and of the religions that preceded and succeeded it in dominating the city. The very name of the Jews' God probably means life. In the Book of Exodus His name is given as I AM THAT I AM—certainly a cryptic phrase. It is said to mean something like "absolute existence," which is what the medieval Jewish philosopher Maimonides considered it to mean, both it and the proper name of the Jews' God, which is variously written as Jehovah, Jahveh, or Yahweh. Yahweh, the last, is probably closest to the original. The word itself sounds like breath. Its root comes from the Hebrew word for "to be," and if it does not mean "I exist," it means "I bring into existence." Either way it means life.

And life was what the Jews worshipped. Like the Muslims who were to come to Jerusalem later, they protected life by surrounding it with a structure of laws. The only way to deal with life in a threatening universe was, they believed, through observance of Yahweh's laws. "See I have set before thee this day life and good and death and evil"; they were told when they received the law at Sinai, "in that I command thee this day to love the Lord thy God, . . . to keep his commandments and his statutes and his judgments that thou mayest live. . . . Therefore choose life, that both thou and thy seed may live." The Muslims were to hear the same thing, in a simpler way. "Everything is perishing but His face," the Koran says. Allah is immortal, man is mortal and powerless, and only through total identification with His will can man survive.

This was the belief of Jews in Jesus' time and it is still their belief. But at the time there was also another response among them, not so much to protect life as to overwhelm death, to gain immortality. This desire for endless life inevitably made some Jews deny life, in effect, by claiming that life on earth is unreal or meaningless or bad and only life after death important. The early Christians came to adopt this point of view and intensify it. "They that are in the flesh," wrote Saint Paul, "can not please God." And with a terrible yearning, the early Christians and many other Jews denied death too. According to the age's reading of the Bible, death was not natural. It had been imposed on man as a punishment for sin, and it would be overcome with the advent of the Messiah. "Death hath no more dominion," Paul wrote, to Christians who believed that the Messiah had already come.

The end of death's dominion was what Jesus began preaching in Galilee sometime around the year 25. There he gathered a faithful following—"the multitude," "a great multitude," "an innumerable multitude," says the Bible again and again. His teaching had an overwhelming power to move people, and it was made even more overwhelming by his followers' belief that he was the Messiah, and by demonstrations that served to confirm their belief. Some of these demonstrations, healing the sick through faith, are reported as miracles in the Bible. Others are scarcely reported at all, healing the angry through preaching love, the avaricious through preaching charity, the desperate through preaching hope. His teaching was predicated on the concept that the law of Jerusalem was about to be superseded. The city's preoccupation with ritual defilement was meaningless. "There is nothing from without a man that . . . can defile him," he said, "but the things which come out of him, those are they that defile the man." Now that the Messianic Age had arrived, love had taken the place of law. Jerusalem's prophets had always said it was more important.

This was not a message that would endear Jesus to the temple establishment in Jerusalem. He came to the city at Passover in the year 29, for the last of his visits there. By now, Jerusalem was no longer ruled by Jews; Herod had died the year of Jesus' birth. A few years after his death, Rome had abandoned even the pretense of independence for Judea. Herod's kingdom was divided into fourths, and Jerusalem, its turbulent center, was placed under the rule of a Roman procurator. During the Passover feast, Jerusalem was crowded with scores of thousands of pilgrims. In the city or in nearby villages they rented rooms in which to sleep and enjoy their communal meals. Some without accommodations slept in huts on the surrounding hills or in the open air, pleasant at the springtime feasts of Passover and Shavuoth and pleasant again during the autumn Feast of Tabernacles. Both townsmen and peasants were accustomed to sleeping in the open anyway, on the rooftops during the summer heat or in the fields at harvest time to guard the crops. To accommodate the numerous pilgrims (and their animals which also took up space) temple sacrifices were performed in three shifts, with the great court of the temple emptying and filling up again each time. To watch over the pilgrims, especially during these turbulent times when a man rumored to be the Messiah had ridden into the city on a white ass, as the Messiah was supposed to do, the Roman garrison stationed in the Antonia tower overlooking the temple court would be at its most vigilant.

The week before the feast, as the great crowds were arriving, Jesus stayed in the village of Bethany over the crest of the Mount of Olives, and from there went into the city daily to preach in the temple. There, if the gospel is to be credited, he attacked the moneychangers (disrupting their business by the way at the height of their season) and expelled them from the temple courtyard. One scholar suggests that this was one move in a planned rebellion to be led by Jesus against the rich, the Sadducees, and their Roman allies.

On the eve of Passover, Jesus and his followers, like thousands of their coreligionists, purchased one of the thousands of lambs that had been driven to the city for the occasion. Jesus, as the leader of the group, drove the lamb to the shambles just north of the divine altar and in front of Yahweh's temple, to be sacrificed to Yahweh that day as the next day he, the slaughterer, would be slaughtered, too. The lamb's innocent throat was cut, the blood collected for God, the carcass skinned, the innards thrown into a reeking pile for burning on the altar, and the good meat set aside to be brought to the room hired for the Passover meal and there roasted and eaten, along with bread and wine at Jesus' Last Supper.

From the hill that is today called Mount Zion, the site of the Last Supper, Jesus walked through the city and out an eastern gate down across the valley of Kidron to the foot of the Mount of Olives. There he and his followers were to camp out that night in a garden called Gethsemane. The authorities had been disturbed by his presence in Jerusalem. They had been watching him, but now they had no way of knowing where he was among the immense crowds until an informer told them.

In the darkness, a few hours after he had arrived at Gethsemane, he was taken prisoner and brought to the house of the High Priest near where he had celebrated the Passover feast, and there imprisoned overnight. At dawn, he was led northward, across the city to the Antonia fortress, and tried before the Roman Procurator, Pontius Pilate. Found guilty, he was scourged and then, carrying the arm-beam of his cross, he was walked in procession westward halfway across the city, wearing a sign that said, "Jesus of Nazareth, King of the Jews," to indicate the crimes of which he was guilty—sedition, rebellion, setting himself up as the Messiah. Three times before he reached the gate leading to the place of execution, he fell. He was hoisted on to the cross and nailed to it and there he hung for three hours, his lingering death witnessed only by a few of the curious (in Jerusalem men were not accustomed to defile themselves by contact with death), by the Romans in charge of the execution, and by the women among his followers (the men, fearing arrest, stayed away). Today the paths that he followed in the city are marked by a Basilica at the site of his agony in Gethsemane and a shrine at the place of the institution of the Eucharist, a chapel of his condemnation, a church of his flagellation and his crowning with thorns, chapels at all the places where he fell and at the place where he met his grieving mother, a Catholic chapel of the crucifixion, a Greek Orthodox chapel of the crucifixion, the stone where his corpse was laid and anointed, the sepulcher in which he was put to rest and where, his followers proclaim each Easter Sunday, he rose again "from the dead to trample down death by death, from weak become strong, from mortal become immortal, from the crucified Jesus become the risen Christ."

Sedition, rebellion—a great many Jews of Jesus' time were guilty of the same crime. In Jesus' lifetime, shortly after Herod had been laid to rest on a purple-draped bier of gold embroidered with jewels, a revolution broke out sparked by the rabbis of Jerusalem who inaugurated public mourning at the temple, not for the late king, but for his late victims, youths who had been executed just before the king died for attempting to remove a great golden image of an eagle that Herod had placed over the temple gate as a tribute to Rome. When soldiers were sent to the temple to quiet the rabbis, they were stoned. Another troop was sent after the first. A riot broke out in the temple court and thousands of worshippers were massacred. Roman troops came down from Syria and took over all the city's formidable fortresses. An army of Jews came against them and began to besiege the Romans. As usual, Rome got the upper hand. The Jews again were massacred, parts of the temple cloister were destroyed, the temple treasure was looted, and Jerusalem placed under the control of a Roman procurator.

One of the early procurators—it was Pontius Pilate—made the mistake of ordering his troops to bring their ensigns into the city, ensigns displaying the image of the emperor who was worshipped as a god. The Jews pleaded with him to remove the graven images, and when Pilate refused, they insisted. Citizens gathered in the marketplace were warned that they would be massacred if they continued to oppose the procurator. The Jews bared their necks for the slaughter, and knelt down before the Roman soldiers. ". . . sooner ready to be slain," Josephus reports, "than that their law should be transgressed. Hereupon Pilate was greatly surprised at their prodigious superstition and gave order that the ensigns should be presently carried out of Jerusalem." When he requisitioned temple money for the worthy purpose of building aqueducts, he was faced once again with a Jerusalem mob. This time he did not back down and there was another massacre.

There was a near riot shortly after Jesus' crucifixion when the emperor Caligula sent orders that his statue be set up in the temple and worshipped as a god; but peace was maintained thanks to the good sense of the official who was procurator at that time, and who managed to evade the order. A few years later there was another riot in the temple, at Passover, when one of the Roman soldiers, traditionally stationed there during the festival to guard against trouble, got angry for some reason at the natives, hitched up his tunic, and turned around to display his bare bottom to the crowd of worshippers, accompanying his indelicate demonstration with, Josephus says, "such words as you might expect upon such a posture." The Jews responded with such actions as you might expect at such a provocation, and the Romans responded in a predictable manner too. The battle led to a massacre, and the massacre to a stampede; together they accounted for thousands of casualties. That was in the spring. In the autumn a party of Galilean Jews en route to Jerusalem for the Feast of Tabernacles got into a squabble with some Samaritans. A little war broke out between Galilee and Samaria, for Galilee was even more tumultuous and prone to rebellion than Jerusalem, and the rest of the country was not far behind either place. Hearing of the war, the Jews gathered in Jerusalem for the festival marched northward in arms to the aid of the Galileans, despite pleas for restraint by the leading Jews of the city who, dressed in sackcloth and ashes, begged them to stop, fearing Roman reprisals against the city and temple. Around the year 45 A.D., the citizens of Jerusalem were invited to a public exhibition of the head of a prophet Theudas, who had annoyed the Romans and aroused the Jews by promising that the River Jordan would open and the Jews would be able to walk across dry land to freedom, away from Roman tyranny. A few years later another prophet came into Jerusalem and promised the people that God would annihilate the Roman garrison and establish his own kingdom. He led his followers to the top of the Mount of Olives where they awaited the end of time. For them it came when Jerusalem's Roman garrison ascended the Mount of Olives and annihilated the prophet and his band.

There was unrest everywhere. Bands of Zealots gathered together, vowing to serve no master but God, vowing to end Roman rule, to bring on the violent time that would usher in the end of the world. They took to the hills of Galilee swooping down on the rich, gaining strength and numbers as the years went by and as Roman taxation became more burdensome, for Roman taxation, never light, had become almost unbearable. The procurators coming to the country were interested only in squeezing out enough to make a sizable fortune before they had to return home. As taxation increased, hatred against the rich increased, for the majority of the rich were on the side of order, and order in this case meant Rome. There was hatred of Jew against Samaritan and Greek, hatred which was reciprocated fully as Samaritans fought the Jews and as the Greek cities of Palestine chipped away bit by bit at the civic rights of their Jewish inhabitants. There was hatred of Jew against the small band of Christians which had gathered in Jerusalem, hatred marked by stoning and riots; and there was fierce hatred of Zealots against Jews who counseled accommodation with Rome. In Jerusalem a band of assassins called Sicarii, or dagger men, cut down Jews they considered too friendly to the Roman cause. If captured by the Romans, they managed to purchase their freedom by bribing the procurator, raising ransom money by robbing the rich. The procurator set them free and then recaptured them, doubling his profits when they were ransomed again.

In the countryside peasants were forced off the land by the repressive Roman taxation. In Jerusalem, there were pitched battles in the streets between the adherents of rival candidates for the high-priesthood, and strikes by the temple workers. The Levite families that baked bread for the temple and mixed incense went on strike, not against Yahweh for whom they performed these services but against his earthly representatives the priests, demanding higher wages. The priests imported scabs from Alexandria to bake the bread and mix the incense (how the strikebreakers could make the incense according to the proper secret formula remains a mystery). In the year 64 A.D. after the finishing touches had finally been put on Herod's temple, there was massive unemployment in Jerusalem. Hundreds of men were thrown out of work and the authorities provided a make-work program for them: repaving streets of the city with white stone left over from the temple project, and then, probably, cutting grooves along the paving stones so that chariots could drive over them without too much discomfort and clatter. But in time Jerusalem ran out of streets and paving stones and the authorities ran out of money, and Rome ran out of time. In 66 A.D. the great rebellion began, the war that was to have such calamitous effects on Jerusalem and the Jewish nation, the most terrible war of all antiquity, with the greatest toll in lives and in destruction.

The occasion for the beginning of the revolt was given by the Procurator Florus, a Roman even greedier and even less sensitive than his predecessors. He decided to appropriate part of the temple treasure on the pretense, which deceived no one, that the government needed it. In Jerusalem, young men with a dangerous sense of humor began satirizing his avarice by taking up a collection for him. They walked through the streets and the marketplace with baskets on their arms, pleading for contributions for the Romans. The people of Jersusalem may have been amused, but Florus was not. From the Roman capital of Caesarea on the coast he marched an army up to the city to punish and plunder it. He was met by a submissive delegation of citizens who were full of apology, but before they could apologize, they were sent home. The next morning Florus, enthroned in the palace that Herod had built, summoned the High

Priest and the prominent men of the town before him, and called on them to surrender the young delinquents. The Jews begged his pardon, but reported that it was impossible to find the guilty youths. Besides, they were young; naturally a city as big as Jerusalem would contain a few youthful hotheads. Then they indiscreetly added, it might be wiser to placate a rebellious city than to feed its rebellion by finding the boys and punishing them. That, unfortunately, was no way to talk to a Roman. Florus immediately ordered his soldiers into the marketplace to plunder, treating Jerusalem like an enemy town captured in war. The Romans broke into the houses of the rich and looted them, ran their swords through anyone foolish enough to venture into the streets, pulled people, including women and children, out of their houses and brought them before Florus for judgment. He ordered them whipped and crucified.

The Romans withdrew from the city to allow the Jews to think over the grievous situation they had got themselves into, and immediately a civil war broke out in the streets of Jerusalem between rival Jewish factions—those who wanted to maintain peace with the Romans, no matter what the price, and those who were eager for open war. The peace party started the civil war. They hoped to batter the war party into submission so that they could then make peace with Rome. Jerusalem's strongest point, the temple, was held by the war party; the doves attacked but failed to take it. Without the temple in their possession, the peace party was unable to re-establish the daily sacrifice for Caesar and the Roman people; its omission was tantamount to a declaration of independence, and of war. The Roman garrison, besieged in the Antonia fortress, was captured and executed by the people of Jerusalem. In the lower town, the ancient City of David, the High Priest's palace was looted and burned, and the High Priest was assassinated. The old Hasmonean Palace beside the temple was looted and burned, too. All public records of indebtedness that the mob could lay its hands on were destroyed. The Rebellion had begun in earnest.

An immense assembly of Jerusalem's citizens was convoked in the courtyard of the temple; leaders were elected to be placed in command of the various fronts where Roman attacks might be expected. In charge of Galilee was a member of the priestly caste, Joseph ben Mattathias, Josephus, who has left us a stirring, if one-sided history of these years. The Jews hoped for aid from their coreligionists abroad, and from the Parthian enemies of Rome. There were futile riots between Jews and gentiles in Alexandria, but no help came from the Diaspora or from the Parthians. Efforts to defend the country were hampered by discord among the Jews. For the defeat and virtual massacre of the peace party in the early weeks of the war did not put an end to factional strife. The Zealots, who wanted to fight the war to the finish, struggled to gain command of the fighting from the moderates. The moderates saw how suicidal it was to battle Rome, and seized every opportunity to diminish the war's intensity, hoping to salvage the country with a gentle defeat. Josephus followed this policy in defending Galilee. He eventually surrendered to the Romans, becoming a pet of the Roman generals, Vespasian and Titus, who were in charge of prosecuting the war. As a result, the moderate leaders were assassinated or disgraced as traitors and the Zealots succeeded in taking over the direction of the war.

Once the Zealots had attained control of the Jewish cause, a three-cornered civil war broke out in Jerusalem among three Zealot generals, a civil war undignified this time by any ideological pretexts. One band of Zealots controlled the temple, and continued to perform the daily sacrifice while fighting off its rivals. A second group, driven out of Galilee by the Roman victories, controlled the rest of the city. The factions were so consumed by hatred of each other that despite the fact that a Roman siege was imminent, one of the Zealots' groups set fire to immense supplies of grain in storehouses around the temple to keep them from falling into the hands of their rivals. From this sort of insanity, the city's small congregation of Christians fled. Like the Zealots, they were certain that the end of the world was at hand. But they did not believe, as the Zealots did, that its end would be hastened by the bloody death of the righteous in Israel fighting against the Romans. They abandoned their houses and their meeting places and made their way to the town of Pella, east of the River Jordan.

It took the Romans a few years to pacify the countryside; even then the pacification was incomplete, although it did free the Roman armies for the attack on Jerusalem. Finally in the spring of 70, an immense army marched up to Jerusalem and surrounded the city. It was Passover time, and the Roman army was joined by another army, pilgrims come to sacrifice at the temple—for the last time as it turned out.

The city the Romans began to besiege was one of the best fortified in the world. On three sides it was protected by deep ravines with high walls above them. The only flat land was on the north and here there were three walls protecting the city, one within the other. Inside at the city's highest point was another stronghold, the temple, best fortified of all and protected on the north by the formidable Antonia fortress.

The Roman army set up camp on the highest hill in the vicinity, one legion on the Mount of Olives and the rest on Mount Scopus, northeast of the city, from which they could survey all Jerusalem. To construct machines with which to assault the walls, the Romans cut down all the trees surrounding the city. Much of the landscape remained denuded until the twentieth century when the Jews began planting trees again. Roman siege towers and battering-rams were moved up against the wall. Although the Jews attempted to set the machines on fire, within fifteen days they had done their work, and the most northerly wall had been breached. The Jews fought fanatically; the Romans, with more experience but with less zeal ("Inconsiderate violence is madness," their commander, the future emperor Titus, reminded them). "Strength combined with skill encouraged the Romans," reports Josephus, who witnessed the siege from the Roman camp. "A daring spirit, nourished by fear, united with their natural fortitude under calamities, emboldened the Jews." A few days later, when the Romans breached the second wall, the Jews succeeded in throwing them back.

Faced with opposition so fierce, Titus decided to attack the Jews' morale rather than their walls. He stopped the assault, and began to parade his army in full panoply before the defenders to show them what they were up against. The parade—it was a pay parade—was held in the northern part of the city, within the recently captured first wall, but outside the range of the Jews' arrows. It took four days for the parade to finish, for some thirty thousand men to receive their money. All were dressed in full battle array, their breastplates gleaming in the hot sun. The Jews within the city ran to the walls to look. "The whole old wall and the north side of the temple were full of spectators," says Josephus.

The Jews were impressed, but they remained defiant and Titus was forced to resume the attack. When no surrender came, artificial mountains were constructed against the wall. The Jews managed to mine one of them, and set it on fire, and it collapsed with a great noise to the horror of the Romans. The Jews then succeeded in demolishing the others and setting fire to the Roman war engines, too.

Meanwhile, within the city, food had almost run out. Famished citizens gnawed leather sandals and killed their fellows for a piece of bread. A case of cannibalism was reported. At night Jews sneaked outside the city walls to graze in the fields. If they were caught by the Romans, they were crucified; if by the Zealots, they were robbed of whatever food they carried back. Jewish soldiers broke into house after house, seeking supplies of grain, trying to make sure they would be able to eat enough to keep fighting. Anyone suspected of holding out supplies was tortured. The famine was aggravated by the Roman habit of sending captured Jewish soldiers back into the city with their hands cut off. They could no longer fight, but they could still eat. Many Jews tried to flee the doomed city. If they were caught by the Zealots, they were executed as traitors. If they were caught by the Roman soldiers they would be slit open, and their innards inspected to see if they had swallowed any gold coins. Still the Jews refused to surrender. They preferred death, they said, to slavery. God himself was on their side, and He would protect His temple and His holy city.

As the famine got worse, the Romans increased the sufferings of the city's defenders by displaying tempting food outside the walls where it could be seen by the Jews. Soon the defenders were so weakened by hunger that they could no longer sally outside the walls; all they could hope for was to defend what they had. The famine, Josephus writes, "devoured the people by whole houses and families; the upper rooms were full of women and children that were dying by famine and the lanes of the city were full of the dead bodies of the aged; the children also and the young men wandered about the market places like shadows, all swelled with the famine, and fell down dead wheresoever their misery siezed them. . . . Nor was there any lamentation made under these calamities, nor were heard any mournful complaints; . . . for those who were just going to die looked upon those that were gone to their rest before them with dry eyes and open mouths. A deep silence also and a kind of deadly night had seized upon the city. . . ."

With the defenders so demoralized, the Romans began to rebuild their earthworks. This time the Jews were unable to stop them. In July, some four months after the siege had begun, the Romans succeeded in breaching the wall opposite the tower of Antonia. Despite a furious defense by the Jews, they managed to hold onto and then demolish the fort. From that vantage point, the Romans reached the streets of the city as the terrified remnants of the population fled for safety into the temple. For more than a week the temple held out against the Romans' battering-ram that was beating at its gate. Finally the Romans set fire to the gate to force their way in. The Jews retreated into the inner court. The next day the Romans succeeded in entering the inner court, too, capturing and killing great numbers of the defenders. The Jews retreated again, this time into the temple building, where they held out for another day. Around the few survivors who huddled in the sanctuary the outer courts of the temple burned; the next day the Romans came up to set the temple building itself on fire. It was the ninth day of Ab, the anniversary of the day on which the temple had been destroyed by the Babylonians in 586 B.C. Before the flames consumed the building entirely, Titus went into the temple and looked around, as the first Roman conqueror of Jerusalem, Pompey, had done more than a century before. As he left the building, the altar of sacrifices at the front was surrounded with the bodies of the Jews who had died defending the sanctuary. "Round about the altar," wrote Josephus, "lay dead bodies heaped upon one another, as at the steps going up to it ran a quantity of their blood. . . ." Throughout the temple precinct, the Jews were "everywhere slain and everywhere beaten . . . they were weak and without arms and had their throats cut wherever they were caught."

Once the Romans had secured the temple, or rather the ruins of the temple, they carried the ensigns of their legions into it and offered sacrifices to them, slaughtering animals instead of people this time. There were still Jews holding out in the old town below the temple and in the upper city. To gain access, the Romans constructed banks of earth against the hill of the upper city; it took more than a month for them to capture it. They set it on fire along with the oldest part of the city. Some Jews fled to caves and quarries beneath the town and to underground passages beneath the temple and sallied out to attack the Romans, until they, too, were captured or hunger finally forced them to suicide or surrender.

In the temple precinct, an immense herd of starving captives was held under Roman guard. There was food enough for them in the Roman camp, but their captors withheld it and many died of starvation. When food was finally offered to them, some of them died willfully, refusing to take anything from the tainted gentiles. Those among the captives who could be identified as belonging to any of the Zealot bands were executed. The old and the sick were executed. Boys and girls under the age of seventeen were sold into slavery; they would fetch a good price and might end up as house servants. Jews older than seventeen were less fortunate; the mighty hand and strong arm of Rome sent them back into the land of Egypt to work in mines there, back into the house of bondage from which their ancestors had been led forth centuries before by the mighty hand and strong arm of Yahweh. The handsome young men were put aside to be marched through the streets of Rome in chains when Titus celebrated his triumph. "Titus also sent a great number into the provinces as a present . . . that they might be destroyed upon the theatres by the sword and by the wild beasts," Josephus writes. The general took others along with him as he and his army marched off in triumph to Caesarea, Beirut, Antioch, and the other Greek towns of the Levant, giving gladiatorial shows with Jewish captives everywhere he went.

And Jerusalem was abandoned. Yahweh had received another sacrifice. Rome had triumphed, Judea had fallen. The image of the conquered province, a woman mourning beneath a palm tree, appeared on a commemorative coin, struck by the Romans. *Judea Capta*, it said—Judea taken captive. Whatever temple treasures could be found—the temple menorah, a table for shewbread, garments of the priests, the silver trumpets sounded at the morning and evening sacrifice—were taken to Rome, displayed to the citizens of that city and probably placed in the temple of that deity who was so alien to both Rome and Jerusalem, the goddess Pax. When Rome in turn fell sacrifice to history, they disappeared. One report claims that they fell in the Tiber during the disturbances attendant on the conquest of the city in 312 by the first Christian emperor, Constantine. Another says that they were taken from

Rome, along with other plunder, by the Vandals who sacked that city in the year 544. And a third says that they are still hidden somewhere in Constantinople, where they were brought after the Vandal kingdom was overthrown. And someday they may turn up again.

CHAPTER 6

Aelia Capitolina

For Westerners, no matter how objective they may be, it is difficult to see the fall of Jersualem in 70 A.D. as anything but the ringing down of a curtain on the history of the Jews after the dramatic climax of the coming of Jesus. Before the crucifixion the Jews were a nation; after it they became merely a people, with a fate instead of a history. But to the Jews of the time the catastrophe meant no such thing. To them it seemed to be just one more painful reversal in a history that had seen many reversals and part of a mysterious process that would lead some day to the coming of the Messiah. After all the temple had been destroyed once before and then rebuilt; there was no reason why it should not be rebuilt again. And so they set themselves to figuring out the cause of the city's fall and the nation's overwhelming defeat, hoping to speed the temple's reconstruction by correcting whatever sins they had committed so grave as to bring down God's wrath on them. Some blamed the city's fall on the desecration of the Sabbath; others on the neglect of study and the contempt felt for men of learning. One rabbi supporting this position said that Jerusalem fell because the schoolboys played hookey. Others said it had fallen because the Jews of the city obeyed the letter of the law rather than its spirit and failed to temper their dealings with understanding and mercy. Whatever the explanation, the rabbis set themselves to recording the most minute details of the temple services so their descendants would be able to resume them in perfect style once the sanctuary was rebuilt.

Jewish history may not have ended with the fall of Jerusalem but it did enter a new phase. As a result of the temple's fall there was a radical transformation of the structure of Jewish society. The temple priests had lost their function; they and their descendants, many named Aaronson or Cohen, which means priest, became merely a caste with minor ritual obligations but undistinguished otherwise from the mass of Jews. Their aristocratic allies, the Sadducees had lost the basis of their power. There was no longer any Jewish political administration for them to control. Whatever national life remained now centered on the Pharisees, who devoted themselves to preserving the only precious thing the Jews had left, the law which they endlessly studied, memorized, and interpreted. By keeping them a people apart, the law in turn was to preserve the Jews.

In lieu of the temple sacrifice, the rabbis, led by a scholar who had fled Jerusalem during the siege and reestablished an academy at the town of Yavneh near the Mediterranean coast, compiled eighteen benedictions which were to be, and still are, recited daily by pious Jews. Some of the prayers had traditionally been recited during the temple services. Others were new, among them a petition for the restoration of national independence: "Restore our judges as at the first and our counselors as at the beginning." Another beseeched Yahweh ". . . to Jerusalem Thy city return in mercy and dwell therein as Thou hast spoken; rebuild it soon in our days . . . and speedily set up there the throne of David . . . let our eyes behold Thy return in mercy to Zion."

Bereft of Zion and its temple, the Jews entered into mourning. Some even abandoned the consumption of meat, a food that had been sacrificed as part of the temple ritual, and refused to cohabit with their wives. Why, they reasoned, bring children into a world so sinful and distressing. The rabbis thought otherwise, and condemned Jews who turned their backs on life. Man will be held to account, one rabbinic dictum states, for having deprived himself of the enjoyment of the good things the world has offered him. Decrees were published setting forth appropriate forms of mourning: women were to wear fewer jewels and cosmetics; in each new house a patch of wall was to be left unpainted in commemoration of the temple's loss.

Since then the Jews have piously prayed each day for the rebuilding of the temple and the return of their people to Zion. During the Middle Ages, they often wore black to remind themselves that they were "mourners of Zion." Even today at weddings, in the midst of their joy, Jewish bridegrooms crush a glass beneath their heel to recall the temple's destruction. In Europe since medieval times, Jews have been pursued by their tormentors shouting HEP! HEP! the traditional cry of the Jew-baiter; it is an acronym for *Hierosolyma est perdita*—Jerusalem is lost.

For a brief time around 120 A.D. it seemed as though both Jerusalem and its temple might be regained, for an imperial edict was published announcing the restoration of the temple and the reinstitution of sacrifice at Jerusalem. It was a tribute not so much to the religion of the Jews as to their power; Rome wanted their friendship to serve as a bulwark against the threatening Parthians. The Jews were overjoyed, some of the Jews that is. The Zealots among them were dismayed at the thought of the temple and Jerusalem being rebuilt under any auspices other than those of the Messiah. They began agitating against the temple's reconstruction, as did the Samaritans, the Jews' traditional enemies and rivals. The Romans were confused by the Zealots and convinced by the Samaritans, and the project was abandoned. Then, a few years later, the Romans again decided to rebuild Jerusalem, but this time as a Roman rather than a Jewish city. The imperial prescript ordering the work called for a new temple too, but a temple dedicated to

Jupiter and the Emperor Hadrian in the place of the one that had been dedicated to Yahweh.

At this news, the Jews of Judea and Galilee rose in rebellion again. In the year 130, they recaptured Jerusalem, improvised an altar at the site of the temple, and began once more to offer sacrifices there. This revolution against Rome, led by a general called Bar Kochba whom many considered the Messiah, was even bloodier than the first one had been. According to a Roman chronicler of the war 580,000 men were slain and almost a thousand villages razed. By the time the war was finished Jerusalem, already in ruins, was completely destroyed, and Judea had become a desert, depopulated and defoliated. Olives, one of the country's main crops, were not harvested there again for more than a century. Jews departed for Galilee or the coast, or the lands of the dispersion; many priests settled in Arabia where their descendants would influence the birth of a new monotheistic faith. And, it is reported, even the birds avoided Judea; there was nothing for them to eat there. The Romans had won another war.

To eradicate the stubborn nationalism of the Jews, the name of the province of Judea was changed to Palestina, after the Jews' ancient adversaries, the Philistines. The city which Hadrian ordered built on the site of Jerusalem in 135 A.D. got a new name too, Aelia Capitolina, Aelia after Aelius, the family name of the emperor, Publius Aelius Hadrianus—who is usually cursed whenever he is mentioned by Jews—and Capitolina after Capitoline Jupiter, the city's new divine patron. Soldiers of the Tenth Legion, which had been stationed in the region since the fall of the temple, and Palestinian gentiles who would make up much of the city's new population plowed over the entire area of Jerusalem and then plowed a furrow along the line that would be followed by the new boundaries. This was done not with hostility, but rather as part of the traditional Roman ceremony for the founding of a new town. A triumphal arch was constructed in commemoration of Hadrian's victory over the Jews, and a forum built in the northwest quarter, near the site of Golgotha. North of it was the city's main gate, marked by a tall column from which the Romans and later the Arabs measured all distances in Palestine. Today the Arabs still call the gate Bal al-Amud, Gate of the Column, although the column has long since disappeared. To divide the city into neat quarters (which are still discernible today), the Romans laid out two wide colonnaded main streets that intersected at Jerusalem's exact center. Looking down from heaven it must have seemed as though a great cross had been placed over the city.

Throughout Aelia new temples were built. At Golgotha, where Jesus and other criminals had been crucified, rose temples dedicated to Venus, Juno and Jupiter. Jupiter Capitolinus was honored at a shrine built on the site of the temple of Solomon. Also honored there was Hadrian, whose statue, placed upon the site of the Holy of Holies, received divine honors. Over one of the gates was carved the figure of a boar or swine, the totem of the Tenth Legion. As a graven image flaunted above the gate of the holy city it was abhorrent to Jews; but it was even more hateful as the figure of an unclean beast. No Jew was permitted to enter the city. Any who did enter would be crucified. The only time they were allowed there was on the ninth day of the month Ab, when for a fee paid to the Romans, they could approach the site of the temple and mourn its destruction on the anniversary of that melancholy event, reciting the Book of Lamentations, crying out, "O my heart, my heart, how it grieves for the slain! My bowels, my bowels, how they yearn for the slain!"

Now in Jerusalem the sacrifice of Christ was celebrated instead of the sacrifice of animals. From the time of Jesus' entry into the city in the year 29, until the beginning of the great Roman siege, there had been a Christian community there. Jerusalem's Christians were all Jews who worshipped at the temple and gathered together for their own services in their own synagogue. To outsiders it appeared at first no different from the synagogue of any separate group of Jews—tanners, Galileans, emancipated slaves, or fellow-travelers of the Essenes. But eventually anti-Christian persecutions began. The first Christian martyr Stephen was stoned to death outside the city walls. Saint Paul was brought to trial, accused of sacrilegiously bringing a gentile into the temple's inner court. The leader of the city's Christians, James the venerable brother or cousin of Jesus, was stoned for preaching the new religion. Nevertheless the Jerusalem Christians maintained their identity as Jews, causing a serious rift in the young church. Outside Jerusalem Paul had been summoning all men to follow Christ even if they refused at the same time to follow Jewish law. "There is neither Jew nor Greek," he preached, "there is neither bond nor free, there is neither male nor female: for ye are all one in Christ Jesus." To the Jerusalem Christians this was almost anathema. In the year 49 a precarious compromise was reached at the first Council of the Christian church, a peace conference that took place in Jerusalem between the city's Christians and their fellows who lived outside Palestine. It maintained Christianity as a Jewish sect in Palestine where that would be beneficial and allowed it elsewhere to shake free of its links to Judaism.

The destruction of the temple gave Christians reassurance—if any reassurance was needed—of the eventual triumph of their cause. Its fall, they decided, was just retribution for the crucifixion of Jesus. Obviously God was no longer pleased with the sacrifices that had been given at the temple; a new system had come to replace the old. Now, they believed, the significance of Jesus' sacrifice would be evident to all men. As a result of Jerusalem's fall Christians definitely cast their lot with the world that lay outside Judaism, a religion that seemed to be dead, utterly destroyed along with the temple sacrifice system that lay at its core. To explain their new faith and, incidentally, to dissociate themselves from Judaism and from the rebellious and unpopular Jews, the Gospel accounts of Jesus' life were written, emphasizing the sacrificial nature of Jesus' crucifixion, blaming the Jews for it and exonerating the Roman official Pilate. The Christian view of the fall of Jerusalem—the standard Roman Catholic view until quite recently —was voiced by the early church father Eusebius: "After the pollution caused by the murder of the Lord [Jerusalem] experienced the last extremity of desolation and paid the penalty for the crime of its impious inhabitants."

During the first great Roman-Jewish war, the Jewish Christians of Jerusalem fled to seek refuge across the Jordan. There they remained, and in Aelia a new community of Christians came to take their place. They spoke Greek, not the Aramaic or Hebrew of their predecessors, and they were uncircumcised, for according to Hadrian's edict no circumcised person could approach the city. They worshipped together at the church on the hill that is today called Mount Zion, the place where Jesus had gathered with his disciples at the Last Supper, the place where the risen Christ had appeared and the Holy Spirit had descended on the disciples after the crucifixion inspiring the founding of the Christian church. Originally Zion had been the name of the temple mount. The early Christians transferred the name to their own hill, in order to make the place where the Church had been founded conform with one of the biblical prophecies: "out of Zion shall go forth the law." It is probably the only time that faith has ever moved a mountain.

Aelia was neither the physical nor the spiritual center of Christian life in Palestine. That distinction was reserved for the city of Caesarea on the coast, the administrative center of Palestine. Although Hadrian had hoped to make Aelia important again, it remained a small provincial garrison town. Evidently it requires religious devotion in order to flourish; both Jews and Christians were devoted to it, but neither was strong enough to bring it to life again. The city was hardly affected by the waves of anti-Christian persecution which swept the Roman empire in the second and third centuries. Indeed all Palestine escaped the full fury of these persecutions, primarily because there were still relatively few Christians there. As late as the fourth century, Saint Jerome, living in Bethlehem, complained that there were too many Jews and far too few Christians dwelling in the Jerusalem region.

But as the years went on Jerusalem acquired more importance in the Christian church. In the fourth century, the bishop of the city, a subordinate of the bishop of Caesarea who was himself subject to the Patriarch of Antioch, carried little weight in the councils of the church. By 431 Jerusalem's bishop was himself considered a Patriarch and he claimed primacy over the Patriarch of Antioch. Some time before, the earliest Christian pilgrims had begun arriving in the city. Very early in the third century, the first pious guide book was written describing sites in Jerusalem and Palestine that are mentioned in the Gospels. The author was a native of Jerusalem, named oddly enough Sextus Julius Africanus, which gives us some idea of the mixed origins of the city's population at the time. Enthusiastic churchmen and pilgrims attempted to follow the path of Jesus in the city, among them the Alexandrian philosopher Origen who journeyed to Palestine to "find the vestiges of Jesus, of his disciples and prophets." Through their efforts most of Jerusalem's important Christian sacred places were identified and brought to public notice, and ever since that time they have attracted the veneration of the faithful. Their authenticity has been questioned again and again by later and more skeptical generations, but their identification rests on the most ancient and most reputable traditions that reach back to within a few score years of the crucifixion.

The most prominent of these visitors came to the city about 325 A.D., Saint Helena, Helena Augusta, the mother of Emperor Constantine who had recently converted to Christianity and had made it the official religion of his empire. Helena was as industrious as she was pious. (According to legend she was a British lady, the daughter of a chieftain named Cwl who has been immortalized in folk literature as Old King Cole.) Her visit resulted in the construction of some thirty churches in Palestine on sites associated with the life of Christ. As soon as she arrived in Jerusalem she conscientiously set herself to searching out places connected with—as one pagan-minded Roman chronicler wrote—"the God whom she worshipped." Her pious labors were not inspired by disinterested motives alone; she also wanted to "make thank offerings by means of prayers for her son, now so great an emperor, and for his sons, her own descendants." Helena, "the God-beloved mother of a God-beloved prince" as the chronicler describes her, naturally had fellow feeling for Mary, the mother of God. She commissioned the construction of a large basilica at Bethlehem to commemorate the nativity of Christ. For it her son, the emperor, purchased embroidered curtains and gold and silver liturgical objects.

In Jerusalem Helena sought to discover the most precious relic of the Christian faith, the cross on which Christ had been crucified. Even before she had come to the city she had received a message from heaven telling her where to look for it; when she arrived she was guided by the inhabitants to the exact spot that heaven had indicated. She hired local workmen to dig there; it was one of the first archaeological expeditions in a land that was to see many. But to her disappointment no cross appeared. It was not that the natives, Helena's inspiration, or heaven had been wrong. It was merely that the pagans, seeking to efface all traces of the true faith, had covered the place with so much dirt that it was difficult to arrive at the right level. But Helena, reinforced by a divinely inspired dream, urged the workmen to keep digging, and was rewarded on September 14, 326 by the unearthing of not one, but three crosses—Jesus' and those of the two thieves crucified with him. Along with them were found the "titulus," the tablet Jesus wore as he carried his cross, inscribed by the Romans with his name and his crime, and four nails that had been used for the crucifixion. (Two of them have disappeared from history; the other two were made by Helena into a crown for her son, the so-called Iron Crown of Lombardy which is still preserved in an Italian church.

"An impudent fabrication," one guidebook calls it; "a pious fraud" says another.)

Helena's trove was rich, but it was also embarrassing. Which one was the true cross? The ticklish problem was solved by the ingenuity of the bishop of Jerusalem, Macarius, who suggested to the Empress that all three crosses be brought to the sickroom of a local lady afflicted with an incurable disease. The first cross brought to her had no effect, and the second was equally useless. But when the third cross was taken into her sickroom, she immediately leaped from her bed completely cured. The third, and potent cross was obviously the one on which Jesus had been crucified.

The cross was sheltered in a shrine built on the site of its discovery. Thereafter mass was celebrated daily in commemoration of its excavation, and it was exhibited to the faithful for one week each year on the anniversary of its discovery, the Feast of the Invention of the Cross.

At the site of Christ's sepulcher the pagans had, as the contemporary church historian Eusebius had dolefully written, built "to the impure demon called Aphrodite a dark shrine of lifeless idols . . . offering [there] their foul oblations on profane and cursed altars." The emperor Constantine ordered this temple destroyed and carted outside the city and discarded. But not only was the temple itself polluted; the soil on which it rested and which covered the cave of the Holy Sepulcher had also been tainted. "Inspired by holy zeal . . . [Constantine] issued orders that, having dug up the soil to a considerable depth they should transport to a far distant spot the actual ground, earth and all, inasmuch as it had been polluted by the defilements of demon-worship." The emperor sent a letter to the bishop, Macarius, ordering him to construct a great shrine above the Holy Sepulcher. "Not only shall this basilica be the finest in the world, but . . . the details also shall be such that all the fairest structures in every city may be surpassed by it."

Under the direction of Constantine's deputies, the shrine, called the Church of the Resurrection, rose at the west end of Jerusalem's forum "with choice columns and with much ornament," of marble on the inside and polished stone outside, and boasting, beside the basilica above the sepulcher of Christ, a courtyard and a large cloister with porticoes. "And having decorated it throughout in costly and imperial fashion [the emperor] . . . adorned it with very many gifts of indescribable beauty, gold and silver and precious stones set in different materials." For the ceremony of its dedication, Constantine transported to Jerusalem all the bishops of the church who had been assembled at Tyre for the purpose of condemning a heresy. In the year 335, in September, the bishops, some three hundred in all, marched into the church that was to become Christendom's holiest shrine, and there reenacted with a mass the sacrifice of Christ.

Constantine considered himself "a bishop ordained by God to oversee whatever is external to the church." Much of what was external to the church directly concerned Christians throughout the Roman Empire. The emperor ordered an end to the barbarous punishment of crucifixion. He abolished centuries-old laws that discriminated against the celibate and that had discouraged Christian monasticism; they had been decreed by emperors worried about the empire's declining birthrate. He established a Sabbath to be celebrated weekly throughout the Roman empire; the law was worded in such a way as not to offend pagans who remained a powerful force: "All judges, city people and craftsmen shall rest on the venerable day of the Sun." (A few years later a church council forbade Christians to judaize by resting on Saturday.) The emperor restored church buildings to their congregations; many of the buildings had been taken away from Christians in a persecution. And, most important for Jerusalem, he embarked on a great campaign of church building that would make the holy city as beautiful as it had been before the destruction of the temple of the Jews. Less than a decade after Helena's visit, Jerusalem boasted, beside the new Church of the Resurrection, a church dedicated to Saint Anne, the mother of the Virgin, another at the house of Caiaphas on Mount Zion, a shrine at the tomb of Lazarus in Bethany, and a great, bejeweled cross standing atop Golgotha.

Jerusalem's great program of church building was not interrupted after Constantine's death when Julian the Apostate came to the throne of the empire and restored paganism to favor. But Christians did discover that they now had rivals in the city, the Jews, newly returned to Jerusalem with a building program of their own. In order to destroy the Christian religion which was threatening to overwhelm the ancient Greek and Roman traditions Julian treasured, and to encourage the Jews whose faith might provide a viable alternative to it, the emperor abolished the special taxes that had been imposed on the Jews after the fall of Jerusalem and ordered them to rebuild the temple. "I desire," the emperor announced to his Jewish subjects, to "rebuild by my own efforts the sacred city of Jerusalem which for so many years you have longed to see inhabited [by Jews] . . . and together with you . . . glorify the Most High God therein."

In response to the emperor's command hundreds of Jews came to the city to begin the sacred task. For their labors, the rich among them provided spades and axes of silver. Singing psalms and blessing God for having preserved them to witness that holy day, the Jews dug into the ruins with their precious implements, and carried rubbish away from the site on silken cloths, dyed a royal purple. According to a Palestinian Christian chronicler who a century later described the event, their psalms soon turned to cries of distress, for while they were happily at work laboring to dig foundations for the temple, an earthquake struck, sent by God to drive the Jews away. "Many were caught thereby, some perished immediately, others were found half dead and mutilated of hands or legs, others were injured in other parts of the body." This expression of divine disfavor failed to stop the Jews however. They continued with their work, even after miraculous fire burst from beneath the ground and burned some of the workmen to ashes. Still the Jews kept on, until suddenly the sign of the cross appeared on the garment of each one of them. At that many of them fell to their knees, abjured the faith of their ancestors, confessed the truth of Christianity, sang hymns to Christ and, of course, abandoned work on the temple. The miracle hardly mattered. Six months after the first silver spade was lifted, Julian died. A Christian emperor succeeded him and Jews were once again forbidden to approach Jerusalem—although some managed eventually to work their way in to live in the city.

But Christian pilgrims came and came in increasing numbers as the fourth century progressed. As early as 333 A.D. a fervent French visitor wrote a report mentioning the city's most revered shrines, among them the place where Jesus was tried before Pilate, the stone beside which Judas betrayed him, the column to which he was tied when he was whipped by the High Priest's soldiers, the palm tree whose branches the Jews plucked when they welcomed him to Jerusalem on the first Palm Sunday. Devout researchers continually discovered other relics and other holy sites. A few years later pilgrims could revere the Holy Lance which had pierced Christ's side; it was displayed—the shaft broken in two and mounted in a wooden cross—in a special relic chamber in the Church of the Resurrection. They could also adore the sponge, soaked with narcotic, and the reed for sipping from it that had been offered to Jesus at the crucifixion; the cup, some say of onyx, some say of silver, from which he drank at the Last Supper; the wooden crib in which he rested as an infant; the crown of thorns he wore on his head as he walked for the last time through the streets of Jerusalem; the lamp lighted in his tomb on the Friday he died; the stone on which his body was anointed with oil and cleaned after the crucifixion; the stone that had closed the door of the tomb into which he was laid and which was discovered rolled aside on the third day after the crucifixion.

That stone was cut into two parts each of which served as an altar. It was difficult for the pilgrims to see it or touch it, adorned as it was, according to one of them who wrote an account of his journey, with the offerings of the faithful, "with gold and gems . . . armlets, bracelets, necklaces, chains, rings, head ornaments, waistbands, sword belts and emperors' crowns of gold and gems and very many ornaments given by empresses."

Once again Jerusalem's economy came to be based on the pilgrim trade. Soon most of the city's population was connected with it in one way or another. The most zealous pilgrims could keep busy with religious exercises all day, rising at dawn to visit the different shrines and joining in the services held throughout the day. To guard against boring pilgrims and themselves, the citizens developed a rich liturgy, with church services of various kinds that were soon adopted by churches throughout Christendom. The pilgrims were conducted to the holy places by guides, who spoke with them in Greek and Latin and translated sermons, which were mostly given in a loud singsong voice in Syriac, the natives' language. The guides also piloted pilgrims to shops, where they could buy Jordan River water and holy oil in little flasks made of silver or lead, whose manufacture and sale provided a steady source of income to Jerusalem's citizens. The souvenir flasks were stamped with a cross or a sacred scene, or a representation of a shrine to remind the pilgrim of the sights he had seen during his journey. Those purchased at Jerusalem showed Christ's tomb or the Ascension. The artisans of Bethlehem manufactured for sale in that town flasks depicting the nativity and the adoration of the Magi. Pilgrims who had spent most of their money en route could buy cheaper souvenirs, small terra cotta medallions showing similar scenes. The rich could purchase beautifully enameled crosses containing chambers for the deposit of relics, and the very rich could afford to buy the relics to deposit in them.

Not every relic-hunting visitor was fortunate enough to bring home the nails of the true cross as Helena had, or a portrait of the Virgin said to have been painted by Saint Luke which a later Byzantine empress acquired. But there was a great traffic in relics, the great majority of them fake, and pilgrims with enough money could easily buy a saint's head or at least a finger or toe. Pilgrims too poor to buy them could carry away instead earth from the Holy Sepulcher and many of them took advantage of that liberty. Others managed to acquire splinters of that most potent relic, the true cross which was shaved of innumerable fragments that were carried throughout Christendom. So many were taken that it would seem the cross might well disappear, but fortunately it had the miraculous power of renewing itself. No matter how many relics were taken from it, it never diminished in size. Despite this happy faculty, the authorities decided it would be unwise to try divine favor indefinitely. Eventually priests were stationed next to the cross when it was displayed to make sure no zealous pilgrim kneeling down to kiss the holy relic would bite off a splinter and hide it in his mouth. Pilgrims were forced to revere it from afar. One, named Antoninus Martyr and more scientifically inclined than most of his fellows, inspected it carefully and decided that the wood of the cross was from a nut tree; but he was unable to determine which kind.

Antoninus was probably wrong. The legends pilgrims told each other about the true cross failed to agree on what kind of tree the cross was made from; but none of them say it was a nut tree. According to one Jerusalem story, the wood came from an offshoot of the tree of knowledge that grew in the Garden of Eden, and that as everyone knew was a fruit tree. Another Jerusalem legend claims the wood is a hybrid, part cypress, part pine and part cedar, that grew together from three seeds planted by Abraham.

Such legends appear again and again in the accounts of their journey that were written by pilgrims to Jerusalem. We have a number of these accounts dating from Byzantine times, many of them written by pilgrims as indefatigable in their descriptions as they were in their devotions. One of our chief sources of information for early church practices is the book of a French lady named Sylvia who for pages describes services conducted at the churches in and near Jerusalem. All the pious exercises are there, enough to satisfy the most intense spiritual hunger—psalms in the morning, psalms at the third hour, the sixth hour, the ninth hour or at vespers, the vigils through the night with hymns and antiphons, mass at the great church in Golgotha, mass at the square church of the Mother of God, mass at the sepulcher where Christ rose from the dead, mass at the sepulcher of Lazarus or at the Church of the Nativity; readings, processions, lighting candles, listening to sermons, kissing the cross, the stone of the tomb, the pillar of the flagellation, the holy cup, the holy lance. All this was to bring her and her fellow pilgrims to eternal life in the Jerusalem that hovered in the sky directly above the earthly city, instead of to the gate of hell that pilgrims could see in the valley beneath the city walls. "Go every one of you home now to your cells and sit there for a little while," the Bishop of Jerusalem urged pilgrims and local residents, to rest after such strenuous devotions; and then refreshed, come back "to gaze on the holy wood of the cross, trusting each one that it will profit us for our salvation."

It must have profited many. For they came eagerly and in the hundreds, long and weary distances that would make a modern traveler faint, exhausted. In the fourth century one of Sylvia's compatriots, known as the Bordeaux pilgrim, recorded the entire journey overland from the Atlantic coast of France to Palestine, day by day at a pace of some twenty miles a day with horses changed at post houses each some ten miles apart. The journey was a formidable one. From Bordeaux, fourteen changes of horse to Toulouse; from Toulouse seven to the fortress of Carcasso, the modern Carcassonne; from there three to Narbonne and eight more to Arles; from Arles forty-four over the Alps to Milan; from there over the frontier of Italy to the Roman provinces of Lower Pannonia, Upper Pannonia, Moesia, Dacia and Thracia to the new imperial city of Constantinople—230 changes of horse, 112 days. Across Asia Minor in thirty-three days to Tarsus where, the Bordeaux pilgrim notes, "Here was born the apostle Paul"; and from there to Jerusalem over the same roads Paul had traveled some three centuries before and in about the same time, twenty-five days. It was not, obviously, an easy trip and not one to be undertaken lightly. Later, in less settled times, pilgrims often enjoyed journeying to Jerusalem for reasons that were hardly pious. But in these early centuries, pilgrims were single-minded, desiring only "to adore Christ in those places where the gospel had first shone forth," which is what inspired Saint Jerome who came to live in Bethlehem in the fourth century.

Many pilgrims never left Jerusalem at all, resolving to go to heaven directly from the city as Christ had done. These men and women, Jerome among them, were involved in the ascetic movement that dominated the Christian church in the fourth and fifth centuries when thousands left their homes in the sinful cities to dwell alone in deserts. The center of this movement was Egypt, in the desert east of the Nile; but other anchorites congregated—if self-enforced isolation can be termed congregation—in the wilderness of northern Syria and in Palestine, living in cells within reach, but out of sight of each other, and accessible to a common church and bakery. Anchorites who found that sort of arrangement too crowded retired to the tops of pillars where they perched for years, almost surrounded by heaven. "Tell me, I pray thee," asked one, "how fares the human race; if new roofs be risen in the ancient cities; whose empire is it that now sways the world?"

In Jerusalem and its environs there dwelt an immense population of monks and nuns, many of them in communities, but some living alone atop pillars or in hovels built on the Mount of Olives or in the wilderness east of the city in the hills beside the Dead Sea where the Essenes had maintained their community and where John the Baptist had wandered alone. Many lived in informal establishments called *lauras*, or alleyways, set in rocky gorges between two hillsides that contained numerous caves, each of which housed an individual monastic. One *laura* founded around the year 500 still exists in the desert east of Jerusalem, although fewer than ten monks now inhabit it. Desert monastics prided themselves on their asceticism, their meager diet, their mortification of the flesh. "I kill my body," one monk of the time said, "for it kills me." And although none in the neighborhood of Jerusalem could fail to know what empire then swayed the world, they did manage to turn their backs on the life of mankind, returning to face the world with all the fury of the God-possessed only when they felt obliged to attack some fearsome heresy that threatened the purity of the faith.

Moved by their religious devotion these men and women came from all over the Christian world. Jerusalem itself could boast individual congregations from many lands. "The first men in Gaul hasten thither," Saint Jerome reported, "The Briton . . . leaves the setting sun and seeks a place known to him only by fame and the narrative of the Scriptures. . . . The Armenians, the Persians, the nations of India and Ethiopia and the neighboring country of Egypt . . . Pontus and Cappadocia, Coelesyria and Mesopotamia . . . flock into these places and display to us examples of diverse excellence. Their speech differs but their religion is one. There are almost as many choirs of psalm singers as there are different nations."

In the countryside at Bethlehem nearby, it was somewhat different. "In the village of Christ," Jerome wrote, ". . . all is rusticity, and except for psalms, silence. Wherever you turn, the ploughman holding the plough handle sings Alleluia; the perspiring reaper diverts himself with psalms, and the vine dresser sings some of the songs of David while he trims the vine with his curved knife. These are the ballads of this country." An ecstatic report, like that of a Victorian missionary seeing a biblical patriarch in every long-robed, long-bearded elder of a Palestinian village.

In Bethlehem Jerome lived in a monastic cell and labored at his great task of translating the Bible into Latin, calling on local Jews for help with difficult Hebrew passages. His translation, the Vulgate, is still the official Roman Catholic version of the Bible. Occasionally he left his cell and traveled the five miles or so to Jerusalem; but he did not much like it there. "Sometimes," he wrote, ". . . that we may return the calls of our visitors, we proceed to the doors of proud houses and amid the sneering remarks of the servants enter their gilded portals." He found the hurly-burly of the city distasteful; there were, he noted with pious horror, ". . . prostitutes, actors, buffoons as in other cities." He even saw fit to compare Jerusalem to Babylon.

Before he had come to Bethlehem in the year 386, Jerome had lived in Rome where proud houses, gilded portals, prostitutes, actors and buffoons abounded. There he had been the darling of high society, at a time when preachers were lionized with all the fervor that modern society devotes to painters. Bedazzled by his rhetoric and his religion, Roman ladies abandoned lives of luxury to work for the poor and some even accompanied him out of God-forsaken Rome to live as nuns in the barbarous, but holy land of Palestine. One of these, a wealthy aristocrat with the noble Roman name of Paula, established a convent of nuns next to Jerome's monastery in Bethlehem and even learned Hebrew so that she, like Jerome, could sing psalms in the original. The local reapers did not even do that; they sang them in the vernacular, in Syriac or Aramaic.

When Jerome left Rome he was sadly missed by his lady followers, and in the relentless rusticity of Bethlehem, he must have missed them too despite the consoling presence of Paula and her nuns. (One of the reasons Jerome had originally taken up the study of Hebrew was because he hoped it would help him subdue his baser passions.) "Oh when will that time come," he wrote to one of his admirers, urging her to leave Rome and come to Jerusalem, "when a breathless messenger shall bring us the news that our Marcella has reached the shores of Palestine . . . ? We shall clasp your hands, we shall behold your face, and shall scarcely be able to leave your long wished for embrace." Together, he promised her, we shall "kiss the wood of the cross." Marcella, alas, never came. She never had the chance, for she died in 410 a victim of injuries suffered when Rome was sacked by the Goths.

With Rome's fall to the barbarians, hundreds of refugees came east to Jerusalem, to dwell in the city of God, now that the greatest city of man had proved so vulnerable. They came to Bethlehem too, and their advent disturbed that town's rural tranquillity. Jerome complained of the intrusion. Bethlehem's tranquillity was threatened even more by the religious quarrels that racked Palestine and all Christendom at the time. Jerome found himself in the middle of them. As a result of one, he was excommunicated by the bishop of Jerusalem and almost driven out of Bethlehem. In another, his monastery was burned to the ground by heretics and one of his monks was killed. He and his surviving followers, in fear for their lives, fled to a fortified tower for safety. A few years after his death there was a full-scale battle outside Jerusalem when an army of heretic monks tried to keep a newly-appointed bishop from entering the city because they disagreed with his views on the nature of Christ.

In a series of councils, churchmen had been trying to hammer out a definition of what actually had happened in Jerusalem and in Bethlehem three or four centuries earlier when Christ was born and crucified and resurrected. Was his nature human, or divine, or a mixture of the two? Or was it a combination rather than a mixture, a complete melding of the two. Or was it both human and divine, with the human element predominant, or both human and divine with the divine element more important? Was the man who had been crucified in Jerusalem of the same substance as the God who had ordained the crucifixion? Or was it God himself who had been crucified? Or had Christ not really been crucified at all? Had he instead fled his body leaving it alone to suffer on the cross, while his spirit remained free? Or had he suffered fully, as a man dying in agony suffers?

All these possibilities and more were considered in the theological speculation that went on in Jerusalem and the other cities of the East. Most of the speculation and most of the controversy went on in Constantinople and in Alexandria, the intellectual centers of the Empire. In Alexandria even longshoremen on the docks considered themselves experts in theological argument and argued concepts of the nature of Christ the way their modern successors might argue the merits of various football teams. Jerusalem echoed these controversies, and it still does as adherents of the various interpretations, represented by the different Christian sects of the city, compete with each other violently for places among the shrines.

"I hold it to be a sort of mad folly to research into the nature of God," the Palestinian historian and courtier Procopius declared in the sixth century. "Even human nature can not, I think, be precisely understood by man." It was sensible advice, but it was uncharacteristic of the age. Even before the establishment of Christianity as the state religion of the empire the feeling against heresy was so strong that when Christians were thrown into the arena the orthodox would separate themselves from heretics, disdaining to be devoured by the same lion; if by some unhappy chance they should be integrated for a while in death inside the lion, they were sure that they would be segregated again in the afterlife, with the orthodox in heaven and the heretics in hell. After Christianity became the state religion, religious animosity increased. It became confused with political feeling, and in Egypt, Syria, and Palestine resentment against the domination of the Byzantines inspired the adoption of various heresies by the population. In Jerusalem the heretics were persecuted and forbidden to worship at the shrines. The Orthodox emperors tried to suppress them for they mistrusted heretics, and feared that they would betray the Eastern Roman Empire to its Persian enemies. The emperors were quite justified in their fears, for the more they repressed their subjects, the more untrustworthy those subjects became.

In Palestine the large and long-persecuted Samaritan popula-

tion also detested the Orthodox emperor. They periodically rebelled, plundered Christian villages, burned Christian shrines and
attacked isolated monasteries. The Jews also looked to the Persians
as liberators. Under Roman and Byzantine rule Palestine had lost
much of its Jewish population; the center of Jewish life was now
within the boundaries of the Persian empire, particularly in Babylonia, where Jews had an autonomous government and their own
villages and cities. A thousand years earlier the Persians had controlled the entire East—Palestine, Egypt and Asia Minor, and they
had never abandoned their ambitions to reconquer this empire.
They encouraged the hopes of the Byzantines' disaffected subjects,
reminding the Jews that once before Persians had restored the
Jerusalem temple, and the heretics, that Persians like themselves,
had a long tradition of hating Greeks, even if the Greeks were classical rather than Orthodox. As the prolonged Persian-Byzantine
war dragged on in the last quarter of the sixth century, the Jews
became more and more optimistic. Although they were persecuted
wherever Christians were in power, they became increasingly
aware of the rich, powerful and free Jewish community backing
them in Babylonia. Early in the seventh century it seemed as
though their prayers were going to be answered and that Jerusalem
was going to be returned to them. A rabbi in Galilee had a dream
that the Messiah was on his way; when his dream was publicized a
wave of excitement overwhelmed the Jewish population of Palestine. Simultaneously a rebellion broke out in the Byzantine empire,
and the Persians under their Emperor Chosroes took advantage of
it and marched into Syria and Palestine, capturing Antioch and
conquering Galilee. As the Persian army proceeded south towards
Jerusalem, it was welcomed by the Jews of Galilee, who were certain, once again, that this time the coming of the Messiah was at
hand. Jews escorted the invading army from Tiberias, on the
shores of the sea of Galilee, to Caesarea on the Mediterranean and
helped take the town. In gratitude for their assistance, the Persians

promised to place Jerusalem under Jewish rule, once it was recaptured.

On May 20, 614, the Persians took the city after a siege of twenty days. Like so many other sieges of Jerusalem, this one terminated with a dreadful slaughter. Thousands of Christians, many of them monks and nuns, were massacred by the Persians with the aid of their Jewish allies. To the horror of Christians, the Persians refused to bury the dead that were killed in their wars; one tenet of their Zoroastrian religion discouraged defiling the pure earth with unclean corpses. The few Zoroastrians left in Persia today still expose the bodies of their dead and let vultures pick them clean. So the Christian martyrs of Jerusalem were left unburied, until a citizen named Thomas and his wife collected their bodies and braved Persian displeasure by giving them burial; a shrine built over their bones remained a pilgrimage center for centuries. As was their custom the Persians expelled most of the inhabitants of the conquered city and led them into captivity, with the Orthodox Patriarch Zacharias at their head. Along with him they took all the church treasures they could lay hands on, including the relic of the true cross, whose capture by infidels threw the entire Christian world into confusion and dismay. The city was thoroughly looted and, at the urging of the magi who accompanied the Persian army, its churches were burned. Constantine's great Basilica of the Resurrection, the church at Mount Zion where the patriarch had his headquarters, the great church dedicated to the Virgin atop the Mount of Olives—all were destroyed. Only the Church of the Nativity in nearby Bethlehem was spared, because the Persians were favorably impressed when they saw in it a representation of the three magi wearing Persian costumes as they visited the infant Christ.

With the expulsion of the Christians from Jerusalem the Jews took over. One of their leaders promptly adopted the name Nehemiah, in commemoration of the prophet who had left Persia a thousand years earlier to rebuild Jerusalem's walls. The site of the temple was venerated again and there was probably even an attempt, after a lapse of half a millennium, to restore the practice of animal sacrifice. Jews flocked to Jerusalem from the rest of Palestine and from Babylonia.

Within a few years the Persians realized that if they were going to hold the conquered regions of Syria and Palestine, they would have to placate the Christians who were more numerous than the Jews. And so about three years after the city was taken, they executed the imitation Nehemiah and ordered all Jews once more out of Jerusalem, forbidding them—as the Romans had—to approach within three miles of its walls. The Christian chroniclers who gleefully recorded their expulsion attributed it to the hand of God and to the displeasure of the Persians who were angry at the Jews for failing to dig up buried treasure for them, which had reportedly been desposited in the city by the Jews centuries before.

In the year 629, the Byzantines, under the command of their Emperor Heraclius, who had sworn to drive the Persians out of his empire and restore the true cross to Jerusalem, reconquered Egypt, Syria, and Palestine. As Heraclius marched southward through Palestine, the Jews of Galilee went out to meet his army as they had met the Persians twenty-five years earlier. Well aware of the stories circulating against them for the part they had played in the massacre of the Christians of Jerusalem, they pleaded with the emperor for amnesty, which he, in Christian charity, granted. When he arrived in Jerusalem, however, he was met by returned Christians who walked in procession to meet him, censing the air before them. They gave him a tour of the ruins of the city and urged him to reconsider his oath of amnesty to the Jews, to kill them in compensation for the massacre of Christians. The pious Heraclius was reluctant to do so—not out of any consideration for the Jews (a few years later he ordered all Jews in his empire to be baptized); but because he had given his oath. "Unless I uphold this covenant I shall be thought by all men to be a liar, a cheat and a man un-

worthy to be trusted, besides the great sin and wickedness whereof
I should be guilty before our Lord Christ if I were to slay the people whom I had sworn to save, and with whom I had sealed a written convenant."

The answer given to him by the monks of Jerusalem was an
ingenious one. "The Lord Christ knoweth that their slaughter will
be to thee for a remission of sins, and for an atonement for thy
offenses"; and it convinced him. The Jews were punished. Just in
case Lord Christ should not be convinced by the logic of the argument as easily as Emperor Heraclius had been, Heraclius' subjects
promised to undertake for him an expiatory fast each year in the
week before Lent, abstaining from eggs and cheese "as long as the
Christian religion shall endure." Actually, they observed the fast
only so long as the Emperor Heraclius endured. Although members of the Coptic Church in Egypt continued to respect it for centuries thereafter, most of Heraclius' subjects abandoned the custom
at his death, even his subjects in Jerusalem, for the true cross was
back in its place. The city's churches were being rebuilt. Jerusalem
once again was Christian and so it would remain, they believed,
forever.

⟨ CHAPTER 7 ⟩

The Dome of the Rock

On Christmas day 635, little more than five years after the Persians had been driven out of Jerusalem, the Patriarch Sophronius and his flock found themselves unable to visit Bethlehem as they were accustomed to do each year—to prostrate themselves in the Church of the Nativity, pressing their foreheads to the floor while adoring "the renowned manger, by whose operation," as Sophronius wrote, man "was brought upon the word of God." Blocking the road between Jerusalem and Bethlehem was an Arab army, sent by the successors of Mohammed to spread his faith throughout the world. Desert warriors, accustomed to race forward on horseback screaming, with their lances aimed at a terrified enemy, they had emerged from the Arabian peninsula in the years that followed Mohammed's death and had begun attacking the lands bordering the Arabian desert—the Byzantine territories of Palestine and Syria, and the Babylonian marches of the Persian Empire. At first the siege of cities, especially a city as strongly fortified as Jerusalem, was too formidable a task for them; they contented themselves with occupying what lands they could take easily (these were considerable, for both the Persians and Byzantines were exhausted from fighting each other), and they presumed that in time, Jerusalem and other such strongholds would fall into their hands.

To them, as to the Christians and Jews, the city was holy. Mohammed had originally ordered his followers to pray in the direction of Jerusalem; it was only when the Jews of Arabia obdurately clung to their religion and refused to accept him as the final messenger sent by God to refine the monotheism that had been given to their ancestors that he changed the direction of worship, from the stone of the temple at Jerusalem where Abraham had supposedly begun to sacrifice Isaac, to the black stone at The Kaaba at Mecca, which had long been revered by the Arabs. To Mohammed and his followers, Jerusalem was the city of prophets and wonder workers; since Mohammed, the greatest of prophets, had now worked the greatest of wonders by bringing the true religion from God to mankind, it was only fitting that the Muslims, as bearers of the final revelation, should control the place where Abraham, David, Jonah, John the Baptist, and Jesus had received earlier Messages from heaven.

As it turned out, the Arabs never had to risk besieging Jerusalem. After defeating several Byzantine armies sent out against them, they annihilated the picked troops of the Byzantine emperor in the year 636 at the Battle of the Yarmuk east of the Sea of Galilee. When Sophronius heard the report of the battle and realized that Byzantine armies were not about to come back soon to rescue Jerusalem from the Arabs controlling the countryside, he sent an emissary to the Arab encampment at Jabiya in southern Syria, offering to surrender the city, but only if he could hand it over personally to the Arab leader, the Caliph Omar.

Omar, the successor to the successor of Mohammed as he called himself, was in Medina, but when he heard of the offer, he left Arabia and rode on camelback to the encampment at Jabiya, where he awaited the patriarch's delegation bringing a formal offer of surrender. After his terms of surrender had been accepted, he again mounted his camel and crossed over the Jordan to see the city he had just become master of. He set up an encampment on the Mount of Olives, unbuckled his saber and put it aside, and signed a treaty of peace with the Christians of Jerusalem. After the treaty was signed, the caliph ordered his new subjects to conduct him into the city so that he could worship, as earlier leaders of the true religion had, at the site of the temple.

Omar was a humble man. The son of a slave woman, he walked barefoot and customarily dressed in a roughspun and ragged camel's-hair cloak that served him at times for a blanket. A modern Arab print, sold in the streets of Jerusalem, shows him appearing before the city (quite white, although his mother had been a black woman) still mounted on his camel in front of the Damascus Gate, peering down suspiciously as the Patriarch Sophronius bows before him and welcomes him to Jerusalem. Sophronius is not the only member of the welcoming committee. There are other Christians, skull-capped representatives of the heretical Christian sects, and there is a worried looking Jew up on the battlements, Jesus Christ, still holding his cross, looking down at the man whose faith claimed to supersede his.

In response to Omar's pious request, the patriarch began to conduct him to the site of Solomon's temple. But first, according to tradition, Sophronius led him to the rebuilt Church of the Resurrection. It was the Muslim hour of worship and Sophronius courteously suggested that Omar use the facilities of the church for prayer. Omar just as courteously declined and went out into the church courtyard to pray, with the reminder that the Muslims would have had to take the church over for a shrine if the successor to the successor of Mohammed had prayed there. Next he was conducted to the site of the temple, which had lain undisturbed since the Temple of Jupiter, erected on the site by Hadrian, had been overturned by Christians. "Behold your house shall be left unto you desolate," Christ had said of the temple. "There shall not be left one stone upon another that shall not be cast down." Christians had never contemplated building there. Indeed, the place was covered with filth; the inhabitants of the city had been accustomed to empty their slop pails there as a special token of contempt for the Jewish religion; according to one report, jars of excrement were specially transported all the way from Constantinople to be unloaded at the place. To this day credulous Jews believe that the Christians of the time imagined they would earn a reward in heaven for every bucket of dirt deposited there. The place was so covered with filth that it even clogged the entrance; Omar had to crawl on his hands and knees to get in, and the Patriarch Sophronius, his host, followed him. Inside Omar stood up and looked around. "By Allah," the chroniclers report him as saying, "by him in whose hand is my life—surely this must be the Mosque of David of which the apostle spoke to us saying, I was conducted there in the Night Journey." He bent over and picked up some trash, put it in the skirt of his camel's-hair cloak and walked with it over to the edge of the temple enclosure to toss it into the valley beneath. His followers imitated him, beginning the process of cleaning the temple area, excavating the sacred rock and making the site fit for Muslim worship.

The Muslims intended to dominate Jerusalem but not to overwhelm it. According to the treaty Omar presented that day to the Patriarch Sophronius, Jesus' followers were to be allowed to practice their faith freely—obsolete though it was: "In the name of Allah, the merciful, the compassionate," the proclamation begins, with the words that inaugurate every chapter of the Koran and are used as a grace before every meal eaten by the Muslim pious. "The commander of the faithful, Omar ibn al-Khattab, to the inhabitants of Aelia: He gives them surety for their persons, their goods, their churches and their crosses . . . those who live within the town or in the fields and all the community. Their churches will not be occupied; they will not be demolished; they will not have anything in them diminished, not even the least portion. . . . They will not be forced to abjure their faith; none of them will be molested . . ." In return for Omar's, and presumably Allah's, mercy and compassion, the inhabitants of the city bound themselves not to display crosses along the public roads or on the outside of churches, not to bear arms, not to sell wine, not to mourn too loudly for their dead in funeral processions through the public streets, or conduct those funeral processions through a Muslim neighborhood. Why, after all, contaminate the living with the sight of an infidel bound for hell?

The Christians of the city promised further to wear no Arab clothes, use no Arab lettering on their personal seals, take no Arab forenames; Omar wanted to keep the line of demarcation very clear between the Arabs and their conquered subjects. Unbelievers paid taxes which Muslims did not, and there was no sense in diminishing the tax base of the profitable new provinces. For the same reason conversions to Islam were not encouraged—although they were not really impeded; one of the articles of the Jerusalem treaty was a promise by the Christians to refrain from hindering anyone who wanted to convert to Islam. But the Arabs were wary of converts, the great majority of whom probably wished to convert to Islam because it was the religion of the conquerors. In the new Arab domains this was such a problem, religious and economic, that Arabic developed two separate words for conversion; one means a nominal conversion, the other a sincere one. Christianity and Judaism having been, for critical periods, religions of the oppressed rather than of conquerors, did not have to stress this sort of distinction.

One of the first acts of Jerusalem's new masters was to continue Omar's work of cleaning the area around the sacred rock. The rock itself had always been partially uncovered. For years it had been the custom for Jews to come into the city on the 9th day of the Hebrew month of Ab to anoint the rock with oil and recite their prayers before it. The Arabs began to follow the custom regularly, substituting prayers of joy for the Jews' lamentations. For them stones had always been objects of reverence.

In ancient times the Arabs had worshipped stones—or the

Above the gate of a convent outside Jerusalem's walls stands a war-battered image of the Virgin Mary.

Dominating Jerusalem is the Dome of the Rock, built at the site of Solomon's temple. The domed Church of the Holy Sepulchre can be seen behind and to the left of the Dome of the Rock.

Hebrew University

RIGHT: A fanciful eighteenth century engraving shows Solomon's temple, illuminated with a light from heaven.

LEFT: Jews pray before the Wailing Wall.

BELOW: One of the city's numerous Talmudic schools.

LOWER LEFT: The modern synagogue at the Hebrew University.

Scheuchzer, Johann Jacob,
Physica Sacra, 1732-35

LEFT: The entrance to the Church of St. James, the center of Armenian life in Jerusalem.

BELOW: A Russian Orthodox church built in characteristic Russian style.

LEFT: A panorama of Jerusalem can be seen from the window of the church of Dominus Flevit built at the site where Jesus wept foreseeing the city's destruction.

LEFT: A fifteenth century view of the Church of the Holy Sepulchre.

ABOVE: Cells of Coptic monks on the church roof.

BELOW: The entrance to the church, with workmen making repairs.

RIGHT: Seated on a Persian carpet
beneath the stained glass windows
of the Dome of the Rock, a worshipper studies the Koran.

LEFT: At a fountain in the Haram
esh Sharif, a devout Muslim washes
before prayer. Al Aqsa mosque can
be seen in the background.

ABOVE: A stone stairway leads down from the Dome of the Rock to the pavement before Al Aqsa mosque.

RIGHT: An inscription above the door of a house commemorates the owner's pilgrimage to Mecca. At the center of the inscription is a depiction of the Dome of the Rock.

ABOVE: Foreign pilgrims wait for the beginning of the procession that retraces Jesus' route along the Via Dolorosa.

UPPER RIGHT: The procession passes along the Via Dolorosa. Two Stations of the Cross are seen here.

LOWER RIGHT: The Fourth Station of the Cross where Jesus encountered his mother.

UPPER LEFT: The Fifth Station, where Jesus met Simon of Cyrene.

LOWER LEFT: Along the Via Dolorosa souvenir shops are as plentiful as shrines.

ABOVE: Arab men sit outside a cafe in the old city.

RIGHT: An Arab drover outside St. Stephen's Gate.

UPPER RIGHT: A Jewish tinsmith in the new city.

BELOW: Orthodox Jews along a street near the Me'a Shearim quarter.

RIGHT: Jewish teenagers and a heavily loaded donkey on the Via Dolorosa.

BELOW: Arab children playing near the Haram esh Sharif.

Israel Information Office

אושוויץ
AUSCHWITZ

מאידאנק
MAJDANEK

UPPER LEFT: A Muslim cemetery overlooking the Mount of Olives; the church of Gethsemane is at left center.

LOWER LEFT: A memorial to Jews killed by the Nazis.

ABOVE: Jewish tombs dating from Roman times.

BELOW: Modern Jewish tombs on the lower slopes of the Mount of Olives, with the ancient monument called the tomb of Absalom at left.

A heavily veiled Muslim woman carrying a broom walks past movie posters within the old city.

spirits dwelling in stones. As a high point in the pilgrimage to Mecca it is still customary to kiss the stone at The Kaaba. In Petra and other ancient Arab cities, the traditional service of worship involved a ritual procession around a sacred rock. Worshippers fondly stroked the sacred stone with their hands and kissed it, sacrificed animals before it and daubed it with the victim's blood. In the Koran Mohammed condemned this sort of practice; but eventually he succumbed to his compatriots' reverence for the sacred stone at Mecca. And so it was natural for the Arabs to revere the great stone of Jerusalem. Over the years they incorporated Jewish legends about it into their own tradition and invented for it new legends of their own—the most famous that of Mohammed's Night Journey which described how the prophet had one night been miraculously transported on the back of a winged steed from Mecca to the Jerusalem stone, from which he had then flown up to heaven.

Shortly after the Arabs conquered Jerusalem, a simple wooden structure was built to cover the rock. At that time, mosque architecture had hardly developed; a house made of date-palm trunks enclosed The Kaaba at Mecca. But within five decades or so of the conquest, the entire vast pavement that Herod had constructed atop the temple mount was marked off for Muslim worship (the Arabs called the area the Haram esh Sharif—the noble sanctuary or enclosure) and the Caliph Abd el-Malik completed the construction of the famous dome that still stands on the site. The building was designed to rival in beauty the Church of the Resurrection and to stand worthy of comparison with the temple of Solomon, which, impressive to begin with, had been adorned further in pious lore through the ages by the rich imaginations of generations that had never seen it.

To build the shrine the caliph employed Greek-speaking artisans, probably from Syria, who worked in the Byzantine style, raising a high and graceful dome in imitation of the one that stood above the Holy Sepulcher. The exterior walls were covered with white marble (the tiles that are seen there now were not added until the sixteenth century) and the dome itself was covered with gold, which was protected from the elements during the winter season by a cap made of hides. Within, every square inch of the shrine was richly decorated with marble and shining mosaics, except, of course, for the broad expanse of the sacred rock that was the reason for the Dome's existence. Two circles of columns stood surrounding the rock. Many of them were taken from the ruins of the Roman Temple of Jupiter which had stood on the site; others had been carried down from a decayed Byzantine church on the Mount of Olives and then dragged uphill again to the site of the Dome. It took seven years worth of revenue from the entire province of Egypt to pay for the construction.

One reason the beautiful building had been constructed was to show Muslims their religious edifices could compete with those of Christians. To make sure Christianity would have no influence on the Muslims who came to worship in the city where Christ had been crucified, some of the mosaics adorning the interior of the shrine were inscribed with quotations from the Koran intended to put Jesus in his place. "Say praise be to God who has had no son or companion in his government and who requires no helper to save him from dishonor," the faithful were reminded when they looked around the Dome. "God is one and far be it from him that he should have had a son." "The Associators" was what pious Muslims often called Christians contemptuously, scandalized at their daring to associate any other being with the power of God.

There has long been a tradition that internecine Muslim quarrels also played an important role in the construction of the shrine. Supposedly one of the reasons Caliph Abd el-Malik resolved to build it was that Mecca was in the hands of a rival caliph. From his capital at Damascus Abd el-Malik ruled a vast Arab empire that extended from the Atlantic Ocean to the Indus River, but he did not control the holy cities of Arabia. For the first nine years of his reign, all Muslims fulfilling their religious obligations of pilgrimage to Mecca had to go into the territory of his rival al-Zubair, elected caliph by the populace of Mecca and Medina, who resented the fact that their cities, once the centers of the Arab empire, had been eclipsed by Damascus. Al-Zubair insisted that all pilgrims visiting Mecca swear allegiance to him as caliph of all Muslims, instead of to Abd el-Malik. At this the caliph of Damascus refused permission for any of his subjects to go on a pilgrimage to Mecca. Naturally enough they were confused, torn between obligations to their earthly ruler and their heavenly one. To ease their distress, the story goes, Abd el-Malik decreed that the rock of Jerusalem would thenceforth substitute for the sacred rock at Mecca, and he built the beautiful Dome to house it. His obliging subjects resolved their doubts and took to circumambulating the rock within the Dome, as they had walked around the rock at Mecca, but here they walked in the opposite direction.

Jerusalem never became the center of Arab rule in the province of Palestine—or Falastin as it was now called. Like the Romans before them who made Caesarea the capital of the country, the Arabs gave spiritual predominance to Jerusalem, but decided it was unwise to give it political power as well. It would be unwise too to concentrate the country's sparse and militarily valuable Arab population in the hill country of Jerusalem, which could be controlled from the desert anyway. But the coastal plain was a different story; it was more difficult for the Arabs to control, and so a new capital, called Ramleh was established there and populated with Arabs.

Official policy called for the Arabs to rule conquered lands from military camps in the countryside, such as Ramleh was at first, ghettoes where they could live by themselves, with lives made pleasant by captured wealth and captured women, following the true faith and uncontaminated by contact with unbelievers. During the first generation of Arab rule in Palestine, this policy was followed with a fair measure of success. But by the second generation it collapsed and the Arabs began to integrate with their subjects.

The process was hastened by the fact that the conquering Arabs had managed to collect such extensive harems and to enjoy them so well, as befits conquerors, that they produced an extraordinary number of sons. These youths were considered authentic Arabs but refused to act like them and be bound to life within a military camp. Theoretically, the Arabs were stationed in the conquered provinces and had no right to move about freely from town to town without permission; but as the threat of rebellion or Byzantine reconquest receded, freedom of movement became more possible, and more and more Arabs moved out of Ramleh and the other camps and into the cities of Palestine.

During the first century of Arab rule Palestine was underpopulated. Many Christian refugees had fled to seek shelter in Christian territory. Even the Jews left their villages, obliged by their Arab overlords to abandon their fields and settle in the port towns along the coast of Syria. There they, unlike the Christian population of the ports, could be relied upon to defend the country against an invasion mounted by the Byzantine fleet, which the desert-dwelling Arabs feared far more than they did the Byzantine armies. (On the other hand the Jews were unreliable when Greek ships stopped by offering to ransom Arab captives.)

After the conquest of Jerusalem, the inhabitants of the city were joined by a few followers of Mohammed and a garrison of Arab soldiers. The garrison consisted of Yemenites from the southern corner of the Arabian peninsula, which had itself been conquered by the Muslims only a few years earlier. These people had a long tradition of urban life and were more accustomed than many of the other Arab soldiers were to Christians and Jews; Yemen had, in the recent past, been the home of both a Christian and a Jewish kingdom. It is likely that the Yemenites set their stamp on the Muslim community of the city, giving it a sort of genteel cast which it maintained for centuries. The Muslim inhabitants considered themselves "neighbors of Allah," and in general they acted accordingly. "In no place will you meet with people more chaste," wrote a tenth century chronicler, a native of the town. "Wine is not publicly consumed and there is no drunkenness. The city is devoid of houses of ill fame, whether public or private." Jerusalem also boasted a modest but respectable intellectual life. Certainly the city never became a great intellectual center of Islam like Damascus, Cairo, or Baghdad (a few centuries after the Arab conquest, there were more than a hundred bookshops in Damascus), but it was always to be an important center of piety—not just the thoughtless devotion that has been so common in Jerusalem, but the sort of profound and informed piety that inspired individual scholars and communities of the faithful to come from other parts of the Arab world to settle in the city, bringing their wives and children with them.

As Muslims were told by their religious leaders, Jerusalem united the advantages of both this world and the next. Depopulated though the region was at first it was still rich. Eventually the province of Falastin provided the caliph with revenues equal and sometimes even greater than those of the region of Damascus which the Arabs considered "the paradise of the earth." In the five centuries since the last Jewish rebellion against Rome, the province had recovered much of its fertility (it was not to be ruined again, this time almost for good, until the crusades). In the fields around Jerusalem, peasants gathered bountiful crops of barley. Both corn and barley were raised on the Mount of Olives, beneath the church marking the site of Jesus' ascension and the mosque which commemorated the place where Omar encamped. The land produced an especially flavorful honey, from bees which fed on thyme blossoms. The Arab chroniclers do not give us a report of milk to accompany the honey; but they do make note of the cheese of Jerusalem, which evidently was famous. The grapes grown in vineyards in the valley of Kidron right outside the city walls were enormous, as those other desert wanderers, the Hebrew spies who visited Canaan so many centuries earlier, had discovered. The city could boast, according to a chronicler, of "all the fruits of the lowlands and of the plains and of the hill country, even all those of the most opposite kinds; such as the orange and the almond, the date and the nut, the fig and the banana, besides milk in plenty, and honey and sugar." The farmers of the Jerusalem region exported jars of olive oil, raisins, cotton, apples, and pine nuts; and the craftsmen of the city made needles and mirrors, and glass oil jars for use as hanging lamps. By the tenth century they also had workshops for the production of rosaries, which had been introduced to Islam as an aid to mystic devotions by Muslim mystics from India. From Jerusalem at the time of the crusades, they were introduced to Western Christianity, and their manufacture in the city became bi-religious. Only the Jews, of all the people in Jerusalem, failed to be hypnotized by them.

Each year on September 15 there was —until the tenth century at least—a great trading fair at Jerusalem. Merchants came from as far away as Italy to visit the fair; spices and silks were purchased and carried to the west where they might reappear the following year at the famous fairs of Bar and Troyes in the French county of Champagne, to be traded from there to England or Scandinavia. Caravans of camels, horses and asses flocked into the city. There were so many animals they soiled the streets, making it difficult for pedestrians to walk without stepping into their droppings. One pious seventh-century Christian visitor reported that each year, as soon as the fair was over, divine providence sent a mighty rainstorm to wash the streets and clean the holy city.

Throughout the early centuries of Muslim rule Christian life flourished in Jerusalem; indeed Christians were treated with such consideration that one tenth-century Muslim complained that they and the Jews had the upper hand in the city. The Muslims trod lightly on their subjects. So long as they paid their taxes and deferred humbly to their Muslim masters, Christians were left in peace. Christian churches retained their autonomy. Between 726 and 836, there were three church councils in Jerusalem to deal with the problem of icons, which partly under Muslim influence, had come to be considered by some in the Orthodox church as works of idolatry. Although the councils were held in Jerusalem, under Muslim control so to speak, the church fathers decided each time that graven images were acceptable, indeed indispensable for Christian worship. As the centuries went by and the number of converts to the dominant religion increased, Christians did find themselves supplanted by Muslims in the city government offices at the Citadel, or Tower of David, at the western end of Jerusalem. But they still formed a large proportion of the officials of Palestine, and a larger proportion of the population. Not until after the crusaders had come and gone were Muslims a majority in Palestine.

Along with crops of barley and corn the Mount of Olives still produced monks and nuns; despite the destruction wrought by the Persians, numerous convents of ascetics and monastics remained. The Orthodox among them were now cut off from easy contact with their Byzantine coreligionists; but Orthodoxy was not what a great many Christians in Palestine and Syria wanted contact with anyway. For members of heretical sects the Arab conquest had been a blessing since the Arabs tolerated them more than the Orthodox Byzantines had. In some ways the Arab conquest proved beneficial for the city's Orthodox too. The patriarch of Jerusalem had always claimed primacy of a sort as head of the church in the city where Christ himself had led Christians; but he had always deferred to the Patriarch of Constantinople, the head of the imperial church. Now he was more independent. Cut off from the Byzantines, the patriarchs of Alexandria and Antioch achieved more autonomy too. Thus a precedent was set for the splintering of Eastern Orthodoxy into national churches, quite unlike the churches of the Catholic West.

The Christians of Jerusalem were unhappy at one thing however, the enforced takeover of many of their holy places by Muslims. Among other places, the sites of the ascension and of the Last Supper were eventually requisitioned for Muslim worship. Omar had promised Christians that they would be enabled to keep control of their shrines. But the promise was not kept. Every significant Muslim shrine in Palestine has been constructed on the site where a Christian or Jewish holy place had previously stood. Of course the Christians themselves had taken many of them over from the Jews, and the Jews from the Canaanites, and the Canaanites from the neolithic indigenes.

Muslims thought nothing strange in this takeover. They considered all the biblical worthies to be prophets of monotheism; since Islam is, they believed, the only authentic monotheism, it was logical for Islam to ingest everything associated with the religion's earlier and less perfect forms. Muslims themselves submit without question to whatever God decrees, and since God had decreed that Islam is the only true faith, they saw no reason why Christians and Jews should not submit too. Islam itself means "submission" or "surrender" to the unimaginable power of heaven. For Muslims nothing exists outside Allah's will; Abdel or Abdullah, "slave of Allah," is a name they chose for their sons. They considered it almost blasphemous to say as Christians do, "Thy will be done, on earth as it is in heaven," as if it were possible that God's will not be done. And so Muslims felt free to incorporate into their own faith whatever they could. Whatever did not fit they ignored.

The Church of the Resurrection or Holy Sepulcher was left alone; it was never considered sacred by Muslims, although they did build a mosque outside it at the spot where Omar was supposed to have prayed. Muslims believe that Jesus was never really crucified, even though Christians have built a religion around that event. According to Islamic tradition, Jesus did not actually have to suffer the indignity of crucifixion, but was taken up to heaven before he died, with Judas Iscariot substituted for him on the cross at Golgotha. So Muslims pay scant attention to any site connected with Jesus' death or his resurrection and what attention they do pay is contemptuous. Muslims in Jerusalem usually referred to the Church of the Resurrection as the Church of Shit—*al Kumamah*—a play on the word *al Kayamah*, the resurrection, which is what Christian Arabs were accustomed to call it.

There is no record that the Jews in Muslim Jerusalem were so indelicate in their references to the church. They tended to ignore it. One Jew of the time who does mention it referred to it simply as "a place of worship . . . containing the sepulcher of *that man.*" The Jews had settled in Jerusalem as soon as they could after the Arab conquest. There may even have been Jewish tribesmen from Arabia in the armies that conquered Palestine. One condition the Christians of Jerusalem probably made in surrendering their city was that Jews be excluded from it. Whether or not Omar acceded to their demands is questionable. In any case Jews arrived in Jerusalem very soon after the Arabs did. Seventy families came from Tiberias on the Sea of Galilee and settled in the southwest part of the city close to the Wailing Wall, in the region that today is the Jewish quarter.

These Jews were permitted to build a synagogue near the Wailing Wall and to pray freely at the site of the temple. But when the Muslims built mosques on the mount, transforming it into a great Islamic shrine, they were excluded. As a consolation they purchased fields on the Mount of Olives, facing the temple mount and there performed their festival rites overlooking the holy place. Especially painful to them was the establishment of a Muslim burial place on the mount, which in the years when the temple stood could not according to Jewish tradition even be approached by anyone who had had contact with a corpse. "The spiters of the Lord . . ." they mourned, "Ammonites, Moabites, Ishmaelites, Edomites and Hagarites came bringing coffins and all kinds of unclean things . . ."

Nevertheless, the Jews were relatively well off in Jerusalem, although there were times, when the government was weak, that they were exposed to the fury of Christian mobs. But just as frequently Christians suffered outrages at the hands of the Muslims.

157

Their churches were desecrated, their shops and houses pillaged; as the number of the Jews increased they expanded their holdings and established another Jewish quarter on the opposite side of town, the northeast, which remained the center of their activities until the time of the crusades. Jewish settlers came from Yemen, a land to which their ancestors had fled following the destruction of the temple by Titus. Scholars came from Europe and studied at a Talmudic academy that was supported, in part, by contributions from the sultan of Egypt. In the tenth century there was a great influx of Persian Jews, who emigrated to Jerusalem for economic as well as religious reasons. At that time Persia was undergoing a depression so severe that it inspired a great emigration of Muslims from Persia, too, who found Palestine and Syria more attractive than their homeland. Soon Persians were a majority among the Muslims in Jerusalem, and on both sides of the Wailing Wall, within the Muslim enclosure and on the outside where the Jews gathered, Persian was heard almost as frequently as the two sacred languages, Arabic and Hebrew.

The Jews of Jerusalem formed a class of artisans and farmers. Many worked as dyers and tanners; others served as the bankers of the city and supervised the quality of the coins in the mint. Some few, twenty men, were allowed access to the Temple mount. They were employed at the Dome of the Rock to sweep up after the crowds came for the summer and winter pilgrimages, and to care for the fountains at which the faithful washed five times each day before prayer. Along with the privilege of approaching the temple site, these men and their families had the more concrete advantage of being exempt from the head tax imposed on every unbeliever in the Arab empire. Also exempt were the Jews who made glass lanterns and wicks for the sixteen hundred lamps that illuminated Jerusalem's Muslim shrines, and provided for the Muslim worshipper a pale reflection of the light cast by Allah over the heaven and the earth.

With the Muslims in control of Jerusalem, it was easy for

Jews to come on pilgrimage. There was freedom of movement throughout the farflung Muslim empire where most of the Jews of the time lived. It had always been traditional for Jews to go on pilgrimage to Jerusalem. Now the tradition was strengthened by the fact that pilgrimage was a major religious obligation for Muslims too, and Jews in exile have always done their best to imitate the practices of their gentile neighbors.

Christian pilgrims continued to come too. Of course they were no longer permitted to ride into the city on a horse or a mule; they could ride up to its gates but then they were obliged to dismount and enter on foot. The Muslims would not allow any Christian—native or foreign—to ride into any city under their control. Having left the West with its triumphant and militant Christianity, they arrived in Jerusalem to walk in the footsteps of Christ. To their dismay they found themselves following him more closely than they had anticipated, for like him they were despised and persecuted in the city. Still they had the chance to gaze in wonder at the room in the Church of the Holy Sepulcher that showed heaven on one wall and hell on another, and to kiss its altars and shrines, and its holy icons that were covered with glass to keep off dust and smudges.

In the year 797 a number of Christian pilgrims arrived in the city from Aachen with passports authorized by the caliph of Islam, Harun al-Rashid of Baghdad. They had been sent by Charlemagne to bring back relics from Jerusalem for his court. They returned with a great trove, including perhaps the two splinters of the true cross that were crossed themselves and embedded in a jeweled reliquary, which was hung around the emperor's neck when he was buried. After he received his relics, Charlemagne sent another emissary to Jerusalem with money for the local Christians. In return for his generosity (according to one tradition) the emperor received the keys to the Holy Sepulcher sent by Harun al-Rashid as one great potentate to another. With the keys came the title of guardian of all Christian holy places in the Holy Land.

The story is probably a medieval fabrication designed to explain why the Roman Catholics, and particularly the French, felt they could interfere freely in the affairs of the Holy Land. But it was believed devoutly by the crusaders. Their tradition even had Charlemagne, in full splendor and accompanied by an army of 80,000 men, visit the Holy Land on a pilgrimage. To prove it there is a stained glass window at Chartres that depicts the expedition. At Jerusalem, the tradition reports, Charlemagne knelt at the Dome of the Rock while an angel came down from heaven with a precious relic for him, the foreskin remaining after Jesus' circumcision, which Charlemagne brought back to Chartres, where it was venerated in medieval times. Eventually the tale was accepted as true even by the Arabs, but of course they gave it a different cast. An Arab chronicler reports that the King of Rum, the Roman Emperor, once came to Jerusalem as a pilgrim, but timidly and in disguise so no one would recognize or harm him.

Most of the pilgrims who arrived in the city were not Christians or Jews however, but Muslims, who came to circumambulate the sacred rock from which Mohammed had risen to heaven, to stroke it with their hands and bow down in prayer beside it. They set out from the ends of the Islamic realm, from as far as India and Spain, accompanied according to tradition, from the moment of their departure to the moment of their return home by ten thousand angels who hovered about them as they walked, and prayed to Allah for their souls. Most of them traveled not only to Jerusalem but to Arabia; they came to see Jerusalem en route as they fulfilled their real religious obligation of pilgrimage to Mecca. Before leaving home, or as they traveled, they read or listened to the pilgrim guide books that were written—especially in the later Middle Ages—to extol the values of pilgrimage to Jersusalem and the glories of the city. Along their way they had ample time to reflect on the advantages that would accrue to them as pilgrims: every prayer offered at Jerusalem was worth 25,000 times as much as a prayer offered elsewhere—except of course at Medina and Mecca, the two holiest cities of Islam, where prayers were worth 50,000 and 100,000 times as much as those uttered in an ordinary town.

Once the travelers arrived at the gate of Jerusalem they donned *ihrams*—the simple white garments characteristically worn by Moslem pilgrims. They found lodgings and then proceeded on a tour of the holy places, touching their foreheads to the ground in each place. From shrine to shrine they followed a strict route that was carefully fixed so as not to cross the traditional route of the Christian pilgrim. They began at the Dome of the Rock. There they circled the sacred rock and prayed, that is, performed a certain number of *rakas*, the traditional Islamic rite of prayer. In performing the prayer, the worshipper bows down, kneels on the ground and prostrates himself with his forehead and his hands to the ground, reciting all the while Koranic verses proclaiming the glory of God. After fondling the sacred rock, and inspecting the mark of Mohammed's foot on it, the pilgrim descended beneath the rock to see the place where part of it hovers in mid-air, having attempted to rise up to heaven after Mohammed, only to be held down by the Angel Gabriel. Prayers were recited at various spots beside the rock where according to tradition Abraham, David, Solomon and Elijah prayed. The pilgrims inspected the horns of the ram which Abraham had sacrificed at the site and the crown of the kings of Persia that had been captured by the Muslims. Eventually both relics were taken to Mecca.

Once he completed his visit to the Dome of the Rock the pilgrim proceeded to the place where Mohammed was carried up to heaven. After the crusaders were expelled from Jerusalem this site was marked with a building called the Dome of the Ascension. (This is not to be confused—though confusion seems inevitable—with the small domed building called the Dome of the Ascension atop the Mount of Olives that marks the site where Jesus ascended to heaven. To add to the confusion that building, once a church, is now a mosque.) Then the pilgrim proceeded across the pavement of the Haram esh Sharif to the eastern wall overlooking the Valley of Kidron to pray beside the Gate of Mercy, which today is called the Golden Gate. It marks the site where David supposedly prayed for and was granted forgiveness for his sins. At the gate they could inspect the pillars which, it was said, that earlier Arab pilgrim, the Queen of Sheba, brought up to Jerusalem to present to King Solomon; and they could try to peer over the wall to see the path on the southeast side of the city along which, legend said, some day a Christian army would come to take Jerusalem away from the Muslims. Christians came, once in 1099 and once again in 1917, but both times they entered along another route. And when the Jews returned to Jerusalem in 1967 to take it back for their turn, they entered at another gate, too. Still the Muslims customarily kept the gate closed, just in case.

From the Gate of Mercy, Muslim pilgrims walked south to a great structure, almost as beautiful as the Dome of the Rock and dominating the entire southern section of the Haram. This was al-Aqsa, "the Further Place," an immense colonnaded hall that served as the main house of prayer for Muslims in Jerusalem, for the Dome of the Rock is a shrine rather than a place of assembly. Here the worshipper's eye was dazzled by an enameled dome, intricate carving on the wooden ceiling, marble walls, fine carpets, and hundreds of marble columns supporting the great roof, most of them taken from old Byzantine buildings. Around the walls were cupboards containing gifts offered to the mosque by citizens of various towns in Syria and Iraq. The pilgrim found the cupboard from his home town and prayed in front of it. He made a special prayer in front of the *mihrab*, or prayer niche, of Zachariah, a recess in the southern wall before which Zachariah, the father of John the Baptist, and Zechariah, the Old Testament prophet (the Muslims confused the two), were accustomed to pray, facing Allah's holy city of Mecca with the foresight appropriate to prophets. From the *mihrab* of Zechariah who, if he really could see the future might have had mixed feelings at the reverence paid him, for his main mission in life had been to assure the exiled Jews that their temple would be rebuilt on that site, the pilgrims went back to the eastern wall of the Haram. There they inspected the throne of Solomon, where that king had supposedly sat to watch genies at work constructing his temple.

After completing their devotions within the Haram esh Sharif, the pilgrims descended to the wall outside to see the place where the Angel Gabriel had made a hole with his finger and tied up Buraq, the winged horse with a woman's face and peacock's tail, on which Mohammed had ascended to heaven. This holy site must have confused pilgrims. According to one tradition it was outside the southern wall of the city beneath al-Aqsa Mosque; but some authorities claimed it was at the western wall of the Haram enclosure, the Wailing Wall of the Jews, who doubtless favored the first possibility since so many of their other shrines had been taken over already. From whichever sacred hitching post he chose, the pilgrim ascended the Mount of Olives hurrying past the monks' cells to see the places where Omar encamped, where Jesus ascended to heaven, and where mankind will be judged at the end of time.

Aside from these prescribed sites, pilgrims also went to drink or bathe at the health-giving springs in the village of Siloam outside Jerusalem. There they could inspect the hospital built by grateful patients who had been restored to health. Endowments given by the pious supported the entire establishment, including the physicians' salaries. The waters were especially beneficial for chronic ailments, but for them to work effectively the patient had to be totally immersed. These and other waters of Jerusalem supposedly tasted better and were more healthful than those anywhere else in the world. Pilgrims were assured that their quality was enhanced by the fact that an underground stream mixed them with the waters of the spring of Zamzam in the holy city of Mecca, adding further medicinal benefits. For the delight of pilgrims and patients there were also beautiful gardens at Siloam; the Arabs were famous for their gardens.

Pilgrimages were also made to all the local sites associated with

the life (but not the death) of Jesus to whom the Muslims attributed the performance of even more miracles than Jesus' own
followers did. Visitors went to the area beneath al-Aqsa to see the
cradle where Jesus lay, and to light a lamp in his honor at the site.
There, too, nearby, they saw the marks made on a pillar by the Virgin Mary as she held onto it during her labor. Then they leaned
over the Haram wall above the valley of Jeshoshaphat with its
thousands of graves to try to hear the sound of the condemned
groaning in hell. The natives assured visitors that the sound could
be heard, but one eleventh-century traveler from Persia tried to
catch it and reported that he couldn't hear a thing. The tomb of
Rachel on the road to Hebron was visited and then Hebron
itself—a town which the Arabs called *al-Khalil*, "the friend," after
the patriarch Abraham, the friend of God, the ancestor of Ishmael
as well as of Israel, Arab as well as Jew, and a prophet revered as
the first monotheist. Later when the Crusaders took over Hebron
they called the town St. Abraham. There pilgrims ate a meal of
lentils and olive oil, handed out gratis to all the faithful from the
proceeds of a pious endowment established by a rich and devout
Muslim. He was imitating Abraham who there had invited to din-
ner three angels who had come calling on him one day. There were
no free meals in Jerusalem, however. In that town the pilgrims had
to pay for everything they got, to the benefit of the inhabitants. It
was a native of Jerusalem, an Arab scholar of the tenth century,
who said, "The holy land is truly a mine of profit both for this
world and the next." He knew what he was talking about.

The religious life of the Jerusalem Muslims was centered at al-
Aqsa Mosque, which had been constructed around the year 710 on
a site where a hospice for Christian pilgrims had once stood and,
long before that, the royal palace of the kings of Judah. Here Muslim citizens of the town came to recite their prayers and listen to
the reading of the Koran. Here, too, they listened to discussion of
the *hadith*, the "traditions" of the Muslim faith which had developed after the Koran had been written and which, like the Talmud

of the Jews, attempted to resolve contradictions in the holy scripture, derive new principles from it, and provide rationalizations for
disobeying precepts that were difficult to follow. A favorite point
of discussion among the learned at al-Aqsa was, naturally enough,
the location of the *kibblah*, the direction in which faithful Muslims
were supposed to face when they prayed. Once it had been Jerusalem; now it was Mecca, and Muslim scholars stretched their wits
trying to figure out how long Mohammed had prayed toward
Jerusalem before he switched the direction of prayer, why he had
changed, and what were the relative advantages of praying toward
one city or the other, citing all the while various authorities to support their arguments. All agreed that now it was proper to face
Mecca; but in the future, they maintained, on the Day of Judgment, the sacred Black Rock of Mecca, toward which Muslims
prayed, would come as a bride to Jerusalem and the two directions
of prayer would be miraculously united.

To the sacred enclosure surrounding al-Aqsa Mosque the
Muslims of Palestine brought their children to be circumcised just
as centuries earlier, the Jews may have brought their children to
the Temple mount. Some of those same children returned years later
as corpses. From all over Palestine dead bodies were carried to
Jerusalem for burial. Sometimes before being interred they were
carried to the pavement before al-Aqsa to rest for a few hours. The
custom may have been an imitation of a Christian practice, for
Christians brought the corpses of especially pious or distinguished
people to the Church of the Resurrection, to celebrate funeral rites
at the site of Golgotha, where Christ himself had died.

On certain days Jerusalem's pious Muslims supplemented worship in al-Aqsa with prayers in the Dome of the Rock. On those
mornings the servants of the shrine cleaned and perfumed the
sacred rock and the building itself with a special wash of rose water, mixed with powdered saffron, musk and ambergris. The formula was carefully prescribed, recalling the special perfumes used
at the temple of the Jews, and the days on which it was used were

fixed, too. These days were Monday and Thursday, the same days on which the Jews of Jerusalem used to visit the temple to pray. Occasionally a sultan passing through the town joined the servants in their labor, humbling himself to wash the shrine and anoint the sacred rock. When the cleaning was done, ten functionaries stood outside the doors and invited the populace to worship. People in Jerusalem claimed they could tell just by walking through the streets on Mondays and Thursdays which of their fellow citizens had been to the Dome to pray. The odor of the perfume used there was so strong that it clung to the worshippers long after they left the shrine.

In the year 1016, the Dome of the Rock collapsed, as a result of an earthquake. It was soon rebuilt but Jerusalem's Muslims were filled with trepidation; surely the disaster was a bad omen and a sign of divine displeasure. To the Christians of the city, on the other hand, the fall came as no surprise and they greeted it with satisfaction, for they saw it as divine retribution for Muslim persecution of Christianity. A few years before they had had the misfortune of seeing their great shrine, the Church of the Resurrection, destroyed at the command of the caliph of Egypt, al-Hakim. In the year 1009, the agents of the caliph had entered the church, ordered the priests and worshippers to leave, and set fire to the place.

The caliph was a madman, a paranoid, who hated Christians and Jews, women and dogs, and persecuted them all. He ordered all the dogs of Cairo to be slain—why it is not clear—all the women to remain indoors, all the Jews and Christians to wear black garments. Non-Muslims were forbidden the solace of alcoholic beverages, and all vines in the vicinity of Cairo were destroyed. An order was issued that all churches and synagogues in his empire be destroyed. According to one contemporary historian, the caliph's brain had dried up, and no one dared pour rose-oil into his nose to moisten it again and restore him to sanity.

The Christians of Jerusalem were especially hard hit by his madness, perhaps because the caliph's mother had been one of them and his maternal uncle had been a bishop in the city. Not only was the Church of the Resurrection burned down, but all Christians were forbidden to come to the city on pilgrimages. The persecution lasted until Hakim was assassinated in 1021. Soon the church was rebuilt by the emperor of Byzantium who, as one Arab chronicler wrote a few years later, "sent ambassadors with presents and promises of service and concluded a treaty in which he stipulated for permission to defray the expenses of rebuilding the church . . ."

In 1034, less than two decades after the collapse of the Dome of the Rock, another ominous earthquake destroyed the cupola again. After it was rebuilt, the city was startled again by its destruction in 1068 for the third time by yet another earthquake. The Muslims of the city were horrified; the Christians rather pleased, and members of both faiths exercised their ingenuity speculating as to what it all meant. In 1071 the answer seemed clear to them. The Dome's triple collapse portended a setback for the Arabs and the coming of the Seljuk Turks who conquered Jerusalem in that year. The Seljuks, a rough and terrifying Central Asiatic race recently converted to Islam, were building an empire for themselves upon the disintegrating body of the Arab empire. And upon the Byzantine empire, too, for in the year 1071 they had also defeated a great army sent against them by the Byzantines. Soon much of Asia Minor was under their control.

In Jerusalem the Seljuks had little respect for Christian shrines or for the rights of Christian citizens or pilgrims, this despite the fact that the pilgrim trade had come to be of great importance to the city once Hakim's ban against it had been rescinded. Europe was enjoying a cultural and economic revival that encouraged pilgrimages. In the year 1064, 7000 European pilgrims had come to Jerusalem as part of just one group, and they were by no means the only arrivals. But the Seljuks began to interfere with the pilgrims, refusing them entry into the Holy Land or into Jerusalem. Pilgrims' tales of Seljuk atrocities began filtering back to Europe, some of them highly colored, but many true. In the popular mind they were confused with the atrocities of which Hakim had been guilty. The Byzantine emperor appealed to the West for aid against the Turks who were threatening the conquest of his realm, the last bastion of Christian power in the East. His appeal was echoed by calls for revenge against the Turks from individual pilgrims who had journeyed all the way to Palestine only to be sorely oppressed as they were performing their religious observances. In the West, Christians were ready to heed their pleas; in the East, the Arabs were demoralized and distraught. For the fall of the Dome of the Rock might mean more than the destruction of Islam's great shrine in Jerusalem and more than the coming of the Turks. It might portend the very end of Islam's existence in the city.

"God Wants It"

J ERUSALEM is the center of the earth," the pope declared in
1095 to an audience of churchmen and nobles who had gathered to
hear him preach in the French Cathedral of Clermont, "the land is
fruitful above all others like a paradise of delights. This spot the
redeemer of mankind has made illustrious by his advent, has beau-
tified by his sojourn, has consecrated by his passion, has redeemed
by his death, has glorified by his burial. This royal city, however,
situated at the center of the earth, is now held captive by the enemies of Christ and is subjected, by those who do not know God, to
the worship of the heathen. She seeks therefore and desires to be
liberated, and ceases not to implore you to come to her aid."

Pope Urban II had come over the Alps to France to attend a
church council at Clermont and address his appeal for the deliverance of Jerusalem especially to the French nation, the "race of
Franks, . . . race beloved and chosen by God." "Let your quarrels end," he told them, "let wars cease and let all dissensions and
controversies slumber. Enter upon the road of the Holy Sepulcher,
wrest that land from the wicked race, and subject it to yourselves."
Although the pope's appeal had been directly inspired by the request for aid sent to him by the emperor of Byzantium, Urban

cared little about rescuing the Byzantine Empire from the Turks. He cared more about the opportunity to rescue the Eastern Church from itself; for the schism that had been festering for centuries between the Eastern and Western branches of Christianity had broken out into an open and seemingly final rift in the year 1054, when the pope of Rome and the Byzantine patriarch of Constantinople had acrimoniously excommunicated each other. With the patriarch of Constantinople went the patriarch of Jerusalem and the other churchmen of the East. Now the Bishop of Rome was alone—which was where he had always wanted to be; but his solitary glory was ignored rather than applauded by the Eastern Orthodox Church. A crusade would, he hoped, gather the eastern lands and churches safely into his fold. As it turned out, Jerusalem was almost all that he got, for Jerusalem became, as a result of the crusades, the center of a Roman Catholic kingdom for more than a century. Desirable as Jerusalem was, it was small pickings compared with Greece, Asia Minor, the Balkans, Russia and the rest of the East, which was what Pope Urban really wanted to gain.

Still, the possession of Jerusalem, the city of peace, the city of Christ, provided ample satisfaction, as well as spiritual reward. Its possession brought peace to the pilgrims, peace to the hearts of the faithful, even a measure of peace to the lands of Western Christendom. "Let quarrels end; let wars cease," the pope had urged. If the warrior class—so fecund of sons but not of peaceful ways to keep them occupied since war was almost their only pastime—was busy elsewhere or smaller, Western Europe would be much more tranquil. France, Germany, England, Italy had been plagued by petty wars. Clerics strove to impose a "peace of God" on the quarrelsome knights, and when a "peace of God," banning attacks on innocent priests, churchgoers, farmers, and merchants, did not work, then a "truce of God"—which forbade all warfare on Sunday and which was later extended to cover a long weekend beginning on Wednesday at sunset. For achieving peace on earth, or, at least, that portion of earth which was Roman Catholic, a crusade

was much more effective than a truce or even a "peace of God."
Sending the bellicose faithful off to Jerusalem "with the assurance
of the reward of imperishable glory in the kingdom of heaven" rid
western Europe of thousands of knights, who left their homes with
the intention of gaining peace in heaven by making war on earth.
They left their homelands peaceful, but everywhere they went
they brought war. Under their overlordship the history of the
Kingdom of Jerusalem was a century-long horror story of raids
and counterraids, battles and burnings. The lands through which
they traveled eventually recovered from their pious attentions; but
the land where they stayed, the Holy Land, was ruined.

The men who were to cause this ruin responded immediately
to Urban's appeal. *Deus vult, Deus vult*—God wants it—they
shouted. One story reports that within a day of Urban's speech,
news of it had traveled miraculously to every part of France from
Clermont at the center; soon thousands were setting out for Palestine, after having been blessed by village priests, offering themselves as sacrificial victims to God, indicating their purpose by
painting the sign of the cross on their foreheads, branding it on
their flesh, or sewing it on their garments, on the breast to indicate
that they were going forward to Jerusalem. Few of them would be
fortunate enough to return home, with the cross of the crusader
sewn, this time, on their backs.

The knights among them considered themselves God's vassals.
Warriors themselves, they thought of Christ as a warrior, rather
than as a shepherd as earlier and later Christians were likely to do;
and they thought of themselves as his army, going out to fight in a
final apocalyptic battle against the forces of evil. And although
they knew they might die when they ran forward into battle
crying "*Deus vult*" they expected, living or dead, that their Lord
would reward their devotion by bringing them to Jerusalem.
Which Jerusalem it was many of them neither knew nor cared. For
they had little capacity for differentiating between the Jerusalem at
the center of the earth and the New Jerusalem at the center of

heaven. They had been hearing of both for so long, and so inter-changeably, that they easily confused the two. Similarly, they con-fused their earthly and their heavenly reward. The streets and buildings of Jerusalem were made of pure gold and the walls were set with jewels, as it says in the Book of Revelations. They had seen representations of this on the walls of their churches. It seemed to them perfectly logical that the wealth of the city should be enjoyed by faithful Christians, particularly by crusaders willing to sacrifice their lives for the city. For many the pursuit of the kingdom of heaven was by no means their only aim. They were seeking kingdoms on earth as well, or at least principalities, and many succeeded in acquiring them when they arrived in the East.

Within two years of Urban's plea, some sixty to a hundred thousand crusaders had made their way across Europe to Constan-tinople. A good many of them were knights from northern France, Flanders, England and the Norman kingdom of southern Italy—regions which bred a surplus of warriors. The warriors were well organized; there were four armies of them under the leadership of prominent knights, one Raymond, Count of Toulouse, another Godfrey de Bouillon. There was also a less organized but probably more devout army of starving peasants and out-of-work farm laborers who were aroused by the preaching of a monk named Peter the Hermit, and there was even a troop of witless folk who marched off to Jerusalem behind a goose whom they believed to be inspired.

The knights and the mercenaries or soldiers under their com-mand lived by plunder, for that was their trade, and so they man-aged to survive quite well all the way across Europe. The peasants, who had found it hard to survive at home, had a worse time abroad. Peter the Hermit's following gradually disintegrated as the crusad-ing armies slowly moved across the continent; scarcely a handful of them ever reached Jerusalem. Some crusaders, in another group, got only as far as the Rhineland. There they decided that it was silly to travel so far to fight for Christ, when they could despoil and destroy his enemies right at home in Europe. They marched south through the Rhineland and attacked Jews in the cities of Cologne, Worms, Mainz, Speyer and wherever else they could find them, burning synagogues and murdering the murderers of Christ who had sought refuge in them. Soon other crusaders, who still intended to continue on to Jerusalem, joined them in the pogroms. Many of the Jews attempted to defend themselves, but they were ineffectual, weakened by the fasts they had undertaken hoping to avert the crusaders. The crusaders who were most fierce in attacking the Jews were also fiercest in attacking and plundering other innocents en route to Jerusalem. As a result, it was these crusaders who suffered most of the casualties when the crusading armies began to encounter difficult going in Hungary, where the populace took up arms against them. Contemporary Christian moralizers saw their destruction as just retribution for the massacres of the Jews.

In Asia, the crusaders really began to run into trouble. They had to fight their way almost mile by mile through the land of the Turks. By the time they reached Syria, their numbers had diminished considerably, and those who finally succeeded in battling their way down to Jerusalem were something like one ninth or tenth the number that had set out. No more than 13,000 men reached Palestine to be welcomed by the Christians of the country. In the year 1099, at the time of the crusaders' arrival, Christians made up half the population of the country, but Jerusalem contained no Christians at all for they had recently been expelled from the city by the Muslims who feared they would support the invading army rather than their Muslim overlords. They were accused by the Muslims of sending letters to the pope and to the kings of Europe requesting the crusades.

In 1092, after the short-lived Seljuk Empire fell apart, Palestine had once again become a border region contested by Egypt and by the Seljuk successor states in Syria. In 1098 it had been reconquered by the Egyptians, and when the crusaders arrived there were Egyptian banners flying over the citadel and over the walls of Jerusalem. The defending army consisted of about 1000 men, mercenaries from the Arabian peninsula and from the Sudan —Ethiopians, the attacking crusaders called them. On June 7, when the crusader army came within sight of the city, the soldiers dismounted from their horses and knelt, weeping with joy and religious devotion. But as they marched on, their tears turned to tears of sorrow for they discovered that the Muslims had poisoned the wells surrounding the city to deprive the invaders of water. There was little wood also. This meant it would be difficult to make siege engines, which considerably disturbed the crusaders' plans, for the walls of Jerusalem were thick and high, as difficult to assail as the fortress of heaven. The construction of battering-rams, catapults, assault towers on wheels and, of course, scaling ladders, required wood which had to be brought on the backs of camels all the way from Samaria. Nails came from the coast, having been transported to Palestine by Genoese seamen. Large pieces of timber could not be carried on camelback, and so the crusaders, instructed by Genoese craftsmen from the ships, built an assault tower of small pieces of wood fastened together as securely as possible. For their good services in the capture of the city, the Genoese later received trading privileges in Jerusalem and a street of their own in which Genoese law applied. They also had the account of their contributions engraved on a golden plaque which was placed in the Church of the Holy Sepulcher.

The crusaders' siege towers might be shaky but their faith was not, even though the first assault on the city was unsuccessful. After the setback the crusaders' fighting ardor was increased by pilgrimages to accessible shrines. They climbed the Mount of Olives to visit the site of Jesus' ascension and went down to the River Jordan to bathe in the waters where Christ had been baptized. Saints and angels, they assured themselves, fought alongside them. Daily, priests and monks attached to the army preached sermons reminding the crusaders why they had come. For the benefit of those who forgot the sins of the infidel for a moment, the Muslim soldiers defending Jerusalem provided convenient reminders. They removed as many crosses as they could from the churches within the city, set them up on the walls and entertained themselves by desecrating them; not being content with making vulgar gestures or spitting at the crosses, they urinated on them, too. These outrages inspired the attackers with a pious fury and a resolution to extirpate the devils, or the devil's servants, who could perform such deeds. But fury and resolution alone proved insufficient to take the city and the siege dragged on for week after week in the dry hot summer.

It was not until one crusader reported a dream which revealed that the Christians would never capture Jerusalem unless they fought for Christ's glory rather than their own, that the delay was explained to the army's satisfaction. To atone for their selfishness the entire crusading army marched in solemn procession around the walls of the city, barefoot and singing hymns. The inhabitants of Jerusalem stood on the walls laughing at them. They were laughing, as it turned out, almost for the last time, for little more than a week later, after a steady bombardment of rocks and fire and battering-ram attacks lasting two days, crusading soldiers pushed a siege tower up against the north wall and succeeded in setting a fire so fierce it drove the defenders away. At noon the first crusading troops made their way over the wall and into the city, to be followed quickly by thousands of others. For almost a century thereafter a cross erected on the wall marked the site where the Muslim defenses had been breached.

There were at the time some forty thousand inhabitants in the city, Muslims and a sizable colony of Jews. Almost all of them were massacred. "Many were pierced to death," one chronicler writes, ". . . and wildly hurled down from the wall. . . . almost ten thousand were decapitated. If you had been there, you would have seen our feet bespattered to the soles with the blood of the slain. . . . not a single life was spared. . . . our squires and the poorest infantry troops, learning of the Saracens' cunning, slit the bellies even of the slain to extract from their bowels the bezants that they had swallowed while alive. After a few days, they piled up the bodies in a great heap and burned them in order to find the coins more easily among the burnt ashes."

The slaughter was incredible. This chronicler records that the crusaders' feet were bespattered to the soles with blood. Other chroniclers report the blood flowing more copiously, reaching to the crusaders' ankles. Yet another historian of the time raises the blood level to reach as high as the fetlocks of the crusaders' horses —and these horses were not small and dainty, but destriers, or chargers, heavy and large. The Jews of Jerusalem were led within their synagogue which was then set afire. A few who had managed to escape were sold into slavery, thirty for one coin—as a reminder of the thirty pieces of silver Judas had received for selling Christ. "The Germans conspire to descend upon us and evil reports of them confound us, and we know not what to do," a Galilean Jew had written a few months earlier upon hearing of the coming of the crusaders into Palestine. The man was misinformed; the crusaders were most of them not Germans, but they acted toward the Jews as the Germans would one day act. "It was indeed the righteous judgment of God," wrote another Christian chronicler, exulting over the death of the Jerusalem Muslims, "which ordained that those who had profaned the sanctuary of the Lord by their superstitious rites and had caused it to be an alien place to His faithful people should expiate their sin by death and by pouring out their own blood to purify the sacred precincts."

Part of the purification process involved picking up anything in the city without an owner, or with an owner who then had but a few moments left to live. The crusaders rushed through the streets and, according to previous plan, each of the knights who was intending to stay in the city set about trying to find a suitable residence. When a house caught his fancy, he marched into it and took possession, hanging his shield above the door as a mark of ownership. Any inhabitant so unfortunate as to remain in the house was slaughtered to make sure there would be no dispute over title. Late-comers had to take any house they could find without a shield over the door. The city had been a rich one, and it took some time before all the booty was collected and enough of the enemy had been slaughtered. Then the real object of the crusade could be achieved.

Weeping—like the Jews who returned to the city in the sixth century B.C. and again in 1967, and as Muslims will doubtless do if they ever conquer it again—the Christians walked through Jerusalem in a solemn procession, barefoot, like penitents, along the *Via Dolorosa*, pausing now and then to bend down and kiss the pavement over which Christ had walked. Before the Holy Sepulcher the barons who had led the crusade fell down and touched their faces to the floor. "Oh what an hour craved by us all," the chronicler Foucher of Chartres, who was there, wrote. "What a moment to be remembered beyond all others."

Among the Arabs, however, there were other exclamations, other tears. "We have mingled our blood with tears . . ." one of them wrote, "what eye can close its lids in sleep indifferent to events which would wake all sleepers?. . . Will the chieftains of Arabia sit down under such an insult? Will the warriors of Persia submit to such debasement?" The answer was yes. The rival caliphs of Baghdad and Cairo dutifully put on garments of mourning to commemorate the massacre and the rape of the Jerusalem shrine; but each caliph thought it incumbent on the other to reconquer the city, and neither was going to extend himself with an all-out effort to seize it if his rival might possibly benefit from its recapture. With the lesson of the Jerusalem massacre before them, the Muslims and Jews in towns along the Palestinian coast resolved to fight to the death against the crusaders. But one by one the coastal towns were taken, beginning in the year 1101 with Haifa, the strongest and the most inimical to the crusaders because the majority of its inhabitants were Jews.

A few months after the conquest of Jerusalem, an Arab army came up to the Gaza region from Egypt. Troublesome Arab raids continued along the pilgrim route connecting Jerusalem with the coast. No part of the crusader domain was more than a few miles from Muslim territory. And so the crusaders decided, despite church pressure, to choose a soldier rather than a bishop for their ruler. After a good deal of the negotiating, disagreement, and bargaining that was to mark the feudal system of the Kingdom of Jerusalem through its lifetime, they selected Godfrey de Bouillon as king of Jerusalem. But Godfrey refused to be king; only Christ, he said, was worthy of the title of King of Jerusalem. He chose, instead, to be the "Advocate," or "Defender of the Holy Sepulcher," and remained so until his death a few years later. (As soon as they had the chance his less modest successors took the title of king.) Godfrey also refused to have his coronation ceremony in Jerusalem, reluctant to wear "a golden crown in the place where Christ had worn a crown of thorns." And so he was named Advocate of the Holy Sepulcher in the Church of the Nativity at Bethlehem. Godfrey paid homage to the newly elected Patriarch of Jerusalem, a Machiavellian Italian churchman who had got himself chosen head of the Jerusalem Church though he was already the Archbishop of Pisa, and he promised the Patriarch to surrender Jerusalem to the church as soon as he acquired another town of comparable value for himself—Cairo, Alexandria, Damascus, any of them might do. None were conquered, however, and Godfrey continued ruler of Jerusalem for the few remaining years of his life.

Jerusalem, on its part, was happy to make do with Godfrey, if the only alternative was to come under the direct rule of the church. The Greek Orthodox were especially relieved for the triumphant Catholic Church bore heavily on them. They had hoped to live untroubled under Christian rule and welcomed the crusaders with processions and psalms as the invaders marched south through Palestine. But once Jerusalem was taken, they found to their dismay that they were under the control of a rude and alien race, who were just as contemptuous of the Orthodox religion as the Muslims ever were. Latin priests took over the Church of the

Resurrection and refused to allow the Orthodox or any other Christian sect to use it, or any other church in the city, for masses. The Latins even changed its name. With the realism, materialism and lugubrious concern with death characteristic of Western men, they called it, as Westerners still do, the Church of the Holy Sepulcher instead of the Church of the Resurrection, or *Anastasis*, the name given it by the Orthodox with their innocent and hopeful spirituality. Barred from the church, the Orthodox refused to divulge to the Catholics the location of its treasured relics, including the True Cross which had been removed and taken to safety before the siege of the city began. So the crusader priests put them to torture until the hiding places were revealed. The Greeks eventually returned to the church but only as guests. Their restoration came about as the result of a miracle, or rather the interruption of a miracle: the Holy Fire, which supposedly comes down spontaneously from heaven at midnight just as Easter begins to symbolize the resurrection of Christ. From it the faithful light their Easter candles, as they still do in Jerusalem and in all Orthodox churches today. But that Easter in 1101 they failed to light them, for the Holy Fire refused to descend. This convinced the Latins that they had been wrong to forbid the Greeks access to the church; almost two years later, when the Greeks and the other non-Catholics were restored to their rights in the church, the fire miraculously lit again without mishap.

Despite the resumption of Greek services in the church, the Latins retained all of the powers and treasures of the Orthodox patriarchate in Jersualem, and for almost a century Eastern Orthodox Christians in the land remained under the control of Latin priests and patriarchs. Those who refused to accept their new spiritual leaders were forced to pay a special tax, imposed throughout the crusader kingdom on heretics, Muslims and Jews. The Latins did manage to prevail on one Eastern group to join with the Roman Church—the Maronites. And they continued, for a while at least, to have high hopes for the reunification of all Christians with the help of Catholic force, if Catholic faith proved unsuccessful. Foucher of Chartres saw the crusades "as a step towards the union of nations."

But the longer the crusaders remained in Jerusalem, the more tolerant of others they became. Even non-Christians benefited. Within the Kingdom of Jerusalem, Christians and Muslims were eventually allowed to marry. One patriarch of Jerusalem was so ecumenical that he performed the wedding ceremony of a Christian knight and a Muslim lady. The pope in Rome heard about it and was outraged and he reprimanded the patriarch. His reprimand could stop marriages with Muslims but it could not stop liaisons. The patriarchs themselves tended to confine their attentions to Christian ladies, but other Western settlers played the field. The number of half-castes in the Kingdom of Jerusalem continued to rise. (The Westerners' blond, blue-eyed descendants can still be picked out among the Arab population of Palestine; the Israelis call them crusaders.) Heretics, Jews and Muslims were encouraged to stay in the environs of Jerusalem, although not in the capital itself, for the region was dangerously underpopulated. A few even managed to bribe their way in to live within the city walls. Muslims were comfortable so long as they paid a tithe of their income to the Roman Catholic church, an annoying tax indeed, but one that was palliated somewhat by the fact that, even though it was going to support an alien creed, taxes were lower for Muslims in the Kingdom of Jerusalem than they were in neighboring Muslim lands. And both Muslims and Jews were allowed to visit Jerusalem as pilgrims. The Muslims were even permitted to pray unobtrusively in their mosques which had been converted to churches. They consoled themselves for the presence of the infidel with the reminder that Palestine was, according to the Koran, "the land . . . blessed for all human beings," even if the human beings were so ignorant as to worship, as many Muslims believed the crusaders did, not one but three gods—God the Father, God the Son, and the Virgin Mary, the third person of the Trinity.

Within a few years of the conquest of Jerusalem, Christians controlled the entire east coast of the Mediterranean, which was divided into numerous independent or semi-independent countries and principalities, under the leadership of the King of Jerusalem— the nominal leadership, that is, for as in most feudal kingdoms the royal vassals were unruly. A few miles inland were the Muslims— almost as unruly, under the leadership of a group of emirs, atabegs, sultans, who would just as soon join with the Christians as with any of their fellow Muslims if it proved advantageous. On the Christian side there was an insanely complex history of shifting alliances and dynastic squabbles. The prince of Galilee, the king of Jerusalem, the constable of Jerusalem, the lord of Oultrejourdain, the emir of Baalbek, the Grand Master of the Temple, the Arab prince of Damascus, the Christian lord of Sidon, Princess Melisende of Jerusalem, and her sister Hodierna, Baldwin the leper king of Jerusalem, Lady Morphia of Melitene, the vizier of Cairo, the general of the Assassin clan, the Genoese, the Pisans, the Venetians, the merchants of Marseilles, any of them might find himself allied with or at war with any of the others. Amid this kaleidoscope of forces the Kingdom of Jerusalem maintained a precarious existence, its survival dependent on the arrival of fresh and fanatical recruits from among the knights of the West. Its fate was linked to the continuing rivalries between the Arabs of Cairo and those of Baghdad and Damascus, between Venice and the other Italian trading towns, between the Latin Christians and the Orthodox, the German knights and the French. All jockeyed for a predominant position. All combined and betrayed each other in the most unpredictable fashion.

At the center of the kingdom, spiritually and politically, was the city of Jerusalem, whose possession was ostensibly the only *raison d'être* of the realm. This sacred prize the Christians adorned with all the fervor that their fellows in Europe were devoting to the beautification of *their* cities. The twelfth century—when the crusaders held Jerusalem—was a great age of urban development.

The Venetians had begun the construction of the vast Basilica of Saint Mark, and were decorating its interior with golden mosaics. In England cathedrals were being erected at Canterbury, Winchester, Durham and Norwich, the last begun a few months after Pope Urban issued his appeal for the first crusade. In the great Russian city-state of Novgorod the first onion-domed churches were rising. France, the land from which most of the crusaders came, was witnessing the heyday of Romanesque architecture. The crusaders brought their civilization's love for fine building to Jerusalem. It seemed hopeless for them to attempt to restore the city to the glory it had enjoyed a few hundred years earlier, before the Persians destroyed the great churches of the Emperor Constantine and his successors. Nevertheless, they labored to build structures that were worthy of the site.

They began with the Church of the Holy Sepulcher. Golgotha, where Christ had been crucified, and the stone where his body had been anointed before its entombment were marked by small chapels. The crusaders joined these to the main part of the church but left a space above the Sepulcher open to the sky to which Jesus had risen from his tomb. A Romanesque façade was built, Romanesque walls and porches, and a bell tower. Bas-reliefs showing Christ's entry into Jerusalem, the Last Supper and other biblical scenes were commissioned in France and transported to Palestine to be placed over the twin doorways that gave access to the church. Within, the walls were adorned with golden mosaics in the Byzantine style, like those that can still be seen at Saint Mark's in Venice and in the churches at Constantinople, "pictures of the prophets and of the Lord Messiah and of the Lady Maryam his mother, and of John the Baptist," as one awed Arab visitor reported. The rebuilt church was dedicated on July 15, 1149, half a century to the day after Jerusalem had been reconquered by the Christians.

Long before the new church was completed, the crusaders made other changes in the city. They took over both al-Aqsa

Mosque and the Dome of the Rock, turning the latter into a church. Believing it to be the original temple of Solomon, they revered it almost as much as they did the sites associated with Christ's death and resurrection. They regilded the dome and topped it with a large cross, built an altar within, and surrounded the sacred rock with a wrought iron railing, portions of which are still standing, to keep pilgrims from chipping off bits to take home as souvenirs. On the wall they hung an icon of the founder of the shrine, Solomon. Al-Aqsa Mosque they used first as a royal palace and then as a dormitory for knights. Nearby they established a monastery of Augustinian canons, perhaps on the site of a building that had been used before as a residence by a brotherhood of Muslim mystics. The public squares of the city were adorned with fountains, new palaces were built with gardens and frescoed halls, and sculptors were set to work carving capitals for hundreds of columns erected along the city's colonnaded streets and squares. Some of the designs showed Muslim arabesques, others Christian imagery, others some of the themes that had adorned Jerusalem in antiquity: imaginary winged beasts like the cherubim, or struggles between wild animals and heroes, like the Jews' Samson, or Gilgamesh of the Babylonians, or the Greek Herakles, heroes the crusaders admired and strove to emulate. One of the crusaders, Richard the Lion-Hearted, was even portrayed by a medieval painter wearing his crown, but wrestling with a lion like Samson or Herakles.

To this beautiful city came knights from all over the crusaders' domain to attend the High Court of Jerusalem, the parliament of the kingdom. Many of the high lords made their homes in Jerusalem, abandoning their estates in the countryside to the care of bailiffs who remitted rents to them in the capital, while they enjoyed its pleasures and endless political intrigues. These knights and most of the city's other Westerners, or Franks as they were called, spoke French, a French that was still in the process of formation, and that, in Palestine, was diluted with many local words. By the second half of the twelfth century there were about twenty-five thousand Franks living in Jerusalem and thousands more who were of mixed Frankish and native descent. Not all the Franks were Frenchmen; there were a good many Italians, and a number of Germans who were disappointed when they arrived in the Holy Land to find the influence of their nation inconsiderable. In Jerusalem the Genoese and Venetians lived by themselves in separate streets, as did the Maronites, Copts, Greeks and Jacobites. Venice and Genoa, along with Amalfi, Pisa, and Marseilles, also maintained their own quarters in the main ports of the crusader kingdom. The Franks were joined in Jerusalem by their allies, the Armenians, who came in the train of various Armenian princesses betrothed to crusaders or arrived as members of armies enlisted to fight against the Saracens. The Armenians settled alongside their compatriots, monks who had long dwelt in the southwest corner of the holy city, in the area that has, since the time of the crusades, been known as the Armenian Quarter. Sometime in the twelfth century a few Jews also arrived, having purchased the right to dwell in the town and practice the trade of dyeing, a trade which they apparently monopolized in the region and which was of considerable importance, for textile production played a large part in the economy of the Levant.

The markets of crusader Jerusalem were located approximately where they are now, at the center of town and along the main north-south street. In the midst of them stood the *bursa*, the purse or bourse or money changers' market, located between the Church of the Holy Sepulcher and the temple from which Jesus had expelled the money changers more than a thousand years earlier. At the *bursa* pilgrims and merchants could exchange Venetian, Byzantine or Saracen coins for the coins of the Kingdom of Jerusalem depicting the king and the Tower of David, the Dome of the Rock and the Church of the Holy Sepulcher. There was a street of the bakers, close to the Holy Sepulcher, and a street of the furriers (where, it is reported, one visiting crusader knight was slain as a

result of a quarrel while playing dice). Another street was called
Malcuisinat—bad cooking; there are still cook shops at the site.
There was a cattle market in the shadow of the south wall, a sheep
pen by the east wall near the ancient Sheep Gate, and to the un-
doubted horror of Jewish and Muslim pilgrims, a pig market in the
western part of the city.

Strong walls surrounded Jerusalem; the crusaders had refortified them after taking the city. They were patrolled by guards
under the direction of the viscount, who was in charge of maintaining order in the town and supervising tax collectors. The citadel
called David's Tower, the last stronghold in the city to yield to the
crusaders, was strengthened; the city's walls were heightened; and
a royal palace was built alongside the tower—a luxurious dwelling
place furnished with gold and silver dishes, porcelain imported
from China, soft carpets and damask hangings to guard against
Jerusalem's harsh winter cold.

Jerusalem was owned in its entirety by the king, and the inhabitants were his vassals. He also owned all the land surrounding
the town, along with the towns of Acre, Nablus, and perhaps Jaffa,
Tyre and Ascalon as well. A large percentage of his income came
from taxes levied on products transported across the territory of
his kingdom between the Arab lands and the Mediterranean. But
much of the wealth of the realm was controlled not by the king or
his nobles, or by the Italian traders, but by military orders and the
church, both of which held vast estates throughout Palestine and
even in Europe. The patriarch of Jerusalem was especially rich.
Many villages and some large towns were owned lock, stock and
barrel. Jericho belonged completely to an abbey at Bethany. When
the Arabs reconquered the country, the villages and estates were
redistributed to Arab nobles and Arab religious foundations.

A good deal of wealth came, as usual, from the pilgrim trade.
Considerable sums of money were made feeding and housing the
pilgrims. The Jerusalemites made a little more money by selling
their women to the visitors—weary men who had journeyed long

and single-mindedly toward their goal—offering, as one contemporary chronicler wrote, "their sisters, their daughters and even their
wives for the pleasure of pilgrims for money." They also picked up
a little extra cash by selling the pilgrims slaves, boys as well as girls,
to serve their masters in and out of bed. And of course they sold
pious souvenirs for a good price—such as sacred oil from the lamps
of the Holy Sepulcher.

Unlike their predecessors and successors in the city, the crusaders were very careful however not to mulct pilgrims, for pilgrims also defended Jerusalem, fighting against the Saracens as
faithfully as they visited the shrines. Even the uncertain ethics of
the day did not permit biting the hand that helped as well as fed
you. Like Israeli Jerusalem for so many years, the crusader city
was always aware of the fact that it was a besieged outpost. At the
time of the crusader conquest the surrounding region had been
emptied of its population, and when the Franks arrived in Jerusalem, they were, according to one chronicler, too few "to fill a
street." In the years after their arrival continued appeals went out
to Europe for immigrants to help Christendom hold on to its bulwark amid a sea of Arabs. These were, in a way, quite similar to
the appeals Israelis have made for more Jewish settlers to come to
the country from the lands of the Disapora. Many of the messengers who traveled throughout Europe calling for settlers were
returning crusaders, well aware of the advantages of life in the
Kingdom of Jerusalem and of the grave need for settlers. Unfortunately, by their very presence in Europe rather than in Palestine,
they acted as reverse advertisements for their cause, no matter how
fervently they voiced it.

Recruits were constantly needed; casualty rates were high
among crusading knights, even after Western armor and fighting
tactics had been adapted to the exigencies of the region. Many
knights who came as pilgrims fought only a season or two and then
left. Few came as permanent immigrants. Those who did had to

undertake an expensive voyage by sea, for the overland routes were too perilous for individuals or small groups. The sea voyage brought some knights but very few peasants since it was far too expensive for most of them to undertake. And, although knights were necessary to the crusader cause, peasants were needed more to make the crusader kingdom of Jerusalem viable. A few peasant colonists did arrive from France and, even more valuable to the cause, remained as peasants on the land; but there was always to be a shortage of Franks in the countryside. Out of a total of a million inhabitants in all the crusader states, there were probably only about fifty thousand westerners—about half of them in Jerusalem. And so, unlike the Zionists, the crusaders made the fatal decision to leave the heavy work to local Arabs while they lived the lives of lords, if they could, in fine town houses in the capital.

Of course no other decision was open to them. It never occurred to these medieval gentlemen that they could live on the land as well as off it. They were, in the most pejorative sense of the word, imperialists, colonialists, exploiters out to seize whatever they could although they seized it with the most pious motives. They came into the land not, as the Jews did two thousand years before and nine hundred years later, searching for a place to settle (though Arabs are fond of comparing crusaders and Zionists); rather they came looking for a place to take over. The crusaders wanted to recreate in Palestine a society such as they were accustomed to in their European homelands, a society with warrior chieftains, each protecting and exploiting his own petty domain. It was a society such as the land had not seen since Canaanite times when Canaan was divided into tiny principalities, and which it would not see again until the eighteenth century when Turkish power was disintegrating.

For centuries younger sons were sent out to the East to make a fortune, to "wrest that land from the wicked race and subject it" to themselves the way the conquistadores went to America and the

British to India, the way whites went to the Congo in the nineteenth century and still go today. Other recruits—again like conquistadores or the whites in India or the Congo—were criminals
who chose exile rather than prison or even execution. Some of the
crusaders were pious and large-hearted men, but most were not.
Although they were fanatically religious, they were as greedy and
as brutal as if they had never even heard of Christianity. Heirs of
the less attractive aspects of the European tradition (the more attractive aspects had hardly been born yet), they had the same sense
of values as children or as characters in a "western" movie. They
smelled bad, they were unshaven and they howled as they ran into
battle, a sound made somehow more chilling by the fact that the
words howled were *Deus vult*. One crusader hero entertained himself by cutting off the heads of Arab prisoners and roasting them,
to make the enemy think that he ate them.

These men had a limited idea of pleasure; their idea of fun-and-
profit was a raid. The crusader lords kept careful watch on the
movements of the Bedouin so that they could ambush them and
steal flocks. Raids into enemy territory were a major source of income for the fledgling Kingdom of Jerusalem under its second
king, Baldwin I. Baldwin and his army would cross the Jordan and,
like western cattle rustlers, round up what livestock they could
from the Arab inhabitants—sheep, goats, and camels—and then
ford the shallow river with them and return to Jerusalem to sell the
loot. Admiring chroniclers recorded the king's exploits, and there is
a medieval manuscript illumination that shows him crossing the
Jordan with one haul. Baldwin's income was also supplemented by
going out to battle with the Arabs, not to destroy them or gain territory, but to win captives, whom he would then offer for ransom.
The Arabs considered the crusaders uncivilized brutes, animals,
good only for fighting, which was something they did superbly.
The crusaders took full advantage of the fear they inspired. To
show his strength Baldwin I decapitated a camel with one stroke of

his sword in front of a terrified Arab. He was so feared and hated that for centuries after his death Arabs passing by the site near Gaza where he was killed in a skirmish were accustomed to throw stones at the spot.

The crusaders most feared and hated by the Arabs were the members of the monastic orders, Templars and Hospitallers, whose hundreds of recruits from all over western Europe vowed poverty, chastity, and obedience, and promised to fight the Saracens at every opportunity. In time these monastic orders became the mainstay of the Kingdom of Jerusalem's defense. The Templar's original concern had been escorting pilgrims safely through the land; the Hospitallers' had been providing housing for pilgrims at the shrines; but fighting quickly became the major business of both orders. The Templars had their headquarters in the Dome of the Rock—Solomon's temple—which gave them their name. The Hospitallers maintained elaborate headquarters near the Church of the Holy Sepulcher. Unable to confine their hostility to the Muslims, they carried on a long and bitter quarrel with the patriarch of Jerusalem and his adherents, making a special point of ringing their own church bells very loudly whenever the patriarch was preaching. To remind the patriarch of their animosity and their power, a group of Hospitallers at one time invaded the Sepulcher of Christ and fired arrows in the church terrifying worshippers and priests.

The military orders became the chief landowners in the crusader domains, or as they were called, *Outremer*, "beyond the sea." As they defended the Kingdom of Jerusalem they impoverished it, for their holdings were considered ecclesiastical property and were thus untaxable. In many ways they, or at least the Templars, were similar to the Muslim orders of warrior monks that developed at the same time and whose fortresses can still be seen along the North African coasts, where they defended the inhabitants of Barbary against the raids of Christian pirates. Both Muslim and Christian orders had the same fighting temperament, the same parochial pride, the same homosexual habits, and the same inclinations toward mysticism, which came to the Templars under the influence of Muslim thought.

The Templars and Hospitallers, like all the other crusaders, felt free to wage war or conclude peace without regard for the policy of the Kingdom of Jerusalem as a whole. They were constantly going out to raid the enemy, stirring up Saracen reprisals even though, as the twelfth century progressed, the crusaders were becoming weaker, and the Saracens stronger and more united. It was not the military orders, however, but a crusader lord, Raynald of Châtillon, Lord of Kerak and Moab, who embarked on the raid that was to have the most serious consequences for the future of Jerusalem and the entire crusader kingdom. In the year 1183, Raynald launched a fleet of ships from the northern end of the Gulf of Aqaba and led his men southward along the coast of the Arabian peninsula, raiding the coastal towns, and plundering caravans proceeding along a coast that had been secure for centuries. Not content with economic gain, Raynald sought spiritual profit as well by sinking Muslim pilgrim ships that were bound for Mecca, and announcing that he was planning to conquer that sacred city, convert it to the Christian faith and rule it himself. Muslims might countenance the taking of Jerusalem, but Mecca was another story. The entire Arab world was outraged. The more pessimistic feared that Raynald's raids heralded the end of the world; others, more vigorous, saw that it could herald the end of Christian rule in Palestine, or at least the end of Raynald himself. Chief among these was Saladin, the sultan of Egypt, part Turk part Kurd, the ruler by 1185 of a new empire, surrounding the crusader states, that had been slowly built up by himself, his uncle and his grandfather.

As soon as Saladin had assured his rule over the valleys of both the Nile and the Tigris-Euphrates, he turned his attention to the crusaders. Unlike previous Muslim rulers, who had controlled less territory and had less energy, he was successful in his attacks. By 1175 the Kingdom of Jerusalem was almost a shambles under the rule of Baldwin IV, who was not only a child but a leper, and completely unable to control or inspirit his vassals. The year 1177 marked the last time that a Frankish army carrying the True Cross into battle was able to defeat the Saracens. From then on, defeat followed defeat. By the time the leper king died in 1185, the life of the kingdom was precarious indeed, for Raynald's raid in 1183 had made Saladin resolve to drive the Crusaders out of Palestine.

In 1185 the Franks managed to negotiate a truce which for a while ensured their survival; but they survived only on Saladin's sufferance. The precarious truce was broken in 1186, foolishly, by Raynald of Châtillon, who captured and plundered a caravan traveling through his domain en route from Cairo to Damascus, from one of Saladin's cities to another. The caravan was too tempting for Raynald to resist and when he was called upon to make amends, he was too avaricious to restore the booty. Saladin declared the truce had been broken, and proceeded to the attack.

On July 4, 1187, at the hill of Hattin, near Tiberias in Galilee, Saladin met the crusader forces—including a large body of Templars equipped by and paid with money sent to Palestine by Henry II of England as a token of his remorse for the murder of Thomas à Becket. The Christian army was destroyed, the Muslims capturing the relic of the True Cross which had been carried into battle under a canopy accompanied by a group of priests, like the ancient Jews' Ark of the Covenant. Numerous Templars and Hospitallers were taken prisoner, and Raynald of Châtillon; Raynald, Saladin decapitated with his own sword. The Templars and Hospitallers, "the worst of the infidel race," as Saladin called them, were executed one by one—while the sultan watched—their heads cut off by members of Muslim religious orders and by the cadis and other spiritual leaders who accompanied the Saracen army. "Every day," wrote a Muslim chronicler in Damascus after the battle, "Christian heads were seen arriving, as numerous as watermelons." Along with them came the relic of the True Cross to be kept captive in the city for years thereafter, and an icon of the crucified Christ which was triumphantly carried through the streets upside down, as the populace cheered. "A splendid and beneficent year, a blessed age," wrote another Arab, "Monotheism avenged itself on the doctrine of the trinity." At the end of September came the climax of that splendid and beneficent year as Saladin led his army up to Jerusalem.

There were about five thousand Christian soldiers remaining within the city, but only a few of them were knights, including thirty bourgeois who had just been ennobled to help cope with the emergency. In the months since his victory at Hattin Saladin had made himself master of most of the country. He had already summoned the inhabitants of Jerusalem to his camp on the Mediterranean coast and demanded their surrender. But they refused, and they remained resolute even when the sultan moved his army up to take a siege position on the plain west of the city, and began to attack the walls near the Citadel of David with his army of some 60,000 men. Five days later, for religious and tactical reasons, he moved his camp to the Mount of Olives where Omar, the city's first Arab conqueror, had encamped; from there he could see the entire city spread out beneath him. This time he resumed the attack on the northeastern corner of the walls where almost a century earlier the crusaders themselves had breached Jerusalem's defenses. Emissaries from the city climbed the Mount of Olives to his camp and begged for terms, threatening to burn down the Muslim shrines in the city and slay all Muslim prisoners unless they were allowed an honorable surrender. Saladin granted it to them, offering to let the Frankish population of the city depart for a ransom— ten dinars for each man, five for each woman, and one for each child (native Christians were allowed to remain free). This was too much money for the city's poor to raise, and so the crusaders' representatives haggled with the sultan until they agreed on a sum of thirty thousand dinars in exchange for seven thousand poor Christians who were unable to afford the regular ransom. That worked out to little more than four dinars each.

Those Franks who could purchase their freedom paid the ransom and left Jerusalem. To free seven thousand of the poor 30,000 dinars were raised to meet Saladin's demands. Much of this money came from the treasuries of the Templars and Hospitallers—although the Orders' leaders surrendered it only reluctantly; part had been money sent to Jerusalem in contrition for the murder of Thomas by Henry II of England. Once this money was paid there were still thousands of poor Franks who were doomed to slavery. Despite this, the Roman Catholic patriarch left Jerusalem after paying his own ten dinar ransom and those of the priests, deacons and canons who served under him; along with him went his wealth, carts full of gold, plate and rich carpets. The Muslims were shocked by his inhumanity. Saladin's brother was so moved by the sight that he offered to purchase the freedom of a thousand poor Christians himself, thus shaming the patriarch into matching his offer, almost, by volunteering ransom money for seven hundred more. Saladin, not to be outdone, then announced that he was freeing all the aged captives, as well as husbands who had been able to raise money to free their wives but not enough to free themselves too. Widows and orphans who were going into slavery he endowed with silver in compensation for their lot. He also ordered that the ransomed prisoners be repatriated to Europe on ships from the Italian trading towns, but only after he had taken precautions to ensure that their fellow Christians, the shipowners, would not sell them into slavery or jettison them on a barren coast in order to take on a more profitable cargo. And despite the example given by the crusaders when they conquered the city, he ordered his men to kill no one, and to steal nothing. They obeyed.

With banners flying the Arabs marched into the city, proceeding directly to al-Aqsa Mosque and the Dome of the Rock to pray and purify them of the sacrileges perpetrated by the Christians. As one of their number climbed up to the top of the Dome of the Rock to wrench off the cross that had stood there for almost a century, the soldiers of the Muslim army cheered. It was October

2, 1187, the anniversary of the day on which Mohammed from that same place had ascended to heaven mounted upon the magical horse Buraq. "What a wonderful coincidence!" exclaimed a Muslim chronicler, the biographer of the hero Saladin. "God allowed the Muslims to take the city as a celebration of the anniversary of their holy prophet's Midnight Journey. Truly this is a sign that this deed was pleasing to almighty God . . ."

CHAPTER 9

Via Dolorosa

Now that they were in control of Jerusalem once again, the Muslims did their best to expunge all traces of the recent Christian occupation. The icon of Jesus was taken down from the door of the Dome of the Rock. New mosaics were commissioned for the mosque of al-Aqsa. Both buildings were purified by being washed down with rose water, and al-Aqsa was cleansed thoroughly of all the impious remains that the Christians had left there. (Reportedly the Knights Templar had utilized the mosque as a latrine. Being only human they had doubtless used part of the building in this mundane, but necessary way. But sacrilege stories are never lacking whenever Jerusalem changes masters, and they were accused of so defiling the entire building.)

After much competition for the honor among religious leaders, a preacher was selected to deliver the sermon at the ceremony that was to be held to celebrate the reconquest of Jerusalem for Islam. Standing before a vast throng assembled for the occasion in the Haram esh Sharif, and before Saladin himself, who wore robes unadorned by any signs of rank to demonstrate his humility, the preacher described at length the virtues of the city of Jerusalem and praised Allah for having restored it to its rightful owners, for "the silencing of the bells and the expulsion of the priests." He apologized to his audience for not reciting every passage in the Koran that begins with the formula "Praise be to God"; there were too many such passages for him to repeat that day. And so he contented himself with his own variations on the theme. "Praise be to God who hath magnified Islam by his aid and humbled the Associators by this glorious victory. . . ," he declared. As the Jews had when they evicted the Syrians from the place during the time of the Maccabees, he praised God for having "purified his consecrated house from the filth." Not only God was praised; Saladin and his soldiers, many of them Syrians, were lauded too for having "renewed the times of the introduction of Islam, those holy times. . . ." "All the chief angels shall exult over you," he promised them, "and the most intelligent prophets and apostles. . . ." "Purify the rest of the earth from these impure," he urged them, ". . . cut off the heads of the infidels; destroy their root from the earth."

With the sanctuary restored to its original purity, Saladin proceeded to deal with Jerusalem's other religious affairs. He requisitioned the crusader church of Saint Anne in the northeast corner of the city—a church that was built, according to one account, leaning slightly to one side just as Christ had leaned while he was nailed to the cross—and established in it an institution for the study of the Muslim religious law. Income for the school's upkeep came from very productive *waqfs*, or religious endowments, based on abandoned crusader estates. The funds of the *waqfs* were later siphoned off for other purposes, and the church eventually returned to Christian worship, but Saladin's inscription dedicating it to the study of the Koran still stands over the door; and Saladin's name has been given by the Arab inhabitants to the area of the town that surrounds the church. The conqueror also established a hospice for pious Muslims in the palace of the Christian patriarch. The tomb of Mary, Mother of God, was converted—in several senses of the word—into a chapel dedicated to Abraham, the first monotheist. Plots of land on the Mount of Olives were distributed to the Muslim faithful, and the fertile plain of El Baqa, southwest of Jerusalem, which produced a profitable crop of grapes, figs and apples, was given as an endowment to the hospice of the Sufi mystics.

The Church of the Holy Sepulcher was closed to Christians. One of Saladin's lieutenants urged him to destroy the building completely, but the conqueror ignored his pleas. After much deliberation, he eventually permitted the reopening of the shrine, giving custody of it to the Syrian Jacobites, whom he supposed would be the least troublesome of the native Christian sects. He was even going to send back to the church the relic of the True Cross, which the Arabs had captured, but he was so distressed by the cruelties of his crusader enemies, that he decided the Christians did not merit his generosity, and kept the relic in captivity.

When Saladin had taken the city, the Catholic patriarch Heraclius left, taking sufficient treasure along to ensure his survival and perhaps his return. He traveled to Rome and the other major cities of Europe, preaching about the loss of Jerusalem before aroused mobs, standing before them dressed in black as a sign of mourning for the city and adding verisimilitude to his sermon by displaying a picture of Christ being beaten by an Arab. Wherever he went his auditors responded; and wherever he did not go, other preachers, most notably Saint Bernard, took up his cause.

The next decades were filled with projects undertaken for the recovery of the holy city. In England a special tax was imposed, called the Saladin tithe. "Each person," proclaimed the law, "will give in charity one tenth of his rents and movable goods for the taking of the land of Jerusalem. . . ." Only knights' arms and armor, and the property of crusaders and clergymen were exempted from the tax. Anyone who refused to pay was excommunicated. Pope Innocent III decreed that all crusaders should have interest cancelled on their loans; and that they should be refunded any interest they had already paid on loans outstanding. The Jews, who had lent them their money, bore the brunt of this pronouncement.

Within a year of Saladin's conquest of Jerusalem, the kings of France and England, who had been at war with each other, made peace and vowed to go on a crusade. In 1189, they, along with the kings of Poland and Bohemia and the emperor of Germany, Frederick Barbarossa, embarked on the Second Crusade. Frederick was accompanied by a troop of German ladies who bore arms like men, giving rise to a legend that an army of Amazons had undertaken a crusade. The emperor never made it to the Holy Land. He drowned en route in Asia Minor, and although his corpse was carried to Jerusalem, most of it decomposed along the way and only his head reached the Holy City. (According to legend, all of him is still in Asia Minor, resting in a cave, waiting for Germany's hour of need, at which time he will arise to deliver the German nation.)

The king of France did reach the Holy Land however, and soon thereafter he was joined by Richard the Lion-Hearted, king of England. Together, they recaptured Acre from the Muslims. Satisfied with this partial triumph, the French returned home, but Richard thirsted for more. After personally witnessing the execution of some three thousand Muslim prisoners captured along with Acre (Saladin had been tardy in sending Richard ransom money for them), the king marched south toward Jerusalem.

Before he even ascended into the Jerusalem hills, Richard despaired of capturing the city. Proposing to acquire it without bloodshed, he offered to marry his sister to Saladin's brother so that the two could rule Jerusalem together. But the lady refused to wed a Muslim and the deal fell through. Richard then made two expeditions in the direction of the Holy City and during one of them besieged it; but he failed to capture it. To ensure Jerusalem's security as Richard approached, Saladin ordered all springs and wells in the vicinity poisoned so the Christians would have nothing to drink.

Roman Catholic settlers in the countryside were expelled from their land; their farms and villages were destroyed, their castles burned to the ground, their olive trees cut down. A special fervor went into the destruction of their vineyards, the famous vineyards of the Judean hills, for the fruit of the vine was taboo to Muslims. The Jerusalem region has not yet recovered from this destruction; it was as complete as that perpetrated by the Babylonians in the sixth century B.C. and by the Roman Wars of the first and second centuries A.D.

Unsuccessful both as a warrior and a marriage broker, Richard left for Europe in October, 1192, and his crusaders soon followed. With the end of the Second Crusade Saladin's conquests were secure, but he did not have much time to enjoy them. In the spring of the following year, he died. His death signaled the beginning of years of strife among his kinsmen and followers for the privilege of succeeding him. The Muslims, as one fifteenth-century Arab chronicler wrote, "exchanged war with the Franks for war with each other." Saladin's empire was divided into a number of principalities. Jerusalem was never the center of one, although the sultans who ruled over the city made a point of paying lip service to its sanctity. Sometimes Jerusalem was ruled from Damascus, sometimes from Gaza, sometimes from Cairo. And at least three times within the century that followed Saladin's death, the city was offered as a bribe to the crusaders by one of the Arab princes of the area in exchange for an alliance against another Arab.

There were continual Christian attempts to reconquer Jerusalem, attempts that became less serious as the years went by. In 1204 there was a crusade that got no further than Constantinople which the crusaders conquered and proceeded to loot. Financially it was profitable; spiritually it was not, for once the crusaders established themselves in Constantinople, they forgot Jerusalem. In 1212 a more highminded crusade was undertaken—the Children's Crusade. Children caught by religious mania left home and began marching to Jerusalem. The pope told them to go home where they belonged. Many of them obeyed; others, heedless or unaware of his advice, embarked on ships for the Holy Land. They were brought not to Palestine but to Algeria and sold into slavery to the Muslims. Under duress many converted to Islam; some who refused to convert were martyred.

In 1218, there was another crusade equally unsuccessful even though it was graced by the presence of Saint Francis of Assisi, who came to the crusader camp in the hope of converting the sultan of Egypt to Christianity. The sultan met with him and listened to him with admiration; but refused to allow the saint to prove the truth of the Christian faith by walking through fire unscathed, and he politely declined to be converted. Francis went off to Jerusalem on pilgrimage, and the crusade ended in disaster. In 1228 there was another crusade. In return for a guarantee of support, the sultan of Egypt ceded Jerusalem to the crusaders for a period of ten years, five months and forty days. They got the city on the condition that Muslims retain control of the Haram esh Sharif, and that "neither walls nor dwellings" be rebuilt. (The walls had been torn down almost four decades earlier during the Second Crusade.)

With the transfer of ownership much of the population left, not only Muslims and the Jews who had been invited back into the city by Saladin, but non-Catholic Christians as well. They knew what to expect once the Franks took over. Just before the allotted time was up, the Christians began to refortify the city, deciding that it was too precious to surrender. The Muslims had to besiege Jerusalem and take by force what they should rightfully have had peaceably. Five years later, in 1244, the crusaders gained control of the city again as a result of a falling out among Muslim princes, but they held it only for a few months. Again a Muslim army conquered it, in the process massacring thousands of Christians—monks, nuns, and laymen, Catholics, Armenians and Greeks. The Muslims set the Church of the Holy Sepulcher on fire, looted houses and shops, broke into the tombs of the crusader kings of

Jerusalem and scattered their bones. By the time they left, Jerusalem was deserted again. The crusaders had finally lost control of it. Christians would not hold the holy city again until the twentieth century.

Later in the thirteenth century the Mongols, whose empire under Kublai Khan reached from China to the Near East, proposed an alliance with the crusaders against their joint enemy—the Muslims. The Mongols offered to provide 20,000 horses, send provisions for the Christian army, and march on Jerusalem from the East while the crusaders attacked from the West. "If you keep your word," a Mongol general wrote to the king of France, "and send troops at the appointed time, and God favors us, when we have taken Jerusalem from these people we will give it to you. But if you fail to meet us, our troops will have marched in vain."

As it turned out, the Mongol troops marched in vain, and Christian efforts to recapture Jerusalem were of no avail. For in the year 1250, a new regime had taken power in Egypt and it proved to be a more formidable opponent to Christians and Mongols than the sultans of Saladin's house had been. For four decades thereafter Egypt's new rulers pursued a systematic and successful campaign of driving out crusaders and Mongols and consolidating their power in the Levant. In 1291 they captured Acre, the last crusader outpost. Although the Mongols invaded Palestine in 1299, and in the next year an Armenian king marched into Jerusalem and held it for a while, the Egyptians were now too powerful for them. Soon it became evident that Christian threats to regain a foothold in the Holy Land and then seize Jerusalem again had become mere bombast. By the year 1305, the Muslims felt secure enough to impose a tax on all Christians, foreign pilgrims and even local residents, who wished to enter the Church of the Holy Sepulcher to pray. Admission was free only at Eastertime and on the Feast of the Invention of the Cross. Until 1517 Jerusalem remained in Egyptian hands. Not since the time of the pharaohs had Palestine been ruled for so long a time from Egypt.

To maintain their hold on the country after the crusaders had been driven out, the Muslim rulers resettled the coastal areas with their coreligionists, repaired roads, built caravansaries, and founded new Muslim shrines at strategic places throughout Palestine—at Acre, Ramleh, Gaza and elsewhere. Each of these shrines was assigned a feast day, and endowments were set aside to support it. The most important of the new shrines was that of Nebi Musa, "the prophet Moses," which was established just east of Jerusalem. Its great religious festival was arranged for the week before Easter to make sure there would be a gathering of well-armed and warlike Muslim pilgrims in Jerusalem at the same time as there was a dangerous assemblage of Christian pilgrims in the town, come to celebrate the resurrection of Christ. A mosque and later a pilgrim's hostel were built, and a populous monastery commanding the road from Nebi Musa to Jerusalem was destroyed so the Muslims could rush back to Jerusalem unimpeded in case Christian pilgrims threatened to take over. The festival, which is still celebrated with great fervor by the Muslims of Palestine, made Jerusalem even holier as a Muslim shrine.

There were, however, other and far more authentic Muslim religious manifestations in Jerusalem. Even before the Crusades the city had become a center of Muslim mysticism. It was chiefly renowned among Muslims as the site from which Mohammed had during his lifetime ascended to heaven, and Muslim mystics attempted to imitate their prophet with ascents of their own spirits, hoping to achieve union, as he had with God. They tried to attain mystical transports by meditating on all passages of the Koran, but particularly on the one that describes the prophet's Night Journey which had taken place from Jerusalem. The great Persian mystic, al-Ghazzali, had come to the city in 1095, the same year in which the First Crusade was launched. He had secluded himself in a chamber in the Haram esh Sharif and there had written his great classic of mysticism, with the unmystical title of *Restoring the Science of Religion*. Throughout the century of the crusades, and for centuries thereafter, his followers came to Jerusalem, holy men, their hearts freed, as al-Ghazzali had described it, "from covetousness of this world and its false appearances . . . their secret thoughts purified of contemplating everything except the divine presence . . ." For God had "revealed Himself mystically to them, with His names and His attributes . . . and had unveiled the majesty of His presence in such a way that their hearts were consumed with the power of the flames of His love; and had revealed Himself in their hearts . . . in such a way that they wandered in the perilous desert of His sublimity and His magnificence. . . ."

Mystics, called dervishes, came to Jerusalem and established themselves in colleges newly built around the enclosure of the Haram, or in houses throughout the city. They loved to lie in the open air in the shadow of the Dome of the Rock, looking up at the heaven to which the prophet had ascended, and repeating over and over to themselves the ninety-nine names of God, counting them off one by one on a rosary equipped with ninety-nine beads: the King, the Holy, the Creator, the Forgiver, the Proud, the Mighty, the Wise, the Abaser, the Exalter, the Just, the Slayer, the First, the Last, the Giver, the Withholder, the Avenger, the Harmful, the Patient, the One of Peace, and of course, the Merciful and the Compassionate. Or they would call out again and again just the one name, Allah. Or a group of them would form a circle and bow and clap, crying, "Allah, Allah, Allah, Allah," for hours on end, until at last they reached Him or dropped from exhaustion. Half-naked, chanting over and over "There is no God but Allah," they led religious processions or prayed nightlong seeking unity with God. Sometimes they attained it, or came so close they identified themselves with Allah, and dared to say, "How mighty am I," or "There is nothing within this cloak but God." But then when sobriety returned they realized that their unity with Allah had been, for all its ecstasy, only an imitation of union with Allah. After all, they were only men.

One result of the crusades had been an increase in Muslim devotion toward Jerusalem, for devotion, as members of all the city's faiths can testify, is often directly proportionate to deprivation. A substantial literature devoted to the glories of Jerusalem developed, many of the books pilgrim guides to the Islamic shrines of the city, written in a flowery style and adorned with flowery titles: *The Book of Arousing Souls to Visit Jerusalem's Holy Walls* or *A Smoothing of the Road for the Visitors of the Mosques.* Pilgrims or Muslim scholars in Cordoba or Samarkand were edified by reading *Diligent Collections on the Virtues of al-Aqsa Mosque, Gardens of Exercise on the Virtues of the Holy House, Marvels of the Holy House,* or *Directions for the Adorer in his Judgment of Mosques.*

After the Muslim reconquest the number of Muslim holy places within Jerusalem's holy walls increased considerably. The years of Egyptian rule saw extensive building in the city. Hospices were constructed for pilgrims of various nationalities and endowed to distribute bread and olives. Schools for the study and interpretation of the Koran were erected along the northern and western edges of the Haram, with an arcaded gallery running along their front, enclosing that sacred space. The Haram platform was repaved and a number of free-standing arcades were built upon it. In a century and a half, almost forty Muslim religious edifices were constructed in the city, monasteries, schools and mosques, many of them connected with tombs of holy men. (Some of these contained a whole body, others merely a hand or head.) For the construction of these institutions, marble was taken from the ruins of ancient buildings. The Sultan's slaves performed the heavy work and skilled stonemasons were imported from Mecca and Cairo for the more demanding tasks. Jerusalem remained merely a provincial outpost, eclipsed by Damascus and by Cairo, the capital of the Egyptian empire and the intellectual center of the Islamic world. But for the first century of Egyptian rule at least, it was a pleasant town, the resort of retired or second-rate scholars and of pious Muslim gentlefolk from the surrounding countryside.

As Muslim life revived in Jerusalem with the expulsion of the crusaders, the life of the Jewish community revived too. Upon taking control of Jerusalem, Saladin had issued a proclamation inviting Jews back to live in their holy city. Their response was enthusiastic. Around the year 1210 more than three hundred rabbis left France and England to settle close to the Wailing Wall. By 1216 there were at least two synagogues in the city, one for Western Europeans and another for North African Jews. But when Jerusalem was given back to the crusaders in 1228 the Jews' situation became precarious; and in the chaotic years around the middle of the thirteenth century they all left. Around 1260, the community was reorganized by the Spanish philosopher Moses ben Nachman, or Nachmanides, who had left Spain after having been required to take part in a disputation before the king of Aragon on the relative merits of Judaism and Christianity. He had made his arguments so forcefully that it would have been dangerous for him to remain in Spain. When Nachmanides arrived in Jerusalem, a Mongol army had just passed through. The city had only two thousand inhabitants; about three hundred of them were Christian and only two of them Jews, both dyers by trade.

Nachmanides found a suitable vacant house, with handsome marble pillars, and requisitioned it as a synagogue, for as he wrote to his son, "the town is without a ruler so that whoever desires to take possession of the ruins can do so." The two Jewish dyers were insufficient to make up a quorum for prayer; they were supplemented by newly-arrived Jewish pilgrims from Syria whom Nachmanides convinced to stay in the city. Together they formed a congregation, a congregation that still survives after many vicissitudes. To join its ranks, Jews came from all over the Diaspora. In the fourteenth century there were about 250 Jewish families in Jerusalem, a good many of them of French origin. "They live there

in happiness and tranquillity," reported a Jewish immigrant to the
city in 1334, "for the royal authority is just and great."

The royal authority was to remain neither just nor great, nor
even authoritative. For more than a century Jerusalem had enjoyed
stability and a degree of peace under Egyptian rule. A few decades
after the end of the crusades, the city was in the happy situation of
being almost without history, or rather without the wars and
turmoil the men of the times considered worth recording as history. But in the year 1388 a civil war erupted that was to last for a
quarter-century. As a result of the war, the Egyptian empire was
plunged into a severe economic depression from which it never recovered. The sultans tried to improve their position by levying
new taxes on their subjects, but the taxes were so oppressive that
they aggravated the situation instead of helping it. Forced purchases were imposed on the rich, and then on the entire population. More than a century earlier, Nachmanides had noted that the
two Jewish dyers in Jerusalem were required to purchase their supplies from the government at artificially inflated prices. In the fifteenth century a list was made of every person in Jerusalem, Jew,
Christian or Muslim; all were forced to purchase olive oil from
government stocks at outrageous prices, and anyone who failed to
take advantage of the offer was tortured. At times only merchants,
or Christians and Jews, were forced to purchase unwanted goods;
at other times everyone was victimized.

Taxes were imposed on the earnings of beggars and of prostitutes. More money came in from the sale of wine and narcotics.
Throughout the realms of Islam, but especially in holy cities such
as Jerusalem, the taking of hashish and the drinking of wine were
frowned upon. Taverns were supposed to be illegal; but the authorities found them and the hashish that was sold on the sly by the
night watchmen of the towns such good sources of income, that
they encouraged and controlled traffic in hashish and wine. Another source of government revenue was graft. The market inspec-
tors who were charged with collecting taxes from every merchant

in every stall in the souks of Jerusalem were accustomed to add a little to the tax assessment to provide a bite for themselves. This was illegal but the practice was so widespread that the government decided to profit from it and tax the tax collector's share of the take. And so the tax collectors received sanction for demanding graft.

As the effectiveness of the government decreased, riots and small-scale wars began to erupt in Jerusalem and the surrounding hill country. The Bedouin and Turkoman tribes, that had in the past centuries been settling throughout Syria and Palestine, freely raided each other's towns and villages and any party of traders or pilgrims so rash as to venture through their territory. In the fifteenth century there were numerous Bedouin uprisings and frequent pitched battles between rival clans and villages. During the fourteenth and fifteenth centuries, the turbulent villages around Jerusalem were almost depopulated, as peasants migrated from the dangers of rural life to seek shelter behind Jerusalem's walls.

The city could boast of quarters of people from different villages and tribal groups, and from foreign lands. There was a neighborhood of Muslims from North Africa, a street called the Street of the Sudan, inhabited by blacks, and another street occupied by immigrants from across the Jordan. Members of three different Bedouin tribes—the Banu Zayd, the Harit and the Sa'd inhabited their own neighborhoods. When the villagers of Salt in Transjordan were engaged in a battle with the Bedouin of the countryside, their cousins in Jerusalem battled in the streets with the Bedouin of the town. When the government executed some criminals of the Banu Zayd tribe outside the city in what was probably one of its rare acts of justice, the Banu Zayd in Jerusalem rose in rebellion and looted shops and houses. All the citizens of Jerusalem were imperiled by these commotions, but Christians and Jews were especially endangered. Their lives were also made hazardous by the constant struggles for power that took place in the higher reaches of government in Cairo. Crowds of beggars, criminals and Sufi mystics took to the streets to support the cause of this or that claimant to the throne. The Sufi, who gathered in Jerusalem in great numbers, were especially dangerous to their fellow citizens. In their religious ecstasy and religious pride, they believed they had nothing to lose by death, and they acted accordingly.

In these centuries, the city attained its final form, with the Jews and Armenians sharing its southwest quarter, other Christians in the northwest quarter, and the entire eastern half inhabited by Muslims. Separating the Muslims from the infidels were the souks and the food markets. The markets were located where they are today, along what had been the main north-south street of the Roman city of Aelia. The souks were at the center of the town, west of the Haram, in covered stalls where, as one admiring European pilgrim remarked "neither rain nor sun can cause annoyance." In them, the makers of straw mats wove their straw and silk, and cotton merchants hawked their wares, as the collectors of rents for religious endowments went from stall to stall gathering their money. Rents from the silk bazaar went to support al-Aqsa Mosque. Those of the paper factory and the public bath were devoted to the support of one religious school; those of the apothecaries' bazaar went to another. As Jerusalem slowly decayed in the fifteenth century, the collectors pocketed more of the rents and gave less and less to the endowed recipients. The silk and cotton merchants sold more cotton and less silk, for now there were fewer rich to buy the fine silks, brocades and damask that prosperous Arabs have always been accustomed to collect the way westerners collect paper money. But the straw mat weavers prospered; there were more poor and the poor bought straw mats instead of carpets.

The decay of the city was aggravated by unfavorable economic conditions throughout the Egyptian empire. Even before the time of David and Solomon, Jerusalem and the other cities of the Levant had stood at the crossroads of East and West. No matter what the political situation was, no matter who was master, the people of the region benefited economically from living in a place that was a center of trade. And they had capitalized on this position by becoming master artisans and by exporting their handiwork. During and after the crusades, Jerusalem's craftsmen made silks and wares of copper. Artisans along the Street of David sitting cross-legged on the floor of their stalls worked in silver and enamel and in gold that was imported from Europe. And Jerusalem was far less important as a craft center than Damascus or Cairo were. But in the fifteenth century, the Levantine cities suffered a blow from which they have never recovered; fine handiwork from other lands began driving their products out of markets where they had long enjoyed a virtual monopoly. Italy led the competition. The Italian cities began producing and selling damask as fine as that made in Damascus, which had given the material its name; now Italian brocades and silks were as rich as those of Jerusalem and Aleppo. It became difficult to sell the copperwork and glass for which the Levant was famous when people could purchase instead Italian majolica ware, or, even more exciting, porcelains from Ming dynasty China.

Meanwhile the Levant's trade in spices and other Eastern luxuries had fallen off precipitously after the Portuguese rounded Africa and discovered a new route to India, a route that bypassed the domain of the Egyptian sultan. For centuries, the Venetians had been coming to Alexandria to purchase spices for trading in Europe; but by 1500 they no longer found it worth their while to make the trip. The Portuguese had been buying up so much of the product at the source that very little was left to reach the Alexandria market where the Venetians could buy it and the sultan could tax it. The sultan sent an emissary to Rome, threatening to destroy the Christian holy places in Jerusalem unless the pope forbade Portuguese trade with India. But it did no good. The Portuguese maintained and even expanded their India trade, and the sultan and his subjects in Jerusalem were that much poorer. The most crushing blow to the Levant trade and to the economic condition of Jeru-

salem came in the year 1492, when a Genoese seaman, who had
abandoned in despair the hope of making a career in the increasingly unprofitable east Mediterranean trade, discovered a new and
even richer India by sailing west across the Atlantic, an India
whose gold and jewels were destined to be routed elsewhere than
Jerusalem.

In the city the last decades of the fifteenth century were a
time of economic collapse, food shortages, natural disasters, and
threats of invasion by the Ottoman Turks who had conquered the
Byzantine empire in 1453 and proposed to conquer the Egyptian
empire too. In 1473 there were torrential rainstorms and more than
three hundred houses crumbled into ruin. Again in 1492 there were
disastrous storms that damaged the Church of the Holy Sepulcher
and drowned monks in the shrine. Caravans approaching Jerusalem
were attacked by the Bedouins. In the 1480's, Jews and Christians
coming as pilgrims to the city along any route but the major Jaffa-
Jerusalem road were advised to disguise themselves as Turks, who
were obvious foreigners, but foreigners with a powerful army
nearby to avenge them if they were harmed. Bedouin raids were
frequent. "They come," one resident of the city wrote, "even up to
the gates of Jerusalem, steal and plunder in the open roads, and no
one can interfere with them. For this reason the district is all
waste . . . and there is neither plowing nor sowing." To add to
the chaos, raids by the ferocious Ottoman Turks disrupted life in
the countryside. "Two Turks could put ten Ishmaelites [Arabs] to
flight," reported one visitor.

In the year 1517, the Turks conquered Jerusalem. Their arrival benefited the city in some ways. The fortifications were repaired—with stones from churches—and the city walls were
strengthened. (They have hardly been altered since and they still
provide a formidable barrier against any invader.) Fountains and
gateways were built and various adornments were added to the
Muslim shrines. But these advances were negated by the ruination
of Christian shrines. One pasha built a chamber for his harem on

the site of the flagellation. Horses were stabled at Pilate's house. Franciscan monks were expelled from much of their property on Mount Zion. Christian sects were taxed atrociously or held up for enormous bribes, and Christian pilgrims were exploited even more ruthlessly than they had been before.

Over all these years the pilgrim trade had been the one favorable economic factor in the city. Annually thousands of visitors were attracted to Jerusalem from the lands of western Europe. The thirteenth, fourteenth and fifteenth centuries were a great age of pilgrimage. People traveled from England to Jerusalem almost as casually then as they would today. Chaucer's Wife of Bath is said to have made three journeys, and she was by no means unusual. In the year 1300, the pilgrimage to Rome became popular, as Pope Boniface VIII inaugurated the first papal jubilee, attracting thousands of the devout to Saint Peter's tomb in the Vatican. Springtime brought English travelers to the new shrine of Saint Thomas à Becket at Canterbury, and in Spain great numbers of French and Spanish worshippers were attracted to a vast, new cathedral at Santiago da Compostella, dedicated to Saint James, the Moor-killer. But the greatest of the pilgrimage sites was, of course, Christ's Jerusalem.

For the most part the pilgrims to Jerusalem were members of religious orders, or prosperous citizens of the rising bourgeois class, or knights who took seriously the religious vows of their profession. Some were merchants, who stopped off in the city while en route to the East; in 1270 Marco Polo came by to pick up some oil from the lamp that burned over the Holy Sepulcher. He wanted it to carry all the way to Peking as a gift for Kublai Khan who was interested in the Christian religion. Many of the visitors were, like the Wife of Bath, wanderers, high-living hedonists, out for adventure. Others like Margery Kempe an English lady who cried and roared with pious frenzy "so loud and wonderful it made the people astonished," were religious fanatics of a particularly unpleasant disposition (Jerusalem has always attracted its share of these). They shocked and amused the inhabitants of Jerusalem with their arduous piety as they had shocked and amused their neighbors at home, and they came to the city without ever leaving the prison of their own tortured heads. Other pilgrims were paupers, dirty and foul-smelling to the annoyance of their fellow travelers, men and women who had been hired to make the pilgrimage on behalf of a pious soul unable to go himself. Others were emissaries carrying the heart of a devout king or nobleman who had asked that it be buried in the holy city. And then there were those, perhaps the great majority, who came to follow a path which they had already followed at home, to seek Jesus whom they had already found.

These pilgrims, and pilgrims with motivations that were different or mixed, and pilgrims who were not even Christians but Jews, generally left for their journey from Venice, a port whose ships' captains had long experience in transporting travelers to the Holy Land. The pilgrims' custom was so important to the enterprising merchants of Venice that the city government carefully regulated pilgrim tours, including the prices, the duration of the journey and the quality of the ship. Pilgrims could even purchase mattresses and pillows for use on shipboard and in the pilgrims' hostel from a Venetian trader who guaranteed to buy them back at half-price after the trip was over no matter what condition they were in. Regular expeditions left for Jaffa twice a year, once after Easter and again about a month and a half later, after Ascension Day. More adventurous pilgrims, people who scorned guided tours perhaps, could leave from Venice at any season on a regular trading ship bound for Jaffa, Alexandria or Beirut.

Aboard ship, pilgrims ate two meals a day, which had been paid for as part of their fare. Some ships had three classes of meals: the highest the captain's table, the second that of the castello, one of the ship's officers, and the third and cheapest, the table of the cook. Jews ate separately of course. Meals were sometimes accompanied by the playing of an orchestra of fife, drum, trumpet, harp

and viols. Those who swallowed the delicacies—"Like the feasts of
Solomon of old," one pilgrim describes them; ". . . feeble bread
and feeble wine and stinking water," says another—and were unable to retain them in turbulent seas, might avail themselves of the
services of the ship's physician who traveled aboard, along with a
surgeon. For the journey the captain loaded an immense amount of
food at each port—sheep, oxen, calves, poultry—for ships might
carry as many as four hundred passengers. Foresighted pilgrims,
and most were foresighted for they could read any number of
guidebooks full of good advice, carried along their own poultry,
including a laying hen, and hams and bacon, cheeses, dried fruit,
spices and twice-baked bread that would keep throughout the
journey. This supplemented the ship's fare.

The pilgrims' supplies could be replenished at each place the
ship stopped. And there were numerous stops: Rovigno, Pola,
Corfu, Crete, Rhodes, Cyprus or any place else where the ship's
captain might take on trading goods in defiance of repeated decrees
issued by the Venetian senate forbidding trade on official pilgrim
voyages. At these ports, pilgrims often had to purchase new provisions even though they might have embarked with enough to last
the entire journey. For thievery among them was rife despite the
pious motives with which the great majority of the travelers had
set out. The thieves may have been emboldened by one of the side
pilgrimages many of the voyagers took while the ship stopped in
Cyprus, a visit to the shrine where the cross of the penitent thief
was displayed.

Prices for the voyage varied according to the sort of food and
accommodation the pilgrim desired. But, as all travelers discover
sooner or later, costs were higher than one had anticipated. "You
can set no limits to your expenses," one traveler reported. "This is
a journey on which the purse can not be kept shut," said another.
To get an accurate idea of how much the trip would cost, pilgrims
were advised to arrange all financial matters before their departure
from Venice. "It is necessary," one of them said, "to have every-

thing written down by a notary at Venice and witnessed." It was difficult to predict how long the voyage would last, a fact that added to the travelers' expenses. The captain might find it profitable to make an extra call at Cyprus to pick up salt, or at Crete to get malmsey and muscatel, or at Alexandria to purchase spices and jewels, particularly sapphires which were usually available only at that port.

Over the centuries in which pilgrimage was popular, the experience of individual pilgrims differed of course; but the main outlines of the journey were about the same, with spiritual rewards and financial and physical perils at every turn. Travelers usually disembarked at Jaffa which sometimes was dangerously deserted, a heap of ruins, and at other times dangerously overpopulated with warlike and unfriendly inhabitants. As soon as they landed, pilgrims enjoyed the benefits of the pardon the church gave to every Christian who traveled to the Holy Land. If they died the moment they stumbled ashore they would be assured of release from purgatory for a certain time. In Jaffa they visited the site of the house where Saint Peter had stayed, and purchased from a local official a safe conduct signed by the sultan who, as one pilgrim wrote, ". . . holds in his hands this entire land of miscreants." The Turks built watchtowers along the road to Jerusalem, often in the neighborhood of old crusader castles; but like most government endeavors in the Turkish empire, the towers were ineffective, and the route remained dangerous.

On the journey inland from Jaffa to Jerusalem, the miscreants were sometimes most dangerous in one village, sometimes in another. They tended to ignore the safe conduct the pilgrim had already purchased and forced him to pay for another. Usually the heads of each religious community paid an annual tax to the government to ensure free passage to Jerusalem for his coreligionists but the government pocketed the tax money and did nothing to help pilgrims on their way. But so long as their purses were open, pilgrims traveling in groups were relatively safe. Individual pilgrims, however, were subjected to every torture a hostile populace could inflict on innocent strangers. Mostly it took the form of robbery or a shakedown; but there were also, invariably, vulgar gestures, spitting, annoying noises, threats, and blows. In the midst of their woes, Christian pilgrims might have received some consolation from the fact that they were not the only ones to suffer from the unsettled state of the land. For two decades around the year 1500, conditions were so dangerous that Muslims were usually unable to go on the annual pilgrimage from Damascus to Mecca; and even in those years when a pilgrimage was undertaken, the sacred caravan was attacked and robbed by Bedouins.

The Christians were in Palestine on sufferance; they were infidels in a Muslim land and they were made to feel their position acutely. At Jaffa they had to check their weapons and hide their wine carefully in saddlebags; its possession was frowned upon by the Muslims who believed in total abstinence, although they sometimes wheedled a drink or two from the pilgrims anyway. Donkeys were hired for the hard journey to Jerusalem and the pilgrims set forth, after innumerable delays and unpredictable charges. When they reached the town of Ramleh about twenty miles from Jaffa, they had to dismount and walk through, often carrying their own baggage, for no Christian was permitted to ride into a Muslim city, and although they were suffered to ride through the countryside, they could do so only on asses, not on horseback. Along their route they were pushed and threatened by bold Muslim villagers and by the Bedouin who considered Christians inferior beings; and they were constantly annoyed, as visitors to Jerusalem still are sometimes, by insolent youths who enjoyed heckling Westerners. But finally they reached the hill that was called Montjoie, Mount of Joy, for from it the traveler could catch his first glimpse of the holy city. They dismounted and knelt, prayed and sang, and they continued to sing hymns as they approached the city, although they had to sing in a subdued voice, for when the Arabs had conquered the city centuries earlier, the Caliph Omar had commanded Christians to keep their religion inconspicuous.

In solemn procession, the pilgrims, many of them barefoot, marched into Jerusalem, and proceeded directly to the Church of the Holy Sepulcher to pray. After a first prayer there, they were conducted to an old crusader hospice near the church or to the Franciscan hospice on Mount Zion, where they would be sheltered for the ten or twelve days the average guided tour remained in the city. Most pilgrims spread out their bedding on the carpets that were provided for them in the hospices and lay down to rest and meditate after their arduous journey. Some, however, went out again as soon as they could to see the holy city, to walk through its streets and pray at its shrines, for they had come to rejoice in Jerusalem, not to rest there. Others went shopping for a hammer and chisel with which to chip off souvenirs from the sacred stones, even though it meant risking excommunication. (This was in the years before the stones were finally hidden behind protective marble screens.) After a long journey in cramped quarters with no privacy at all, others used the free time, the only free time of the entire tour, to avail themselves of that bodily refreshment Jerusalem has usually been able to proffer its visitors. One medieval guidebook provides interested pilgrims with the Hebrew words for "Woman, let me sleep with you tonight. I will give you gold," and then presuming that the answer was yes, the words for "good night" and "good morning" as well. Pilgrims might have been at a loss for the same words in Arabic, a language that was far more useful in the city; but any guide could be enlisted to act as a translator and a go-between.

The next morning the pilgrims arose to follow the Way of the Cross, to pray at the sites of Jesus' passion and to kiss the stones on which they believed their savior had walked—even though certain of the stones they customarily kissed might have been smeared with feces as a joke by high-spirited local Muslims. Although the

Via Dolorosa did not reach its final form until 1855, its route was more or less fixed in the fourteenth century, and fixed so ingeniously that Christians and Muslims could tour their respective holy places without once crossing each others' paths. The pilgrims visited other shrines aside from those on the Via Dolorosa, took an overnight jaunt to Bethlehem (if the road was safe), and a two day excursion to the Dead Sea and to the site of Christ's baptism. This was an agonizing journey in the summer heat, but an interesting one. The route passed through "a way of robbers . . . a country where there are wicked men. We pilgrims," wrote one fourteenth century traveler, "when we went that way, were in great fear." But on the excursion Christians could see Lot's wife, a pillar of salt that was never consumed although wild animals used it as a salt lick. And they could bathe piously in the Jordan where Christ had been baptized (although they couldn't be baptized again; that was a dreadful sin). And they could sing their prayers and watch the muddy waters of the river grow clear at the sound of their holy words.

Back in the city after this trip, some pilgrims measured lengths of cloth against the stone on which Christ's corpse had been anointed; the cloth would serve them as a shroud. Others measured off the altar of calvary or the opening to Christ's tomb with lengths of string which they would bring back as welcome souvenirs for their friends. Others carefully measured the distances between stations of the cross so they could set up accurate stations of the cross at home, where people too poor or sick or timid to go to Jerusalem could follow a replica Via Dolorosa. Eventually, every Catholic church had one, but without the accurate scale of distances, of course. The more adventurous pilgrims did not confine themselves to the major sites favored by Roman Catholic devotion. They visited also the shrines of some of the native Christians, "the Christians of the girdle" as they were called because they dressed exactly like the Muslims but wore a girdle on their robes. And they visited former Christian shrines, now in the hands of Muslims, where prayers could be uttered only with the heart and mind and not with the lips. Chief among these was the mosque built at the spot where Christ had ascended to heaven. There, very close to one wall, was a "column of ordeal." If one could squeeze between it and the wall, one would enjoy remission of sins. In the fourteenth century, one Italian lady pilgrim tried, but couldn't make it, even after she had stripped naked to try again. The boldest among the pilgrims bribed their Muslim guides, put on Arab-style clothing, and penetrated the pavement of the Haram esh Sharif to see the Temple of Solomon. It was a thrilling adventure but a dangerous one, for if they were caught they would be put to death.

Of course it was the Church of the Holy Sepulcher that attracted the pilgrims most. The Muslim authorities had imposed a tax on every Christian entering the place, not only on every individual, but on every visit. But for ten ducats, pilgrims could purchase a pass that allowed entry at any time. (Ten ducats was a lot of money; in 1500 it would buy room and board in Jerusalem for two weeks.) On the guided tours that left from Venice, pilgrims spent three entire nights within the church, after having been warned to devote their almsgiving to Roman Catholic altars rather than to those of other sects. They were locked within the shrine by the Muslim gatekeeper, sometimes as many as two thousand at a time, and there they spent the night, praying, moving from shrine to shrine, singing hymns, kissing sacred stones, and trying as best they could to ignore the distractions that went on within the church. That was not an easy thing to do. There were the pious shrieks of the native Christians, who often jumped up and down and shouted as they worshipped; the snores of fellow pilgrims who had fallen asleep; the clanging of iron that accompanied the prayers of members of the Jacobite sect; the calls of the vendors who set up shop and hawked their wares to the pilgrims (they sold, one pilgrim reported, "cloth of damask, of camlet, and of silk," and they sold as well food, rings, precious stones and of course rosaries, crosses, amulets and relics, real and fake). Some pilgrims picnicked on the stone floor of the church. Others haggled with the vendors trying, unsuccessfully surely, to get a bargain. Others wandered about the church looking at its thousand sights: the stocks to which Christ's legs were chained, the Chapel of Derision, Godfrey de Bouillon's magic sword which leaped from its scabbard to clang against Godfrey's shield whenever danger threatened. Others busied themselves scratching their names or drawing their coats-of-arms on pillars or walls to inform posterity of their visit. All scratched themselves; the place abounded with fleas and lice and it was a rare visitor who escaped their attentions.

Pilgrims who were of noble birth could, for a fee, take advantage of their visit and be dubbed Knights of the Holy Sepulcher before the tomb of Jesus, whom the Middle Ages considered the greatest knight of all. (He may have been only a carpenter, but he was of noble blood on his mother's side of the family.) The new knight might be dubbed by a friend who had accompanied him on the pilgrimage or he might avail himself of the services of a knight stationed at the church, who made his living by dubbing pilgrims and by renting them the two golden spurs and the sword that were required for the ceremony. By the fifteenth century knighthood had become a farce; prosperous bourgeois purchased knighthoods for themselves and their sons the way people nowadays purchase bachelor's degrees. Nevertheless nobles solemnly knelt before the Holy Sepulcher by candlelight and swore by God and the Holy Sepulcher "to protect the widows, orphans, churches, monasteries, and the poor, and do no man injustice."

One of the chief sights at the church of the Holy Sepulcher was witnessed by few western pilgrims—the traditional ceremony of the Holy Fire which Eastern Christians celebrated with uncontrollable ardor. Annually at Eastertime, there were riots at the Church when the mob rushed to light tapers from the Holy Fire, which they believed came miraculously from heaven, as Turkish guards armed with huge clubs beat them in the vain hope of maintaining order. The scene was described by many travelers, most graphically by Henry Maundrell, an Englishman who came to Jerusalem in 1697. His report of the ceremony, which had remained the same for centuries, is written with the disdainful tone of an enlightened Protestant, who is above such antics.

"They began their disorders," Maundrell wrote, "by running round the Holy Sepulcher with all their might and swiftness, crying out as they went, Huia! which signifies 'this is He' or 'this is it'; an expression by which they assert the verity of the Christian religion." [And which, it might be added, sounds curiously like the name of Yahweh.] "After they had by these vertiginous circulations and clamours turn'd their heads and inflamed their madness, they began to act the most antick tricks and postures, in a thousand shapes of distraction. Sometimes they dragg'd one another along the floor all around the sepulcher; sometimes they set one man upright on another's shoulders, and in this posture march'd round; sometimes they took men with their heels upward, and hurry'd them about in such an undecent manner, as to expose their nudities; sometimes they tumbled round the sepulcher, after the manner of tumblers on the stage. . . . In this tumultuous frantick humour they continued from twelve 'til four of the clock."

Finally representatives of the Greek Orthodox and Armenian faiths entered the tomb of Christ to begin the miracle. "The two miracle mongers had not been above a minute in the holy sepulcher when the glimmering of the holy fire was seen, or imagin'd to appear, thro' some chinks of the door; and certainly Bedlam it self never saw such an unruly transport, as was produc'd in the mob at this sight. Immediately after, out came the two priests with blazing torches in their hands, which they held up at the door of the sepulcher, while the people throng'd about with inexpressible ardour; every one striving to obtain a part of the first and purest flame. . . . It could not be long before innumerable tapers were lighted. The whole church, gallerys, and every place seemed instantly to be in a flame. . . ."

By the time Henry Maundrell came to Jerusalem, pilgrim traffic from the west had decreased, partly as a result of the Protestant reformation and partly as a symptom of the change in thinking that had brought the Reformation about. Protestants scorned the cult of relics and the superstitions that always attended pilgrimages, and Roman Catholics came to be somewhat embarrassed by them too. But as the western pilgrims stopped coming, there was an increase in the visits of members of other sects. Russians came from Moscow, Serbs from beside the Danube, Greeks from Constantinople. (In imitation of their Turkish masters, returned Greek pilgrims placed the title "Haj" before their names, the title Muslims earn after a visit to Mecca.) Most of the Orthodox pilgrims were traveling not to a foreign land but merely part-way across the Turkish empire. Not only Orthodox pilgrims came. Abyssinians arrived from their African mountains and Copts came from Cairo. On their return home they could display designs showing the risen Christ or an angel or a cross which they had tattooed upon their arms as a souvenir of their visit and as a symbol of the fiery descent of the Holy Spirit upon them. (Coptic pilgrims in Jerusalem still get tattooed with these traditional designs.) And in increasing numbers, the Jews came too.

Unlike the others they came to the holy city to dwell as well as to worship. In exile they had dreamed of the restoration of Zion and prayed for it six times each day. Silently, whenever the mood was upon them, they would repeat the verses of the 137th psalm that mourns the destruction of Jerusalem. Their women—rich women at least—wore "golden Jerusalems," brooches figured with a view of the city as a memorial of its past and a token of its future glories. But like the city they represented all the brooches were imperfect; for all jewelry worn by Jews was made with some slight flaw to recall Jerusalem's destruction. The longing to return to Jerusalem was fierce, so strong, that men and women were legally permitted to divorce a spouse who refused to accompany them on a trip to the Holy Land.

When Christian pilgrims arrived within sight of the holy city, they sang. The Jews had little cause for singing; they rent their garments, and when they reached a spot from which they could view the site where the temple had stood, they rent them again. Once they reached the city itself, they were welcomed to it by their fellow Jews with a traditional phrase that was lugubrious and hopeful at the same time: "As you have lived to see Jerusalem destroyed, so may you live to see it rebuilt!" Still, destruction was almost all that they saw, as they followed their own Via Dolorosa, visiting their own traditional shrines, along a route that was as carefully defined as those followed by Christians and Muslims. Some of its shrines were not of Jewish construction or even of Jewish origin, but they had been appropriated by Jewish legend nevertheless. A crusader hospital that had decayed under Muslim rule to become a market hall was revered as the palace of Solomon. The citadel of Jerusalem, staffed with Muslim troops, built by Herod and refortified by Romans, Arabs, crusaders, was visited and venerated as the Tower of David, which is what the inhabitants of Jerusalem still call it. The Jews prayed at the tomb of the prophetess Huldah atop the Mount of Olives (actually it was a mosque that had once been a church), and at the tombs of Absalom and Zechariah at the foot of the Mount, and at a palace where a Muslim judge held court and which they considered the home of an ancient convert to Judaism. The last two on their list of seven sacred sites were connected with the temple: the Golden Gate, which they called the Gate of Mercy and which was walled up so that no one could enter, and most important of all, the Western Wall, called the Wailing Wall by gentiles because of the weeping the Jews did there. Their route was indeed dolorous: tombs, a closed gate, a judgment hall, a fortress, a filthy market, and a wall against which they could wail.

The Jews were not allowed to enter the Haram esh Sharif for no infidel was given access; but even if they had been allowed, they would not have gone in for fear they might unheedingly step on the site of the Holy of Holies where only the High Priest could walk. But all the Jewish pilgrims who visited Jerusalem and wrote memoirs of their visits, wrote about the Dome of the Rock, some few with objectivity of a sort. "The Muslims gather there . . . in crowds and dance around . . . as the Israelites used to do," one thirteenth-century rabbi wrote, and then added as a pious aside, "if we may compare holy things with profane." From afar, they venerated the place, gazing at it in relative safety from the roofs of the Jewish quarter.

Most of the Jewish residents of Jerusalem in late medieval times were artisans—tailors, carpenters, shoemakers, goldsmiths— or tradesmen, who maintained shops "in the best part of the city," as one Jewish visitor smugly recorded. Some made their living by calligraphy, copying scrolls of the law for sale to pilgrims; and others rented out rooms for pilgrims—of any faith—and served as guides. Some were pharmacists, and not very good pharmacists at that. According to one visitor, they were men with "no adept knowledge of the art of preparing drugs . . . they simply buy them and sell them again . . . they know nothing of medicine, but are for the most part asses." But there were some good doctors, and men who pursued the study of astronomy and mathematics; obviously these were men of independent means or merchants who dabbled in science part-time. Some of their fellow Jewish intellectuals in the city were swallowed up by the even more entrancing study of the Kabbalah, that intoxicating and mystical Hebrew philosophy that strives to unlock the secrets of the universe. More sober scholars confined themselves to the study of the scripture and the Talmud. Those who devoted their entire time to sacred study were maintained as was often the custom throughout Jewry, at the expense of the community; and all over the Diaspora, collections were taken up for the pious scholars of Jerusalem.

For a time the Jews lived peacefully and piously with, one visitor reported, "no sinful laughter or levity or whoring." They plied their trades side by side with the Arabs and there was little overt animosity between the two communities. According to the Koran, Jews were, like Christians, ignorant, untrustworthy evildoers; but they had been set on their erroneous path by Allah and

Muslims had no call to question Allah's decision. "If God had willed," the Koran informed them, "He would have made you one nation." "God misleads whom he pleases," their preachers told them. And so following the lead of Allah (one of whose epithets is "The Misleader") they suffered the Jews to live peacefully, far more peacefully than they were permitted to in Christian Europe. But as the Egyptian empire decayed in the fifteenth century, this happy situation changed. The entire population became impoverished, overtaxed, insecure, and the Jews, naturally, became the most impoverished, most taxed, and least secure of all. Their synagogue was demolished in a pogrom. When there was drought they were attacked by Muslims who believed that it had been caused by the Jews' sins. In one decade between 1480 and 1490, more than half of the 250 Jewish families in the city departed, fleeing famine and oppressive taxes. Among those Jews remaining, women, and aged women at that, outnumbered men considerably. Meanwhile, corrupt elders of the synagogue sold off many of the houses belonging to the Jewish community and pocketed the profits. On the Jews who remained in Jerusalem they imposed arbitrary taxes, which they also pocketed.

In 1478 an Italian rabbi, Obadiah da Bertinoro, emigrated to the holy city and restored some order and spirit to the community. He was a man of the Italian Renaissance. "In my opinion," he wrote, "an intelligent man versed in political science might easily raise himself to be chief of the Jews . . . for among all the inhabitants there is not a wise and sensible man who knows how to deal affably with his fellow men, all are ignorant misanthropes intent only on gain . . ." Obadiah proceeded to deal affably. Less than a decade after his arrival someone could write of him: "The whole land obeys his words. No one will lift a hand without him." By 1500 the Jewish community had grown again to a respectable size. Many Jews had returned to the city, and their number was augmented by immigrants from Yemen and by refugees who had been expelled from Spain in 1492.

For a time early in the sixteenth century it seemed as though their numbers would be increased beyond measure by the return to Jerusalem of all the Jews scattered throughout the lands of their exile. In Italy some time around the year 1523, a young boy caught a snow-white dove, whose feathers were arranged in such a way that he could read on its body the words "The tribes will soon come back." From Egypt came a report that the Jews were selling their houses preparing for the day of redemption. In Morocco Jews told each other that the Messiah had come. The Damascus Jews learned that an emissary of the ten lost tribes had arrived in the Holy Land to begin the process of redemption; and indeed in Jerusalem a mysterious young man did arrive, a Jew named David, who posed as a Muslim and spent five weeks in prayer and fasting at the site of the ancient temple. In Jerusalem he remained incognito, but when he left the city and came to Italy he declared his real identity: David Reubeni, the son of one king and the brother of another, each of them, he said, rulers of the lost tribes of Reuben, Gad and Manasseh who lived in the distant wilderness beyond India. In Rome he managed to get an audience with the pope, and promised him and Christian Europe the aid of the ten lost tribes against the Turks, who had recently conquered Jerusalem. Then he went to one of Europe's most powerful rulers, the king of Portugal, to beg for weapons. "We shall first take the Holy Land," he told the king, ". . . then our captains of the host will go forth to the west and east to gather the dispersed of Israel." But Reubeni's plans came to nothing. The Spanish Inquisition got him, and the Jews never learned if he was an imposter.

In the next century, however, another presumed messiah arrived, Sabbatai Zevi, an ascetic from Smyrna who came to Jerusalem and inspired the Jewish population with hopes for the end of the world. He traveled about to Egypt, collecting money for the needy of Jerusalem, and then pocketed it for his own needs. Unlike Reubeni or even Jesus he felt quite free to announce himself to his fellow Jews as the Messiah, and a great many of them, unlike their

ancestors, felt free to believe. Even more than Reubeni had, Sabbatai aroused Jewry with hopes of a return to Zion; but here again,
the hopes were vain. The Jews of Jerusalem excommunicated
Sabbatai as an impostor. He fled the city and eventually went to
Constantinople where he converted to Islam.

Persecution, in Jerusalem and the lands of the Diaspora, had
made the Jews especially susceptible to Messianic dreams. The seventeenth century was disastrous for them and the eighteenth century was worse. Like their Christian neighbors, the Jews were in
bondage to moneylenders, "as full of debt as a pomegranate is of
seeds," one of them recorded. The Turks made money by selling
Jews the right to dwell in the city and then made more money
taking bribes to allow a few extra Jews in. (Only a small number
were allowed in, fewer than three hundred families.) There were
constant quarrels between the old settlers and the new, promoting a
kind of old-family snobbishness that has remained a factor in Jerusalem Jewish life. Annually appeals went out to the Jews of the
Diaspora, who were sunk into poverty themselves, for money to
keep the Jerusalem Jews alive. The Jews in exile dutifully paid,
fearing a day when there might once again be a Jerusalem without
Jews; but the Jerusalem Jews acquired reputations as beggars.
When money did come in it was never enough. About 1700, Arab
moneylenders set fire to a synagogue in the city because the Jews
were unable to pay their debts. Except when a rich and benevolent
family helped support the community, the Jews lived close to starvation; but they clung to the city nevertheless. Despite their dire
straits the population even increased.

From the sixteenth century onward most of the Christian
communities of the city were plunged into unrelieved poverty too,
in large measure as a result of the exaction of their Turkish masters. Even under the Egyptians various Christian sects had been
pushed to the brink of extinction in the city by the terrible taxes
that had been imposed upon them. At the time of the Turkish conquest, the Greek Orthodox patriarch of Jerusalem was so impover-

ished that he had to work with his hands to earn money for his food. Egyptian demands had been outrageous but those of the Turks were worse, and as the Turkish empire decayed, they became almost impossible to keep up with. Forced loans were frequently imposed on the Christian sects. To raise money for the taxes and bribes required by the Turkish authorities, the Armenians, the Abyssinians and the once powerful Greek Orthodox fell into the clutches of the moneylenders. Church treasures were sold off. Houses owned by Christians and Jews collapsed into ruins, because it cost more to bribe the Turks for permits to rebuild than to do the rebuilding itself.

The Ottoman government in Jerusalem was headed by a district governor. Under him were a mayor and a cadi, or judge, a mufti, or religious leader, the commander of the Janissaries who were stationed in the Tower of David, and a city council, made up of the town's principal Muslim dignitaries. Upon assuming office each of these gentlemen was given a sum of money, called the "arrival tax" by each Christian community in the city. Gifts had to be given again whenever a new Christian patriarch assumed office, and whenever a major Christian or Muslim feast rolled round. Annually, each community paid the government a tax of 5000 piasters for permission to bury its dead, which was supplemented by a tax of five piasters on every corpse, for even death did not deliver the taxpayer from the hands of Turks. When a new cadi took office all Christian legal documents lapsed. With Alice-in-Wonderland logic they had to be registered again even though they had already been validated once or twice. And of course registration fees for them had to be paid, even though each Christian patriarch had already given the retiring cadi 5000 piasters for "travel expenses." Annually in the eighteenth and early nineteenth centuries, the Turkish pasha of Damascus arrived in Jerusalem to collect his share of the taxes. "Even if the stones and soil . . . were turned into gold and silver," one Christian resident of the city wrote, ". . . it would still be impossible" to give the pasha satisfaction. He came with an army of some 3000 men and tortured or imprisoned leaders of each community that did not meet his exorbitant demands.

After the taxes had been paid, there were still the bribes. In order to do anything in Jerusalem one had to pay a bribe. Early in the eighteenth century, when the Armenian community wanted to replaster the walls of their chief shrine, the medieval Church of Saint James, the labor and materials for the job cost 4827 piasters, but bribes to the Turks for permission for the work to go forward cost almost 12,000. The Turks put everything up for sale. In 1517 when they conquered the city, they appointed members of one Muslim family to a lucrative position, collecting admission fees from Christian worshippers at the Church of the Holy Sepulcher. But soon the price of admission went up, for another Muslim family bribed the authorities to get the post for themselves, and the bribe was so large that it had to be recouped. Eventually two officials were in charge of collecting admission, thus doubling the opportunities for payoffs. Around 1670 the Turks even managed to sell the title of Armenian patriarch to a clergyman who bribed them for it. The Greek Orthodox patriarch of Jerusalem, around that time, usually purchased his office too. The situation became so bad that one eighteenth-century Armenian patriarch wore a symbolic iron chain around his neck and vowed never to remove it until the debts of his community were paid off. Begging for assistance, the Armenians sent emissaries to their rich compatriots in Constantinople who managed to bail them out.

As if the cost of living under the rule of rapacious Muslims were not terrible enough, the Christian sects aggravated their situation by imposing extraordinary taxes upon themselves in the form of bribes that they eagerly paid, first to the Egyptians and then to the Turks, in continual and unprincipled attempts to dispossess rival sects from the shrines and seize control of them for themselves. Disregarding Jesus' prophecy that God will be worshipped not "at Jerusalem" but rather "in the spirit and in truth," the sects competed furiously for the most insignificant privileges at the holy sites to the delight and great profit of the Muslims. Year after year the Muslims impartially sold traditional Orthodox sites to the Catholics, and to the Orthodox guarantees against further encroachments by the Catholics. For a fee they promised one year to benefit the Armenians at the expense of everyone else, and the next year to allow the Armenians to maintain their newly-purchased position. The end result was that all the Christian communities were impoverished, and although shrines changed allegiance with dizzying frequency, no group was aggrandized with the exception of the Catholics. The Catholics were not, of course, any greedier than members of other sects; they were simply more prosperous. After the crusaders had been expelled the Catholics retained no rights at all in the Church of the Holy Sepulcher, except for the right to worship as individuals, a right courteously granted to all Christians by the Muslims, who according to Muslim law owned everything in Jerusalem. Eventually the Catholics acquired the keys to the Sepulcher and exclusive rights to celebrate mass within it and to maintain an altar on Golgotha. By the nineteenth century they claimed ownership of almost the entire church.

Control of the shrines swept back and forth like the tide of faith itself. In 1330 the Georgians, supported by the king of Georgia, tried to take control of the shrine at Golgotha which the Armenians claimed to own. In 1423 or 1424, the Georgian king sent gifts and bribes to the sultan of Egypt in order to win possession, promising an annual tribute of concubines and other slaves if it were granted. The sultan graciously obliged and ousted the Armenians, who were forced to raise money to outbribe the Georgians and regain possession, which they did in 1424. The next year the Georgians repurchased the shrine, and so the Armenian patriarch of Jerusalem journeyed to Cairo and succeeded in buying it back. In 1426 the Georgians bought it again. The Armenian patriarch—a gentleman aptly named Martiros—traveled to Cairo a third time, only to be informed by the sultan (who had already sold Golgotha five times) that this time the Armenians could not afford to top the Georgian offer. So he went disconsolately home and saved his money, and in thirteen years had hoarded enough to purchase an area adjoining the tomb of Christ which was furbished as a church and named "Second Golgotha." A year after the new Armenian church was opened, the Georgian kingdom collapsed, leaving the Georgians in Jerusalem penniless. All their shrines were snapped up by the Greek Orthodox.

With the Ottoman Turks' conquest of Jerusalem, a three-cornered fight broke out among the Catholics, the Armenians and the Orthodox for control of most of the major shrines, particularly the Churches of the Holy Sepulcher and of the Nativity at Bethlehem. The dreadful oppression of the government had reduced the minor Christian sects to utter poverty and rendered them *hors de combat*. Eventually the Copts had only one priest stationed in the Church of the Holy Sepulcher. He never dared leave because he couldn't pay the entrance fee to get in again. No Coptic worshippers ever came to the church; they were too poor to come and only showed up on the two days a year when the church was open free.

In the quarrels the Catholics were supported by France, Spain, and Venice who placed subtle diplomatic pressures on the Turks to favor their cause. The Orthodox were supported by an increasingly powerful Russia, and the Armenians were supported by no one. Of course the Armenians came out third in the race. In 1555 the Catholics acquired the right to rebuild a chapel over Christ's tomb, thus gaining control of it. All non-Catholic religious ceremonies were banned. In 1620 the Turks officially gave Rome sole rights to the Holy Sepulcher and the shrine of the Nativity. But little more than ten years later the Turks gave the Orthodox the same sole rights. In 1690 the Catholics got them back. In 1757 the Greeks got them. The Armenians meanwhile were trying merely to hold on to their ancient shrine of Saint James, which the Greeks were contesting and often acquiring, and to the privilege of hanging lamps and lighting candles near the tomb of Christ. "Never trust the Greeks and Latins," an Armenian patriarch warned his flock in a statement he described as his last testament. "Whereas the Muslims harass us only for silver . . . these do so on account of our holy faith; they are implacable enemies of our share in the Holy Places." He was, alas, quite right.

CHAPTER 10

A New Jerusalem

In the summer of 1798, the agents of the pasha went to the doors of the Church of the Holy Sepulcher and locked up the monks within. Muslim mobs ran through the streets of Jerusalem, plundering Christian shops and houses. An enormous tax was imposed on all Christian inhabitants, supposedly to pay for gunpowder and ammunition to defend the town against invaders. The invaders were the French, who had landed in Egypt to harry the British, to gain a colony in compensation for their Canadian and Indian outposts that had been conquered by Britain, and to win imperishable glory in the East. ("Europe is a molehill," their leader, General Bonaparte, complained.) The Turks considered Christians in Jerusalem to be natural allies of Napoleon, as indeed they were; and Christians were forced to pay for the effort to forestall him.

Napoleon, on his part, also considered the Christians his natural allies, along with everyone else. He issued appeals for aid to members of all three major religious communities in Palestine. He tried to convince the Muslims that he and his army were about to convert to Islam and he wrote a letter couched in Islamic terms to the religious authorities in Jerusalem. To the Jews he promised, in the stentorian voice so characteristic of revolutionaries and of

Frenchmen, the restoration of "Israel's patrimony," the avenging of its "shame," its "yoke of slavery" and its "almost two-thousand year-old ignominy." The Turks took care to see that his appeals remained unanswered. The monks locked in the Church of the Holy Sepulcher had to remain there for 170 days. They were released; but as soon as the French came marching into Palestine 2000 monks and Christian pilgrims were once again held prisoner in the Church. Jerusalem's Christians and Jews were warned that they would be massacred by vengeful Muslim mobs if the French were victorious in Palestine. As it turned out the French were defeated by the Turks and British at Acre and expelled from the country. With their departure, there were anti-Christian riots in Nazareth, anti-Jewish riots in Safed, and in Jerusalem threats to both Christians and Jews until a contingent of British marines came marching into the town to bring order.

Napoleon had left without ever even reaching Jerusalem, but it was really he who was responsible for introducing modernity to the town. For with his arrival in Egypt, the entire East awoke. Grandiose plans for Egypt's economic and intellectual development were drawn up. An Arabic printing press—Egypt's first—was brought into the country (having been plundered by the French from the Vatican, where it had been used for religious propaganda). A survey was made of Egypt's economic resources and another of its archeological treasures. To counter French influence in Egypt, British trading representatives in the Middle East began to build up British power along the coasts of the Persian Gulf and the Red Sea. Exactly as the crusaders had, the French and British attempted to divide up the East. Their competition was to have a profound effect on Jerusalem, for it unleashed the nationalism of Arab and of Jew.

The French and British were joined by others, by Russians and Germans, who also tried to exploit the awakening nationalism of the Arabs. The Germans attempted to use the Jews too for a while. All four European powers began to play an increasing role in the history of Jerusalem, masking each of their political moves under the veil of religion. The Turkish empire was dying; evidently it would not be able to rule Jerusalem much longer. In an age of imperial expansion, the question that occupied the city was a critical one: would the empire that succeeded Turkey in control of Jerusalem be Anglican or Lutheran, Catholic or Orthodox? It occurred to few people that the successors might be Muslims; to fewer still that they might be Jews.

At first the process of change was almost imperceptible in Jerusalem. Early in the nineteenth century Palestine remained in complete chaos, with Turkish power only nominal. Throughout the seventeen-hundreds northern Palestine and Lebanon had been virtually independent. Jerusalem was ostensibly ruled as a dependency of Damascus, but the local governor was almost autonomous, although his power could be exerted only within the city for the countryside was uncontrollable, racked by blood feuds, subject to Bedouin raids and to the whimsical authority of numerous local sheikhs. Palestine was almost depopulated. Conditions were so insecure that the grain harvest was hidden underground in caves as soon as it was threshed. "Outside the walls of Jerusalem," wrote the French visitor Lamartine around 1830, "we saw . . . no living object, heard no living sound, we found the same void, the same silence . . . as we should have expected before . . . Pompeii or Herculaneum. . . . A complete eternal silence reigns."

The silence was broken only by the sounds of local wars among the villages and peasant clans which were constantly feuding with each other. Wars were fought over a few sheep or goats, over an insult, over a previous war. Sometimes hundreds of men were involved in battles in the fields outside Jerusalem, with the men fighting and the village women in the background urging them on with cheers and rousing songs, as citizens safe within the walls looked out scornfully or with trepidation at the yokels foolishly breaking each other's heads. Sheikhs or village champions would be challenged to individual combat, and for fear of being accused of cowardice they had to fight. If they refused battle or seemed afraid, they were mocked at as *siknaj*, "coward," the local Arab pronunciation of Ashkenazi, which in Hebrew means a Jew from Central or Eastern Europe—a group so fearful and so beaten down at that time in Jerusalem that among the Arabs their name became synonymous with timidity.

The peasants lived and battled happily across the landscape under the relaxed rule of the Turks. But in 1832 the Turks were driven out of the country; the Egyptians took over and tried to modernize Palestine. Order was imposed, taxes were raised, conscription was enforced, and rebellion broke out. Thousands of peasants from the region around Jerusalem stormed the city, gaining access to the Armenian quarter through a sewer. They looted shops and raped women—Jewish women, that is, for there were Christians among the insurgents. If only Muslim peasants had been involved, Christian women would have been raped too. The rebels were driven out again by the Egyptians, and the Egyptians were driven out again by the Turks. Nothing seemed to have changed.

Certainly the religious situation remained constant. No matter who was in charge of Jerusalem the quarrels among the sects continued and, indeed, became even more acrimonious. They reached their peak in 1808 when the Church of the Holy Sepulcher burned down. On September 30th of that year, a terrible conflagration erupted: columns cracked, galleries burned, and the great dome collapsed on top of the Holy Sepulcher, which was crushed. The fire had broken out in the Armenian section of the church, and so the Greek Orthodox and Roman Catholics in solemn judgment declared that it had been arson: the fire had been set intentionally by the Armenians in the hope of destroying the position of rival faiths at the shrine. The Greek Orthodox resolved to take advantage of the disaster to gain control of the Holy Sepulcher for themselves. When the Roman Catholics realized this, they had second thoughts about the situation. They decided they needed Armenian help to defeat the Greek effort, and so declared that their first judgment had been an error. The fire had not been Armenian arson after all.

At this time the Greek people were enjoying a revival of national feeling; in a few years they would rebel and liberate their homeland from the Turks. The Church of the Holy Sepulcher had first been built by a Byzantine emperor, Constantine, whom the Greeks considered one of their own; his name has been given to several modern Greek kings. They considered it a Greek church and they freely donated their savings and even sold furniture and household utensils to raise enough money to pay for the right to rebuild it. They managed to purchase the right and then set to work, despite the riots that broke out against them led by the Armenians and Roman Catholics. Muslims hindered them too. The Turkish garrison stationed in Jerusalem revolted, attacked Greek construction workers and destroyed part of the rebuilt church. But the church rose nevertheless, its crusader fabric masked by Greek work done in a sort of semi-classical style, with a few architectural touches that in the West would be called Greek Revival. The tombs of the crusader kings, including that of Godfrey of Bouillon, disappeared under what a Catholic writer has called the "sacrilegious hammer" of the Greeks. "Thus were deleted," says another Catholic writer, "every Latin decoration and inscription." A Greek inscription was put up in their stead proclaiming that the Church of the Holy Sepulcher was completely rebuilt from bottom to top by the offerings of the Greek Orthodox.

As a result of their building project, the Greeks had control of the church, as they still do. During the Greek War of Independence their position was endangered. To maintain it, the Orthodox had to increase their bribes to the Turks. In the decade during which the war was being fought, the debt of the Greek patriarchate in Jerusalem rose from 300,000 to thirty million piasters. At that time orders came to the city from Constantinople for the execution of the Greek patriarch along with several of his subordinates. Fortunately for them, the Turkish governor of Jerusalem could not read the dispatch and the Turkish official who did read it was pro-Greek and suppressed the order.

In the church, the Roman Catholics had lost almost all the rights they had slowly acquired over the years. But the Catholics did not surrender their claims easily. In 1819 a spokesman for the Latin cause listed as Roman Catholic possessions: "The Church of the Holy Sepulcher . . . , the sepulcher of our Lord Jesus Christ which is in the center of the church of the same name. The great and the small cupola with the lead which covers them. The arches and columns which are around them as far as the iron gates placed to mark the line at which the part of the church belonging to the Greeks commences. The galleries and dwellings of the Latin monks which are over the aforesaid arches or columns. The great arch which is surmounted with the cupola which is over the above mentioned iron gates. The chamber which is at the end of the wall of the above mentioned great arch" and so on and so on. But the Greeks were in control and Roman Catholics and other Christians had to content themselves, for the time being, with other shrines and other quarrels.

In 1814 a horrendous war broke out between the Catholics and the Armenians: the Catholics were disturbed by the fact that the Armenians had placed a rug along a passageway in the Church of the Nativity at Bethlehem to deaden the noise that occurred when Catholic monks walked by an Armenian chapel during mass on their way to their own services. The struggle lasted a decade. The rug was laid and removed and laid down again. The passageway was blocked and then reopened. After a few years the combatants turned their attentions to the Mount of Olives, where the Armenians were trying to build a monastery. A mob of Catholics and Orthodox, led by clergymen, stormed through the streets of Jerusalem and up to the Mount of Olives to demolish the Armenian work, and then came back to sing and dance in triumph along the city streets. In 1820, two of the poorest communities in Jerusalem, the Copts and the Abyssinians, had a falling out, which has lasted to this day. The Armenians joined the fray on the side of the Copts expecting to inherit some, or if God was on their side, all of the spoils, a few pitiful chapels on the roof of the Church of the Holy Sepulcher. To impress their position on their adversaries, Armenian ruffians attacked Abyssinian monks, beat them and put iron collars around their necks, collars that could be, and were, tightened with screws.

In the 1840's the Catholics embarked on an intensive campaign for the restoration of their privileges in the holy places. The campaign, which led to a series of international incidents and finally to the Crimean War, was born in Bethlehem, in the autumn of 1847 at the Church of the Nativity when the Catholics discovered that a silver aureole, inscribed in Latin with the words "Here Jesus Christ was born of the Virgin Mary," had disappeared. The Greeks tried to put a Greek inscription in its place. When the Catholics asked the Turks to stop them, the Turkish government refused to pay heed. The Catholics requested protection from the pope, and from Louis Napoleon of France. Soon France, Austria, Belgium, Sardinia and Spain were demanding that the Turks restore Catholic rights in the holy places. The Orthodox, in turn, were supported by the Russians who demanded that the Turks name Russia the protector of all Orthodox Christians in the Turkish empire. Most of the powers involved cared little for Catholic or Orthodox rights at the holy places. They were far more concerned with dismembering the Turkish empire, or with seeing that no other power gained a disproportionate advantage from Turkey's collapse. The most fervent advocates were the Russians and the French. The French wanted to increase their already considerable influence in the East. The Russians longed to seize control of the Balkans, with their large Orthodox population, and gain access to the Mediterranean coast, which they are still attempting to do. In the resulting war the Russians were ranged against France, Sardinia and Turkey, and the British, who were eager to limit Russian power. When the war was over almost nothing had changed in the holy places. The status quo was reaffirmed and an agreement was negotiated for the repair of the dome of the Holy Sepulcher by French and Russian architects with French and Russian money. The Church sadly needed repair for the Greeks had expended so much money early in the century on bribes for the privilege of rebuilding it that they did not have enough left over to make sure the construction was adequately done.

The status quo may have been maintained at the shrines, but the Crimean War signaled the end of the ancient order almost everywhere else in Jerusalem. Before the war, Christians had been forbidden to sound church bells in the city for fear of offending the Muslim populace. The pious were summoned to church by the sound of wooden clappers. But after the war, church bells sounded, and Christian self-confidence grew so rapidly that in 1855 the Catholics set off a public fireworks display in celebration of the papal bull declaring the Immaculate Conception of Mary a dogma. In that same year, the Dome of the Rock and its surroundings were opened to Christian visitors. The first tourist was, alas, an ignoble representative of the Christian faith—Leopold, prince of Belgium, later king of that country, the tyrant responsible for the atrocities that Belgium was to commit in the Congo.

The process of Christian emancipation in the city had been going on for some time, even before the Crimean War. In the 1830's the Egyptians, who were in control of Palestine at the time, had opened the country to European travelers; when the Turks returned Palestine remained open. Protestant missionaries began arriving. As they looked at the city they recited excerpts from the Book of Lamentations, and they listened with a sort of perverse satisfaction to mourners wailing in the streets, sounds they interpreted as the fulfillment of biblical prophecies. Sometimes they uttered lamentations themselves about the vermin and the plague that was rife in the city (touch no one in the streets they were told, and pass all food through water). At first, they addressed their efforts to the Jews of Jerusalem, but that was dangerous and unrewarding work. A ban was pronounced by the rabbis on all Jews who had contact with missionaries, and the first Jewish convert, a man named Joseph, had to be sent to Constantinople for safety before he was baptized in 1838.

When it became evident that the conversion of the Jews was not imminent, missionaries began to devote their efforts to the Arab population. The Arabs did not always welcome their attentions. The Maronite patriarch of Beirut extracted from the government a decree forbidding the distribution of Bibles to Turkish subjects. The missionaries dared work only with Arabs who were already Christian. Muslims who converted to another religion were in danger of death, even though the government announced in 1844 that the Koranic law that called for death in such cases was not necessarily going to be applied.

In the year 1841, Queen Victoria and the King of Prussia agreed to set up a joint Protestant bishopric in Jerusalem. The first bishop was to be a Lutheran German; his successor was to be an Anglican and then the position was supposed to see-saw back and forth. Part of the reason for establishing the bishopric was to provide protection for Protestant missions in the Holy Land; part was an attempt to counter the growing influence of Russia, with its Orthodox, and France with its Catholic interests in Jerusalem.

The establishment of the bishopric was fought fiercely by a group of English religious leaders, including Henry Newman, later Cardinal Newman, who was disturbed by the fact that it increased the distance between the English and Roman churches. It was supported, on the other hand, by imperialists who wanted to promote a British protectorate over the Jerusalem Jews. Unlike the other religious groups of the city they had no foreign state to protect them. The British press discussed the possibility of setting up Jewish colonies in the empty land of Palestine where they would provide a stabilizing and pro-British influence on the moribund Turkish empire. The imperialists were seconded by those who believed that the return of the Jews to Jerusalem, under British auspices, might be expected to herald the second coming of Christ. By happy omen, the first bishop was a converted Jew. His title was Bishop *in* Jerusalem, for the Orthodox patriarch was recognized as the legitimate bishop *of* Jerusalem. Amid all the shrines of the superstitious Easterners the English built for him a comfy Victorian Gothic church set within an English church close, with a garden, Gothic Revival stained glass, birds chirping outside, flowers on the altar, plump kneeling cushions and wall brasses. The Germans quickly disengaged themselves from the agreement, for they found they were playing second fiddle to England in this as in so much else. The English carried on alone and there has been an English bishop in Jerusalem ever since.

With the missionaries came the consuls. In an age that saw little distinction between cross and flag, the two worked hand in hand. In 1839 the first foreign consul, an Englishman, came to the city. In 1842, after the Prussians had set up a bishopric with Britain, they established a consulate too. In 1844 a Russian church official arrived, his title archimandrite, and his task the supervision of all Russian monastic establishments in Jerusalem. In 1847, the Roman Catholics reestablished their patriarchate and the first Latin patriarch since the time of the crusades came to take up his post in the city. (This raised problems for the Franciscans, who theretofore had been the official Roman Catholic representatives in the Holy Land, and now had to share their power.) In 1858, Russia sent both a consul and a bishop, the latter a converted Russian Jew named Levinson.

In time the consuls virtually ruled the city. The local Turkish governor was almost powerless, and incredibly corrupt, and the inhabitants of Jerusalem—Muslim, Christian and Jew—found it advisable to place themselves under the protection of a foreign consul, if they could possibly manage it. Although sometimes they found this role burdensome, the consuls generally welcomed it, for the more influential they were the more powerful their country seemed. The French consul watched over Arab Catholics; the Russian consul asserted a protectorate over the Orthodox Christians and over Jerusalem's Russian and Polish Jews, who found themselves in the anomalous position of being courted in Jerusalem by the Russian government which was persecuting their coreligionists at home. Perhaps because there were few Protestants with whom they could demonstrate their power, the British tended to guard the interests of the minor sects, the Abyssinians and Copts and soon, those of the Jews as well.

The missionaries had spheres of influence, national and sectarian rivalries, quarrels over the possession of choice properties and choice converts. In the 1870's, American and British missionaries divided the entire Levant into spheres of influence. The Americans, as the decidedly junior partner, took the less Holy Land of Syria, the British got the Holy Land proper. (That is why there is a now a democratic and progressive American college in Beirut, and a small, élite British-style school in Jerusalem). Individual missions vied for and sometimes paid for converts and raided each other's flocks. Arab Orthodox villagers found it profitable, financially, if not spiritually, to convert en masse to Roman Catholicism and then relapse to Orthodoxy, and then when money was needed again to offer themselves to the Anglicans. Anglican converts enjoyed the protection of the English consul, Lutherans, that of the German consul. In the troubled land of Palestine this was enough to bring about conversions. Preachers representing churches unconnected with a great power—Mormons, Moravians, Baptists, Evangelists—who came to the city in great numbers in the nineteenth century had little chance of attracting converts.

Under these circumstances missionary work was difficult and full of discouragement. Jerusalem with all its hypocrisies was enough to dishearten even the most dedicated and optimistic soul in that dedicated and optimistic age. Missionaries consoled themselves with the thought that Jesus himself had not got much response in the city. Considering the efforts expended, results were astonishingly meager. It cost one American Protestant missionary in the middle of the nineteenth century an estimated four to five thousand United States dollars to convert one Jew in Jerusalem. And chances were that a good many of the Jews and Arabs who were converted at untold cost to the missionaries' health and spirits were opportunists.

And so the missionaries soon devoted most of their efforts to another cause, the care of the body and the mind. They opened schools and the Arabs of the city, particularly the Arab Christians, came to them freely, and to the church services that were connected with them. Thanks, in part, to these schools, the Arabs of Palestine became relatively westernized and more prosperous than citizens in most other Arab lands. There were hospitals, too, patronized by the missionaries as well as by the natives, for Jerusalem took a great toll on the health of its foreign residents. One hospital was set up by Moravians for the cure of lepers, another was established for the care of Jews. It served kosher food and operated almost at capacity. The "hospital of the enticers," the rabbis called it and they tried to keep Jews away. Their ban frightened prospective patients, who became even more frightened when fanatical Jews ripped from the grave and left naked on the ground the corpse of a woman who had been so disloyal to her ancestral faith as to die in the hospital. By the end of the nineteenth century, the profusion of schools and hospitals made Jerusalem the most advanced city in the Near East, although at the beginning of the century it had been one of the most backward.

Almost as soon as foreigners had been permitted to travel freely in Palestine, the missionaries were joined by the cranks. In Jerusalem, the excesses of Victorian piety reached an excruciating pitch as dotty old English ladies with religious manias and heaven-crazed men came out to make the holy city their home. The city in the nineteenth century could boast of numerous inhabitants who claimed to be Elijah or John the Baptist, sent by God to proclaim the Second Coming. There was a prophet Daniel and even a Jesus or two. Not only Protestants succumbed to these manias. They afflicted Jews, too. Until quite recently, there was a Jewish gentleman who dressed in his best clothes daily and stood in front of a coffee shop called the Café Alaska on the Jaffa road where, his studies told him, the Messiah would arrive. Emotionally akin to him was the English lady who was convinced that Jesus would come to earth again during a certain ten-day period. Each day during that time she took tea for two up to the top of the Mount of Olives to refresh herself after her ascent and her savior after his descent. In the 1870's a Dutch lady, inspired by the verse in the Book of Revelation that promises the salvation of 144,000 chosen souls, paid for the building of an enormous house outside the city walls in which these fortunates could dwell. Often madmen could be seen walking through the streets bearing a cross or crying out "Woe, woe to the inhabitants of Jerusalem." The Arabs, believing that madmen are touched by God, honored them.

The influx of Roman Catholic churchmen was even greater than that of Protestants. Led by the French, it began in earnest after the Crimean War. The French took over the crusader Church of Saint Anne which had been used as a Muslim religious school and then as a Turkish army barracks, and restored it to its beautiful medieval state. The sultan had offered it to them in gratitude for France's aid in the Crimean War. Before that, he had offered it to the English and for the same reason, but they politely declined the gift; the church was too far, they thought, from the Jewish quarter, where English missionary activities were intended to be centered. The French had no such scruples. Beside the church they built a school for the Sisters of Zion, a new order, dedicated to the conversion of the Jews. A long walk outside the city they constructed another French school for prospective converts. On the Mount of Olives arose another convent, and beside it a crypt commemorating the credo, a cloister commemorating the Lord's Prayer (which was inscribed on the walls in 44 different languages), and the foundation of a vast basilica dedicated to the sacred heart of Jesus. An enormous hospice was built to shelter six hundred French pilgrims. It was given the name, Our Lady of France.

As the French led the Catholic church of the West in Jerusalem, the churches of the East were led, often against their will, by Russia. Throughout the nineteenth century Russian pilgrims formed the vast majority of Christian visitors to Jerusalem. Some came overland through the mountains of the Caucasus. Most, however, came by pilgrim ships which arrived in Palestine regularly after the Crimean War. Their presence in Jerusalem provided Russia with an important political foothold in the Mediterranean. To house the pilgrims the Russians built an immense compound outside the walls of the city on what had been the Jerusalem parade ground, the only extensive flat land close to the city walls. "Moskovieh," the people of Jerusalem called it, and a little Muscovy it was, with a Russian-style cathedral at the center, a hospital around it, priests' houses, and hospices for pilgrims—dwellings that were divided into three categories for the three categories of pilgrims: male, female, and wealthy.

To this compound pilgrims began coming at Christmas time and by Easter there would be, by 1900, more than seven thousand of them there. Devout peasants tramped throughout the vast reaches of Russia, sometimes from Siberia or the coasts of the White Sea, begging their keep along the way, promising in return to commission prayers in Jerusalem or to bring back for their hosts some holy souvenir. Finally they reached Odessa or one of the other Black Sea ports from which they would take a stinking and crowded pilgrim ship to Palestine. The fare was nominal; the Russian government subsidized the trip. The more pious the Russians were, the more they would love their Czar. The journey cost only twelve rubles each way and, in the Czar's impoverished land, even beggars could afford it.

Once the pilgrims reached Jerusalem they were fed and housed in the compound. Though weakened by their lenten fast, they traveled on foot to Galilee to visit the places where Christ had preached, and again in the spring heat tramped, singing, along the desert hills to the banks of the Jordan to bathe in the waters where he had been baptized. (The natives sold them soap for their river bath, stamped with the figure of Christ or John the Baptist.) Into the Jordan they walked wearing the linen shrouds in which they would some day be buried and which they had carried with them from Russia to be blessed for a moment at "The Life-Giving Grave," which is what they called the Church of the Holy Sepulcher. From "The Life-Giving Grave," they got on the eve of Easter a flame of the Holy Fire, which, to ensure themselves eternal life, they brushed for a moment against their shrouds and against the skull caps they would wear in their coffins. This fire they guarded carefully in cunningly made lanterns that would protect it from death by wind, and they carried it home with them as they walked across Russia, stopping at the houses which earlier that year had given them shelter, to offer some of the Jerusalem fire in return for their keep. Candles lit with the fire would burn before icons all across Russia.

Of all the Europeans in Jerusalem, the Russians seemed the most devout, the Germans least. True, there was a settlement of German pietists who dwelt in an agricultural colony southwest of the city walls, attempting to live a Christian life uncomplicated by the worldly pressures of their homeland. Nevertheless, much of the German impact on the city seemed political rather than religious in tone, even though the Germans built churches and hospitals like everyone else. The sultan of Turkey was wooing Germany seeking an alliance and aid, and Germany was fully responsive to his blandishments. In 1898, the Kaiser made a much-publicized and very dramatic pilgrimage to Jerusalem to dedicate a German Lutheran church built on the site of a crusader ruin that the sultan had given to Prussia. For the Kaiser's visit all buildings in the town were washed; all dogs exiled. Although there was a local superstition that any Christian who rode through the city gate on horseback would be a conqueror, Wilhelm II insisted on riding into

Jerusalem. His demand put the Turks in a difficult position, catching them between the demands of their histrionic guest and the superstitions of the local Muslim population. They solved the problem by tearing down a portion of the city wall so that the Kaiser could ride into Jerusalem without riding through one of the gates.

The Kaiser dedicated his church, a proper German church with characteristic Teutonic devices prominent in its decor: castle and rathaus repeated again and again, representing the knights and burghers of medieval, crusading Germany and the soldiers and capitalists of the Kaiser's expanding empire. Wilhelm traveled about Jerusalem receiving dignitaries (and a Zionist delegation led by Theodore Herzl) and visiting local points of interest. At one of the English churches he inspected with interest a baptismal font that had been presented by Queen Victoria. "I must telegraph to Grandmama," he said, "and tell her that I have seen her font." The English, the Russians, the French had more than one church in Jerusalem, and so it was unthinkable that Germany should have only one. Having satisfied his Lutheran subjects with one church, the Kaiser ordered the construction of a second for Germans of the Roman Catholic faith. It rose in German Romanesque style on Mount Zion, marking the site where the Virgin Mary supposedly fell asleep for eternity. (It was located little more than a mile from the place where the Kaiser's kinsman, the Czar, had erected an onion-domed Russian church to commemorate the Virgin's ascension to heaven.) Another German building went up atop the Mount of Olives in a commanding position overlooking the city, a vast hospice for pilgrims and missionaries. The structure was so big, so strongly built and so lavishly decorated, that the story went around that it was designed to serve as government headquarters once Germany took over Palestine. Adding fuel to this report were tales of gun emplacements being constructed against the walls, gun parts being brought up to the building site under cover of diplomatic immunity, and the installation of a large searchlight atop the building's tower with a beam so strong it could be seen by ships, or, perhaps, U-boats in the Mediterranean.

Throughout the nineteenth century literati, scholars, artists and archeologists came to Jerusalem on the heels of the churchmen and statesmen. The information they provided has been indispensable for modern biblical scholars. They observed ruins, analyzed place names and traced them back to biblical times. They devoted great care to the study of the customs of the local peasants. All those simpering good shepherds and Rebeccas-at-the-well in illustrated Bibles are derived from their descriptions and sketches. So are the anthropological data that show how closely the peasants of Palestine are connected with the pre-Arab and even pre-Hebrew inhabitants of the land. In Jerusalem, the scholars walked around town, studying the architecture of buildings and the slopes of the land, tracing the routes of ancient streets, poking through the ruins to unearth remains of biblical structures.

Literary visitors came and compiled prolific accounts of their travels—accounts filled with pious ejaculations about the country's state of decay and patronizing descriptions of the superstitions of the natives. Despite its occasional "horticultural decorations," Jerusalem was, one visitor said, "an extraordinary scene of desolation and wretchedness . . . a most repulsive assemblage of decay, dilapidation, poverty, filth and gloom. . . ." The holy sites are mostly "manifestly apocryphal, some are glaringly false or outrageously absurd, and almost all . . . excite an enlightened Christian's pity or disgust."

Numerous such descriptions of the city were published in fine illustrated volumes that came to rest on Victorian parlor tables. It was the great age of the steel engraving, and the work of some of the great artists of the time was used to illustrate these books: Edward Lear who actually visited the city; Turner who did not, but sketched from the watercolors of artists who had been to the east. In 1854, the indefatigable pre-Raphaelite painter Holman Hunt, famous for his religious works, came to Jerusalem to paint biblical scenes "surrounded by the very people and circumstances of the life in Judaea of old days." He was delighted with the local types and used them as models. Jews who posed for him were placed under a ban by their rabbis, even though only a part of their anatomy might appear in the painting—like the locks of a beautiful blond Jewess which served as a model for the hair of Christ. Hunt was followed by other Victorian genre painters who set up their easels to provide the parlors of the west with Arab scenes and views in oil of the Via Dolorosa. It was a far cry from the days in the seventeenth century when the French painter Le Bruyn visited Jerusalem and concealed himself from the Turks as he sketched the town for fear he would be imprisoned as a spy.

The publication of Darwin's *On the Origin of Species* in 1859 had a great impact on Jerusalem, for it inspired biblical scholars, dismayed by the theory of evolution, to intensify their studies in order to prove that the Bible is true. Many of these scholars came to visit and study Jerusalem. In 1865 at Westminister Abbey a group of distinguished Englishmen founded the Palestine Exploration Fund to encourage exploration in the Holy Land. Queen Victoria pledged 150 pounds for the fund; Charles Darwin, who may have unwittingly inspired its establishment, pledged eight guineas, to be paid on the installment plan over a period of three years. In 1867, the fund sent out an expedition to explore Jerusalem, as part of a project to survey all Palestine. Shafts were sunk at various places around the wall of the Haram esh Sharif. The excavation outraged the religious sensibilities of the city's Muslims. The natives who had been hired to do the digging were outraged too, and for more than religious reasons. They were appalled, and perhaps justifiably so, by the English custom of paying men who worked hard more money than slackers, even though Allah had made all men equal. The explorers pursued their tasks conscientiously, but results were meager. Since then archeological surveys have continued in the city, undertaken with varying degrees of professionalism, but they have unearthed no major works of art and few inscriptions of more than routine interest, for Jerusalem has been thoroughly occupied and thoroughly plundered for so many centuries.

The digs that have taken place have been hampered by the amateurism of some of the diggers, by the Arabs' reluctance to disturb the djinns guarding buried treasure underground, and by the greed of the natives who find and sell ancient objects before they can be properly studied, or steal them from archeological sites. After the First World War, an entire Roman staircase was stolen by a building contractor who wanted to use the stones for his own purposes. In 1911, riots broke out because the Arabs suspected two English archeologists of breaking into the sacred area under the Haram esh Sharif. Here, according to Jerusalem tradition, was the foundation stone of the universe and, if it were disturbed, not only the city but the entire world would be gravely endangered. Rumors spread that the Englishmen had found Solomon's ring, which gave them control of the world and unlimited magical powers, and had unearthed the Ark of the Covenant and the sacred vessels of Solomon's temple. "Our rare treasures," a local Arab newspaper called the loot. An excited mob raced through the streets of the city determined to get them back. Jews and Christians took shelter (although there were Jews in the mob as well as Muslims) and there were rumors that the entire English colony of the city would be massacred. Happily, the storm soon blew over.

Archeology has not yet inspired the Christians of Jerusalem to riot, but it has caused great dissension nevertheless. A furious argument has raged over the site of the crucifixion. The Catholics and Orthodox, naturally, tend to favor the traditional site; a good many Protestants scorn it and have sought to find an appropriate substitute. In 1884, the year before the British general and amateur scholar, Chinese Gordon, was killed at the siege of Khartoum, he took a sabbatical leave to pursue biblical studies in Jerusalem, one of his main concerns being the exact location of the hill of Golgotha. Each day he stationed himself on the roof of a missionary's house, just inside the Damascus Gate, and searched the topography of the city for it with his keen military gaze. Finally, he decided on a little hill north of the city, outside the walls and about half a mile away from the Church of the Holy Sepulcher, a hill which he fancied resembled a skull (Golgotha, supposedly, means "the place of the skull"). The general supported his theory with a drawing that showed a skeleton lying across the ancient city of Jerusalem, with the skull at his very own Golgotha and the place where the anal opening would be strategically located at the altar of the Jewish temple, indicating that God had rejected the sacrifices of the Jews. The site Gordon selected came to be called Gordon's Calvary, and it remained a place of pilgrimage for Protestants for almost a decade, until the day the American Evangelist Dwight Moody, decided to hold a prayer meeting there. During his sermon Moody unfortunately got so carried away by his own fervor that he accidentally stepped on the graves of some Muslims who happened to be resting near his feet. His misstep so offended the Arabs that they walled all Christians off the hill.

Archeologists, missionaries, diplomats and pilgrims, kings and cranks all made their impact on Jerusalem, but the greatest impact was made by the Jews who migrated to Jerusalem in increasing numbers as the nineteenth century progressed. Christians enshrined Jerusalem in their hymns; the Jews did that too, but they also enshrined the city in a national anthem. "Let us return," they sang, "to the land of our fathers, to the city of David, our David." Throughout the nineteenth century, as the appeal of nationalism spread across Europe, and Germans, Italians, Poles, Czechs, Norwegians awoke to a sense of their own identity, Jewish nationalism awoke too, and it seemed to the Jews to promise the solution for their ancient woes. Its beginnings were slow. The Jews returned to Jerusalem at first not because of a nationalistic program, but rather as part of a mass movement that only gradually acquired a political ideology. Their return was part of the nineteenth century's mas-

sive redistribution of population, which filled up empty lands all
over the world. This migratory stirring brought more Jews back to
the city than had dwelt there since ancient times. By the time the
first Zionist congress was called in 1897 to plan the colonization of
the Jews in Palestine, Jerusalem had a predominantly Jewish population.

In the eighteenth century, the Jewish population of Jerusalem
had been limited by law to two thousand, although there were usually a few more than that number there. After the Napoleonic
wars, Jews were freer to settle in the city, but for decades thereafter they were not exactly welcomed in the town. Until 1865 they
paid for the privilege of praying by the Wailing Wall. They paid
more rent and higher taxes than other people. Any Jew crossing
the street near the Church of the Holy Sepulcher was forced by
the monks to kiss an icon of the Virgin and a New Testament or
risk death. "O Jew, O Jews," the Greek Orthodox are said to have
sung at Easter time before the ceremony of the Holy Fire, "your
feast is the feast of monkeys. Our feast is the feast of Christ." Still
Jews were relatively free in Jerusalem, as free as they were in most
places in the world, and by 1895 thirty thousand of the town's
fifty thousand inhabitants were Jews.

They had come from all the lands of the Diaspora, spontaneously and slowly. Some came in disguise, like the Jews of Meshed
in Persia, who had been forced to convert to Islam in 1839. They
turned Muslim, went on the obligatory pilgrimage to Mecca and
then proceeded to Jerusalem where they reverted to their old faith.
In the eighteen-thirties, after the French occupied Algiers, Jews
came from Algeria and moved to Palestine as French subjects, under French protection. Emigration from Poland and Austria was
constant, and increased as the years went by. From the domains of
the Czar, Jews came as individuals and in groups. The old had always come to Jerusalem to die, but now young men came too,
motivated by nationalistic feelings. In the eighties pogroms in Rus-

sia gave a strong impetus to the migration. Large numbers of Jews came from Russia and Poland and formed what was probably the largest Jewish community in the city. In 1882, a band of Yemenite Jews decided to return to Jerusalem. They sold their property and booked passage aboard a ship, but when they arrived they got a hostile welcome. The Jews of the city thought them strange, virtual Arabs, and saw them as competitors for the charity money that came from Europe to support the community. The Yemenites camped outside the walls, almost starving until help came from Christian missionaries who provided them with kosher food. They stayed and were eventually assimilated into the Jewish community. Now they are among the most popular of the Jewish communities in the city; their fellow Jews consider them quaint. In 1892, Jews of Bokhara in Central Asia arrived to a better reception. They were relatively prosperous and they established their own suburb outside the walls of Jerusalem, with long low buildings, a school and synagogue, wide streets as befitting immigrants from spacious Central Asia, and special quarters for housing the Messiah if he should arrive too.

The European powers generally welcomed Jewish immigration into Palestine as a progressive force in the corrupt Turkish empire. For the same reason, the Turks got nervous about the immigration and, periodically, the sultan issued an edict ordering its end. Jewish migrants at Jaffa would row to shore and be turned back; they would row back with a bribe and be turned back again, and then again until the bribe was sufficient. Scarcely anyone concerned himself with how the Arabs of the country reacted to the Jewish influx. It was an age of great population movements to the Americas, Africa, Australia, and to Palestine. The oppressed of the old world were pushing toward independence. Unfortunately, their independence was always acquired at the expense of someone else. This was already evident to disinterested observers watching the growth of the United States in the nineteenth century. In the case of Palestine it was harder to see, for the Jews, in Jerusalem and in the rest of the country, were still a long way from independence.

They lived, for the most part, in extreme poverty and squalor, competing with one another for the remittances collected for their maintenances in the Jewries of the world. *Halukkah*, it was called, and every devout Jew in Jerusalem could live off it, if he so desired, in extreme penury. The remittances paid the upkeep of pious rabbis studying the Law, of students who came to Jerusalem to learn from them, of beggared widows, and attempted to keep up with the debts of the community as a whole, debts arising from extortionist taxes imposed by the Turkish government. Around 1840, *halukkah* amounted to about three and a half English pounds per person per year. Traditionally Jews had sent rabbinically-licensed messengers out to wander through Europe and Asia collecting money, but by the nineteenth century that system had become vestigial although it still survives. It was replaced by a centralized collection agency centered in Amsterdam, which forwarded money to Jerusalem. The people of the city made a meager living as craftsmen—cobblers, carpenters, tailors—or as petty businessmen. They were a contentious lot, certain that they were performing a meritorious service by just residing in Jerusalem. As a result they believed that their fellow Jews owed them a living. Fortunately for them, their fellow Jews believed it too, but with less fervor.

In the year 1827, the English Jewish philanthropist Sir Moses Montefiore came to Jerusalem on the first of seven visits. While he was there, he liberally gave money to schools and charitable foundations. On his second visit, in 1839, hundreds of Jews carried petitions to him, climbing up to the Mount of Olives where he had set up camp. (Visitors who could afford it, lived in tent camps outside the walls to avoid the city's discomforts.) Montefiore stood receiving his admirers and granting many of them their wishes, while roped off behind a cordon that had been raised to keep him in quarantine, for a plague had been raging in the city. One result of his visit was the opening to Jews of the tomb of David on Mount Zion, theretofore a Muslim holy place. That made Montefiore popular with the rabbis of the city and he remained popular with them until he made the mistake of going to the Dome of the Rock on a subsequent visit whereupon he was excommunicated for setting foot on the site of the temple. Another result of the 1839 visit was a government decree issued at Montefiore's urging which denounced an accusation that the Jews of Damascus had murdered a gentile child to use his blood to make Passover matzoth. In 1847, another such accusation was made against the Jews of Jerusalem by an Orthodox monk, but thanks to the decree procured by Montefiore the campaign against them came to nothing.

As a result of Montefiore's beneficence and that of another philanthropist, Baron Edmond de Rothschild of Paris, the Jews of Jerusalem began constructing new buildings, just like the Christians. The Rothschild family founded a hospital in 1854, and a girl's school a decade later. Around 1860, Montefiore founded the first Jewish suburb outside the city walls; its costs were defrayed by a charitable American Jewish merchant, Judah Touro of New Orleans. The Jews of Berlin, paid for the establishment of a kindergarten, the Jews of Frankfurt did the same, and the Jews of Odessa established two. Another school was founded by a French charitable organization, the *Alliance Israélite*. It was a bit racy for Jerusalem. The boys attending it were so modern that some of them even wore the fez, instead of the traditional skullcap. At the beginning of the century, the Jews of Jerusalem had possessed only a few dilapidated synagogues, some of them located in buildings rented from Arab owners. By the end of the century, sizable houses of worship had risen and there were dozens of smaller synagogues inside and outside the walls. One of the synagogues indicated a great change in the state of the Jerusalem Jews. Its dome was large enough to rival the Dome of the Rock and the dome of the Church of the Holy Sepulcher.

With the enormous growth in Jewish population, the city

grew too. New quarters were built outside the walls, even though the fields were dangerous and the city gates were locked nightly making it impossible for suburban inhabitants to seek shelter in case of attack. And so many of the suburbs resembled fortresses; they were long stone-built structures arranged around a central court with few windows on the outside and gates that could be defended against assault. Not all the new quarters were built by Jews. A Swiss Christian who believed in prophecies predicting the Jews' return to the city constructed a suburb for them north of the walls, siting it as best he could in accordance with one of the biblical descriptions of the New Jerusalem. By 1870, there were four Jewish suburbs outside the walls. Within twenty years more than a dozen others had been added. Their construction had been made easier by a government edict of 1867 that finally allowed foreign-born residents to purchase land if they became Turkish citizens. Jerusalem grew to the west and north along the Jaffa road. Jews, in increasing numbers, moved from the old part of the city to the healthier suburbs, and some, inspired by new hope for Jewish resettlement of the land, even moved, in 1878, to the country and established an agricultural colony which they called Petakh Tikvah, "the gate of hope." Their place within the walled city was taken by an influx of Muslims, a great many from the Hebron region, who migrated to Jerusalem attracted by the economic opportunities that had arisen with the city's growth. By 1900, more than half of Jerusalem's Jews resided outside the city walls.

By this time, the migration of Jews to Jerusalem had become a political movement, with its chief prophet a Viennese journalist named Theodore Herzl, who, in 1896, proposed the restoration of the Jewish state. A year later, Herzl called the first Zionist congress, to meet at Basel, its aim "to secure for the Jewish people a publicly recognized, legally secured home in Palestine." To Basel came more than two hundred delegates from all over the world, responding to the nationalism that had been stirring for decades among Jews, to anti-Semitism, and to their era's enthusiasm for planning utopias and sending out colonies. "I have the solution to the Jewish question," Herzl wrote, at a time when people still believed that political questions had answers.

To reach their goal and re-establish their state, the Jews devoted equal attention to colonization and diplomacy. Colonization took place regularly decade after decade until the Jewish population of Palestine had grown enormously, and Jerusalem no longer contained the majority of Jews in the country. Diplomacy was equally successful. Herzl went to Constantinople to see the sultan, he talked to the pope, and to the king of Italy. But he pinned his hopes most on the Kaiser, who was so influential in Constantinople and who might be expected to see the advantages in having a strong pro-German Jewish colony in Palestine. In 1898, when the Kaiser came to Jerusalem, Herzl came too to urge him, in that historic place, to take the Zionist movement under his protection. The Kaiser had his doubts. "What future can there be for the people who crucified our Lord?" he is reported to have remarked during his stay in the city. Nevertheless, he received Herzl courteously (they had met before), if noncommitally. "That brief reception," Herzl wrote in his diary, "will live on forever in Jewish history." Herzl was wrong. The help Germany would one day give to Zionism was considerable, but it would be of quite another nature.

Eventually, Zionists came to rely on England rather than Germany. In 1903, the British government surprised the Jews by offering them a large area of Uganda in East Africa for settlement. There was a quarrel among the Zionists. Many, including Herzl, were eager to accept the offer of seeing Uganda as a haven for Jewish refugees from Russian persecution. But the majority, led by the Russian Jews, refused to think of any other home than Zion.

With the outbreak of World War I, a decade after Herzl's death, most Zionists pursued a cautious neutrality. It was evident that one result of the war would be a change in the status of the Turkish empire. If Turkey lost the war, it would be dismembered; if Turkey won, it would be even more open to German influence. But as time went on, Zionists came over to the side of the Allies and worked assiduously to get from Britain some statement of their rights to a homeland in Palestine. Influence was also brought to bear on the Americans, on President Wilson who had been sensitive to the claims of national minorities throughout Europe. Finally, in November 1917, the British government issued an ambiguous, but favorable, statement announcing that "His Majesty's government view with favor the establishment in Palestine of a national home for the Jewish people, and will use their best endeavours to facilitate the achievement of this object, it being clearly understood that nothing shall be done which may prejudice the civil and religious rights of other non-Jewish communities in Palestine. . . ."

Earlier in the war, the British had also promised to support the establishment of an Arab kingdom, which the Arabs believed would include Palestine. Along with this, Britain also signed a secret compact with France, giving France control of Lebanon and of a puppet Arab kingdom in Syria; Northern Palestine was to go to the British and Jerusalem to an international administration of Christian powers, with one Muslim representative.

A great deal of ink and a great deal of blood have been consumed in the discussions and quarrels that resulted from this devious series of wartime agreements in which Britain, France, Jews and Arabs bargained with each other from varying positions of strength and weakness. It is sufficient here to say that the Arabs never really accepted the Balfour Declaration, and that the Jews believed they had finally been restored officially to their national home. Their belief was strengthened when the Declaration was incorporated into the Mandate by which the League of Nations, after the war, gave the government of Palestine to Britain.

In 1917, the British had conquered Palestine. There was a legend in Jerusalem that the Turks would finally leave the city after the death of a certain tree which grew on the site where criminals were executed. Shortly after the issuance of the Balfour Declaration the tree died, the Turkish army pulled out of the city and the British general Allenby entered Jerusalem, on foot like a pilgrim. More prophecies were trotted out for his reception. Jerusalem would fall, tradition said, to a man with the name of a prophet, at a time when the waters of the Nile flowed into Palestine. Providentially, the waters of the Nile had been brought across the Sinai in water-pipes to supply the English army in Palestine, and the General's name, Allenby, could easily approximate the Arab word for prophet—*al nebi*. Standing before the inhabitants of "Jerusalem the Blessed," at the tower of David, the General who had fulfilled these prophecies promised the people of Jerusalem that "every sacred building, monument, holy spot, shrine, traditional site, endowment, pious bequest, or customary place of prayer, of whatsoever form of the three religions will be maintained and protected . . ."

During the war, Jerusalem and the entire country had suffered severely from famine. In the city, Turkish soldiers, ragged and hungry, knocked humbly on the doors of the inhabitants begging for food. The city was full of refugees, for food was still more plentiful in Jerusalem than elsewhere. Hundreds of Armenians came fleeing the Turks to dwell in the fortress-like Armenian convent in the southwest section of town. Hundreds more were to arrive in 1921, when the French army of occupation left Turkey. As soon as the British had marched into Jerusalem, thousands of Arab refugees came too, many from across the Jordan where their descendants have now returned as a result of yet another war. For these starving people, the British brought in food. As soon as the war was over, they brought in playgrounds, too. They built substantial government offices and banks, and enlisted city-planning experts to map the growth of the holy city. West and south the planners pointed and west and south the city expanded. They drew up a plan for a park system, listing the city's green spots (including the garden of Gethsemane). They laid out new streets, (some named, of course, King George Street, and Princess Mary Street), and placed on them street signs in English, Arabic and even Hebrew. Few other moves could have made the Jews feel more at home. A big new archeological museum was constructed north of the city. On a hill to the west rose offices for the Jewish Agency for Palestine, the para-governmental headquarters of the Jews in the country. And on Mount Scopus, overlooking the city on one side and the Jordan valley on the other, rose a Hebrew university. Its cornerstone had been laid even before the war was over, not with one stone, but with twelve, one for each of the tribes of Israel.

Once again, for the first time since the crusades, the city was in Christian hands, a fact that excited a good deal of self-congratulation in the west. Even so Jerusalem was now predominantly Jewish not only in population, but also in tone. The center of gravity had moved outside the walls of the Old City, which remained a picturesque, primarily Arab and religious enclave on the eastern fringe of town, to settle on the Jaffa road, where the Jewish offices and shops were. Even the first British High Commissioner for Palestine was a Jew; "the little Messiah," he was nicknamed by the Jews of Jerusalem, and "the Jewish King." After his appointment he came to worship at a synagogue on the anniversary of the destruction of the temple, making his way over carpets that had been spread along the streets by Persian Jews. He was called up to pray before the congregation and when he recited "Have mercy on Zion for it is the home of our life" he burst into tears. It may be the inauguration of "an era of tears of joy" proclaimed the chief rabbi of the Ashkenazim; "may be," he had to say, for if the Jews of Jerusalem were joyous, the Arabs were not.

From the time the Balfour Declaration had reached their attention, they had become increasingly restive about a Jewish take-over of the land they considered their own. In the spring of 1920 anti-Jewish riots took place during the Nebi Musa pilgrimage that brought numerous peasants from the countryside into Jerusalem. Throughout the twenties, Palestine was relatively quiet, but still ominous enough for the British to try to figure out some formula that would disengage them from the terrible impasse their wartime diplomacy had gotten them into. They were without success, for it was almost impossible to satisfy both parties, and as the years went by, the Arabs became increasingly intransigent, refusing adamantly to become a minority in Palestine.

Arab nationalism had been awakening more slowly than Jewish nationalism, but it had been awakening, nevertheless, since the nineteenth century. Late in the century, the Turkish sultan tried to control it by encouraging religious fervor as a substitute. To this end, he redecorated the Dome of the Rock and constructed a railway to transport pilgrims from Damascus to Mecca. (Its engines were fed with wood from the cedars of Lebanon, which have all but vanished as a result.) The railroad diminished considerably the number of Muslim pilgrims in Jerusalem, for now pilgrims tended to go directly from Damascus to Mecca and back. During World War I, Jerusalem witnessed the execution of Arab nationalists by the Turks. When the war was over, the Arabs, resenting the way in which Europeans were gobbling up their lands, rebelled against the British in Egypt and Iraq, and against the French in Syria.

In 1929, simmering Arab resentment against the Jews and the British in Palestine broke out into open rebellion. The revolt was sparked by a slight change made by the Jews at the Wailing Wall, which was Muslim-owned, although a Jewish shrine. When the Jews placed in front of the wall a screen designed to protect male worshippers from the distractions provided by the enticing sight of their elderly wives praying nearby, the Arabs protested. The British removed the screen and the Arabs, emboldened, began to claim more rights at the Wall, which was sacred to them as one of the places where Mohammed's horse may have been hitched the night the prophet ascended to heaven. Arabs knocked open a door beside the Wall and began using the Wall area, theretofore a rather isolated cul-de-sac, as a thoroughfare. Eventually, there were demonstrations, and riots, and then a full scale invasion of the Jewish quarters of the city. Jews were massacred in Safed and Hebron, and attacked everywhere in the country, often while the British looked the other way. A British commission came out and recommended, as a solution to the country's troubles, a limitation on Jewish immigration, thus challenging the concept of a national home to provide a haven for persecuted Jews.

In the early thirties, with Hitler's rise to power, there was a great influx of German Jews to the country. As a result, another Arab rebellion broke out in 1936; this one, more serious than the 1929 revolt, lasted three years. To end it, the British government, in 1939, announced that thenceforth only 75,000 more Jews would be admitted as immigrants to Palestine. Any further immigration would require Arab approval, which everyone knew would never be given. The Jews of Germany, Austria, Czechoslovakia were already under the heel of the Nazis. The Jews of Poland, France, the Balkans, Russia, Italy, and the Low Countries had not yet been trapped.

Throughout World War II, when one in every three Jews was slaughtered, Britain refused to abandon this policy. After the war, there was no change, even to admit concentration camp survivors. Survivors began slipping into the country anyway as illegal immigrants. In 1946 the Jews' hopes were raised when a joint British-American commission came to Jerusalem and recommended the admission of 100,000 Jews. But the British government refused to accept the recommendation. Jewish terrorists inaugurated a campaign against the British. In Jerusalem, a major hotel was blown up; British soldiers and officials were assassinated; and a small-scale civil war broke out in the country between Arab and Jew, a war complicated by the fact that it was also a rebellion of the Jews against Britain. Finally, in 1947, the United Nations voted to end the British mandate and partition the country into Jewish and Arab states, leaving Jerusalem intact, an island in the middle of the Arab portion of the country governed by an international administration.

The Jews accepted the solution but the Arabs refused. Even before the British terminated their mandate, the war between them and the Jews was raging full force. In December 1947 sniping began in the old city of Jerusalem. By the end of the year there was an Arab and British blockade that kept all Jewish traffic out of the old city, except for a convoy allowed in three times a week with food—and smuggled arms. By March the Jews were in open warfare with the British as well as with the Arabs. By April the British were attacking the Jews with cannon as well as with small arms. In May, the British left, and Arab armies marched into Palestine. Jordanian troops took up positions in Jerusalem and were welcomed fervently by the city's Muslims. On the day Israel declared its independence, all Jerusalem was a battlefield. In the following three weeks 10,000 shells fell on the city.

The Jews were subjected to a twin siege. The Jewish quarter in the old walled city was surrounded, and in the new city the Jews, beleaguered too, maintained their contact with the rest of Israel only through a precarious twisting road, freshly hacked out of the mountainside. At the end of May the Jews in the old city finally surrendered, and thirteen hundred of them, starving and ill, hobbled out between ranks of Jordanian soldiers. But in the rest of the city the Jews managed to hold out, and when, after a series of truces, the war ended with victory for Israel, they were in control of half of Jerusalem.

The United Nations partition plan had given the city to neither party. Nevertheless the Jews insisted on retaining what they had of Jerusalem. Eventually they named it the capital of Israel, although foreign countries do not, as a rule, recognize it as the legitimate capital. Their embassies are in Tel Aviv and Jerusalem has only consulates. Jordan annexed the Arab half of the city, and a wall arose at various points along the border to keep the Jews and Arabs apart.

For almost twenty years Jerusalem remained divided. The inhabitants were within earshot and gunshot of each other, but there was no intercourse between them. Only one passageway, the Mandelbaum Gate, near a house that had belonged to a man with the peaceful name of Mandelbaum, provided access between its halves. Along the border, on both sides of the city, there were soldiers, gun emplacements, and sudden, ominous warnings that said, "Stop! Danger!" The Jordanians painted out Hebrew street signs, taped over Hebrew explanations under the exhibits in the museum. In the Jerusalem Arab newspapers, the word Israel appeared in quotation marks, if it appeared at all. On maps, Israeli territory was marked "Jewish-Occupied Palestine," and the Jewish quarter of the old city was labeled "Ex-Jewish Quarter." That quarter was plundered and almost destroyed, and Arabs moved into its crumbling houses as Jews were moving into Arab houses in their half of Jerusalem and throughout Israel. The population of the old city increased with the influx of Arab refugees from what was now Israel. To house them hundreds of tiny grey stone houses sprouted on the hillsides. Since they were cut off now from the YMCA on the Jewish side of the city, the Arabs built another on their side of the border and named it the Aelia Capitolina YMCA as a reminder of those happy times when no Jews had been allowed to set foot in Jerusalem. On both sides of the city there was a chronic brooding sense of isolation and insecurity. It was especially evident among the Jews. A century earlier the Jews had lived, in Christendom and in the lands of Islam, isolated in ghettoes, hated by their neighbors and in constant fear of physical attack. To end that situation and be like other people, they had resolved to have a nation of their own. Now that nation was isolated and hated by its neighbors and lived in constant fear of physical attack.

"Lo it is a people that shall dwell alone," an early biblical prophecy proclaims of the Jews, "and shall not be reckoned among the nations." As if to disprove that prophecy, the Jewish half of Jerusalem assumed all the trappings of the capital of a small new twentieth-century republic: a parliament building, a national museum, public monuments, parades, political debates. The city may have been an outpost in unfriendly territory, locked out of the rest of Asia by surrounding hostile gentiles, but there was contact with the rest of Jewry. Thousands of Jewish immigrants arrived from Europe and the Arab lands and settled in immense new housing projects that spread for miles over the Jerusalem hills. With their arrival and the city's expansion, Jerusalem's character changed. Now it was no longer a rather sedate and pious university town, but a bustling though small capital city, with a little industry, a night club or two, an underworld and traffic lights. It had reached the twentieth century. Other Jews came as visitors, from America, South Africa, and Europe. They descended from the sky like angels and scattered gold through the streets. The results of their beneficence are visible everywhere in schools, hospitals, university dormitories and synagogues that they built and endowed, and on the hundreds of plaques fixed to the walls of the new buildings to inform the public of their generosity. As a result of their donations a new university campus rose in a valley west of the city to replace the hilltop campus on Mount Scopus that remained inaccessible, surrounded by Arabs.

The university became one of the major industries of Jerusalem. Another major industry was tourism. The Israelis tried half-heartedly to convince the tourist trade that they had a perfectly authentic Jerusalem to show off to visitors, despite their pained awareness that the real Jerusalem, the Jerusalem of David and Solomon, and of Jesus and Mohammed, was unattainable, within sight but out of reach. For the Arabs refused to allow Jews, Israeli or foreign, access to their holy places in the old city. In the Jewish half of Jerusalem, citizens spent an unconscionable amount of time looking past the border into the old city which they could glimpse from many vantage points. The guidebooks to the Israeli half of town list place after place from which a good view can be obtained. Even foreign tourists in Israel, who knew they were going over to the other side, always got caught up in the excitement and took part in the game, peering into the future, spotting this tower and that dome and that hill with all the fervor of a religious fanatic trying to envision the outlines of the heavenly Jerusalem. Else-

where in Israel and throughout the world, Jews at Passover promise themselves that they will spend the following Passover in the
holy city. In Jerusalem itself, Jews said, as was customary, "Next
year in the heavenly Jerusalem!" and then tried to catch a glimpse
of the worldly old city. Even in their homeland, in their capital,
the Jews were still, in a sense, on the outside looking in.

Then, in 1967, on the third day of the six-day Arab-Israeli
war, the city was reunited, when Israeli troops drove past Saint
Stephen's Gate in the eastern wall of the city. (Their orders had
called for them to enter by the Dung Gate along the southern wall,
but they considered that undignified.) Less than a half-hour after
the first Jewish soldier had broken into the old city, the Jews were
at the Wailing Wall, weeping again, but this time with tears of joy.
Once more, for the first time in almost two thousand years, Jerusalem belonged to the Jews.

Israel annexed what had been the Arab half of the city, drawing for the new Jerusalem wide municipal boundaries that reached
eastward over the Mount of Olives and extended south almost to
Bethlehem. "A hasty administrative action!" the President of the
United States declared. "Hypocrisy, demagoguery and blas-
phemy!" said the Russians. "Desist forthwith!" said the United
Nations. A month after the conquest the Mayor of Jerusalem in-
vited the United Nations to make its home in the holy city. The
United Nations, which had never recognized Israel's right to be in
Jerusalem in the first place, did not reply.

The Arabs were dismayed by the Israeli victory. Without
Jerusalem and its surroundings the Kingdom of Jordan was
scarcely a viable nation, but merely the personal fief of its ruler.
The leader of the Muslim pious, the King of Arabia, vowed that
Muslims would never rest until the city was returned to Islamic
control. In Cairo an apparition of the Virgin Mary was seen at a
Coptic church, and Muslim and Christian invalids by the hundreds
made pilgrimages to her there hoping to be healed. She had come to
Cairo, an Egyptian government spokesman said, because she could

not bear to remain in Jerusalem now that the Jews had taken over.

In Israel, however, there was rejoicing and universal agreement that Jerusalem would never be surrendered. Nevertheless, after the victory the rabbis refused to cancel the traditional fast that memorialized the destruction of the temple, and insisted that the Jews continue to wail at the newly regained Wailing Wall. On the fast day, Jews flocked to the Wall from all over Israel and despite the ruling, celebrated a triumphant festival there. To receive the immense crowds the area before the wall was blasted clear—of the slums as the Israelis said, of the Arab homes as the Arabs said—which blocked it. As a result the road to the Wailing Wall is no longer a dead end.

In Israel a new song caught the public fancy. "Jerusalem of gold, of copper and of light," the words went, "to all your songs I am your harp." The Arabs answered with a song of their own, "The Flower of Cities," describing the loss of Jerusalem to the hated Jews. The Arab song became popular in Israel, the Israeli song in Jordan.

Almost as soon as the war was over both the Arabs and the Israelis published a list of enemy desecrations that had taken place in Jerusalem. Arabs showed Israeli gun emplacements on the ruins of Christian Churches. Israelis showed destroyed synagogues, and Jewish tombstones lining the pathway to a Jordanian army latrine. Arab propaganda rather heavy-handedly answered that with pictures of ruined buildings in Jerusalem and quotes from the Book of Lamentations and the Jewish prophets bemoaning the woes of the city. "Zion is a wilderness, Jerusalem a desolation," they informed the Jews and the world. "Jerusalem remembered in the days of her affliction . . . all the pleasant things that she had in the days of old." "Woe to him," they added in the words of the Jewish prophet Habakkuk, "that increaseth that which is not his." History seemed to have come full circle, and it was as mysterious as ever.

CHAPTER 11

The Veronica Photography Shop

JERUSALEM today is a city made of stone. There is stone in the fields, stone in the public park, stone is almost all one sees ascending to the city along the highway or on the railroad. The city walls are of stone, the churches and the houses of stone; and within the shrines, stone receives adoration—the stone that has given its name to the Dome of the Rock, the stone on which Christ's cross was fixed, the stone that covered Christ's tomb. The great shrine of the Jews—the Wailing Wall—is a pile of stone. In the Jews' temple sacrifices were made on stone, and outside it stone was used for killing malefactors, for stoning is a punishment that comes naturally in that rocky land. Stone is everywhere, in the cobble streets or sidewalks, in the ruins of old buildings, and on the sides of new ones. Dressed smooth or left rough, millions of blocks surround the living and cover the dead in acres on acres of graveyards. Wherever there is buildng the leisurely sound of the stonemason's hammer rings through the cobbled alleys and across the rocky fields. As one walks through the streets of the city one is always aware of stone. In the narrow medieval alleys of the old city it arches overhead where the buildings—as they so often do—cross over the streets. Cobbled roads, stairways actually, rise and descend in tiers across the old city's hills. One is hemmed in by high walls, fortress walls, that are pierced by a few rare, iron-grilled windows. The old city itself is hemmed in, by high and massive walls of stone that rise on stony hillsides and in some places on great outcrops of mountain rock.

In the new city too there is only stone; the great hotels, the government buildings, the university's lecture halls and dormitories, the apartment complexes, the railroad station, the movie houses are of stone. The streets are wider here; there is often space between buildings; architectural styles are more various. But here too one walks between looming bulks of stone, down long empty treeless streets of stone that die, eventually, on a rocky field at the edge of the town.

The stone is limestone, Jerusalem stone, honey-colored often, or light pink or pale gray with golden overtones. Thanks to it, the city, so diverse in its people and its ideals and its history, is all of a piece from one end to the other, and from one age to the other, and all of a piece with the rocky hills on which it is built and by which it is surrounded. "The mountains are round about Jerusalem," the psalmist sang; the mountains are mostly treeless now, vast, and bare. They look as though they could easily grow their own Jerusalems overnight; or they look as though Jerusalems had grown upon them and then ebbed to rubble. For the city grows from its earth as no city in the west ever does, where towns are always a different color from their matrix. For all its vaunted links to heaven, Jerusalem seems more firmly linked to earth than any other city does. To match it, its heavenly counterpart must indeed be made of light.

It is beautiful and inspiring and if one has a predilection for believing, the stones and the siting of the city can bring belief alive, despite the deadening effects of the shrines. But the stones are stones of earth. The city is a city of earth. The inhabitants and pilgrims who kiss its stones like to think of themselves as immortal; still they are material beings who will die and crumble into dust.

Their sacred stones smell of urine. Their votive candles cost money. In religious processions they push and shove. On fast days, they have bad breath. Jerusalem on its hills is a half mile closer to heaven than New York or even Rome but here, more than elsewhere, the flesh and the things of the flesh are always in evidence. Perhaps they seem so obtrusive here because the city so relentlessly demands the soul of the native or visitor, rather than his body; and as a result the rebellious body asserts itself.

Devout visitors are appalled by the humanity of the city, by the Pop-Op discotheque, the knife fights in the street between pimps, by the salacious Arabs, the beggars, the sticky hands of the souvenir salesmen, the priests who offer to trade watches. For centuries this has been the reaction to Jerusalem. Jerusalem is worldly and even criminal. It is a rote reaction, on a par with the observation that in Venice the canals smell, in Paris the people are unfriendly. For solace, pious visitors can kiss the stones and look out at the hills, and try to imagine what it was like when Jesus walked these streets. Surely, they tell themselves, it was different; it was a different time and therefore a different city. The most tenacious among them will try to search out the actual path Christ walked down the Mount of Olives, inspect its Sunday school landscape and reassure themselves that the Bible tales are true. Sympathetic guides will point out the actual path to them. There are three paths on the mountain and any one of them will do. As the pilgrims do, the guides live by faith, even if it is the pilgrims' faith and not their own.

The pilgrims themselves, no matter how high-minded they may be, unconsciously become part of the push and shove of Jerusalem—the pageant of superstition for which they condemn the city. Every Friday, on the anniversary of the crucifixion, they gather in separate groups according to religion to follow the stations of the cross, retracing the steps of Jesus. Invariably they cause a noisy and ill-tempered traffic jam, inspiring curses in Arabic which they fortunately cannot understand. The crowd forms in a Muslim schoolyard near the edge of the city, beside a basketball court and opposite Pilate's palace, the site of the first station of the cross. It is Friday afternoon, the Muslim holy day, and so school is not in session. There are no schoolboys inside singing along with their masters to learn texts by heart or gazing with dismay at the wall-map that shows the Arab empire at its height in the great days before the Christians took back Spain and Sicily and the hated Zionists took back "Jewish-occupied Palestine." The pilgrims wander in in tour groups or one by one, along with guides in shiny gigolo suits, and priests, monks and nuns in their habits. Ordinary pilgrims, men and women, often wear newly-purchased Arab headdresses, like little sheikhs. Almost all, clergy and laymen, wear cameras too.

As individual tourists or pilgrims look on, waiting for the procession to begin, members of the religious tour groups busy themselves practicing hefting the cross that they will carry along. How to hold it? Upright like a conquistador taking posession of a new land? Or hooked onto a shoulder as in the Sunday school images of Jesus. After a number of variations are tried, the decision is made: over the shoulder it is, for that seems to be the custom here, even though it wasn't in Roman times—for the upright of the cross was already in place at Golgotha and Jesus only had to carry the crossbar.

The procession is always scheduled to begin at three, the hour of the Passion and a comfortable interval after lunch. But like all parades it is slow getting started, and like all parades, no one in the line of march or the audience ever knows just what it is that finally makes it start. Yet, suddenly, as if to a signal from heaven, a group of monks kneels in a circle in the middle of the courtyard while one of their number leads them in prayer. The tourists excitedly clump together. Brothers and sisters of the various orders move in to stand close to their sibs. The tourists snap their cameras ever more frantically. And the march begins.

Like every other religious activity in this city, it is both ludi-crous and profoundly touching. People jostle each other. Surely some of them are mourning the crucifixion of Jesus. Pilgrim groups walk along the narrow gloomy Via Dolorosa, each pilgrim carry-ing the cross for a time while his comrades try to keep from being bumped by it. As the awful burden is passed from one marcher to the next, a priest or guide will steady it. From the front and back comes the sound of singing. The way is downhill past the place where Jesus was crowned with thorns, past the Chapel of the Con-demnation (Catholic) and the Prison of Christ (Greek Orthodox) to the third station of the cross, where Jesus, for the first time, fell under his burden. Here there is a chapel run by Polish Catholics, and a museum, and inevitably, a souvenir shop. The fourth station of the cross is also Catholic, as most of them are—and it is Polish too, a memorial to Polish war veterans and to Christ's meeting with his mother who had been waiting to see her son for the last time. Nearby the Armenians commemorate the meeting with the Church of Our Lady of the Spasm.

At each station, the crowd halts; priests kneel and pray, sing-ing, and then rise again to continue the march past religious estab-lishments of every sect and nation. The crowd of worshippers surges through the street and as it flows forward a massive traffic jam develops near the main north-south street of Jerusalem, where another crowd equally intent is walking along in another direction —the Muslims of the city whiling away their Sabbath by strolling through the market streets. The traffic jam is aggravated by the fact that three of the stations of the cross are out of the way, on the roof of the Church of the Holy Sepulchre, and require that the pilgrims who go to them double back after the visit retracing their steps in order to get to the street that leads to the site of Golgotha.

At the crossroad a policeman directs traffic, with unintelligible shouts instead of a whistle, and attempts to separate the pilgrims going to stations six, seven, and eight from the pilgrims who have already been there, and all the pilgrims from the inhabitants of the city irreverently going about their business. The rush becomes similar to that of a New York subway crowd, as complex, brutal and competitive as Jerusalem's spiritual tangle. Pilgrims stumble and fall. To their terror and surprise they are caught up in the vicious pushing that is the normal way of life within the walls of the old city, the uncontrolled egotism that has been endemic in Jerusalem throughout history (as Pope Paul VI discovered in 1964 when he tried to push his way through crowds along the same route). It is the exact opposite of Christianity.

Confronted with it, many of those following the stations of the cross decide to skip two or three of them: Jesus' second fall, Jesus' third fall, Jesus' meeting with the charitable ladies of Jerusalem who offered him a sedative to drink. Instead they can stop at an Arab café to have an orange soda or a beer, waiting out in the street on little straw-seated stools, until the rest of the procession returns.

When the pilgrims finally reach the Church of the Holy Sepulcher, the end of the Via Dolorosa, and climb the steep and narrow stairway that leads up to the hill of Calvary, the Chapel of the Crucifixion becomes as noisy as an airport waiting room. There are the same echoing marble floors, the same excited international crowds, even the same heavenly expectations. Pilgrims walk about the shrine, chatting, taking each others' pictures with flashbulbs popping, pushing to the front of the line to get near the sacred stones. They genuflect, some weep, and on a long marble bench beside the half-Orthodox, half-Catholic double chapel bemused Protestants sit looking on, smug and a bit envious. Here they are outsiders. The chapel of Golgotha is dark, although hundreds of lamps and candles try to light it and their light is reflected by golden mosaics on the ceiling and by the gilt cloaks of dozens of icons.

The Orthodox have the true site of Golgotha, the stone where the cross was fixed (beside it the Latins must be content with the place where Christ was nailed to the cross), and they guard the holy stone beneath slabs of marble and cover it with an altar made of marble too. "Popery has contrived to hide the *place* where the Redeemer died as completely as she has done the *person* of the Redeemer himself," wrote an indignant nineteenth-century Presbyterian missionary. But the place can still be seen. In the marble floor is a circular opening, bordered by a narrow band of silver that has been polished bright by the kisses of pilgrims. Beneath is the naked rock of Calvary, and the pilgrim or tourist can reach down with his hand to touch it, one more stone in a city made of stone and surrounded by hills covered with stone. Only the most resolute infidel can fail to be moved; and to the devout, afterwards, Rome with all its sanctity, or any other Christian shrine, will always appear faintly pretentious.

Downstairs in the tomb of Christ, worship is focused on the Messiah; but in the place where he died, he shares the devotion with his mother, who appears prominently in both the Catholic and Orthodox chapels, and in the space between. In the Orthodox chapel she is relatively subdued, her body, like that of so many holy figures in the church, half hidden behind a screen of silver, with only the holiest parts—her face and her hands—left naked. (More than a thousand years before Mary lived, the Babylonians followed the same principle in decorating sacred images; although they covered the face and hands with precious metal and revealed the more profane parts of the body. But of course they did not revere virgins.) The Catholic Mary seems much more powerful than her Orthodox counterpart a few feet away. She is shown in a mosaic above the Catholic altar standing erect, mourning over her son who lies before her nailed to his cross; through a trick of perspective and the accident of the colors used she appears much larger than he, much more powerful and more godlike. As if this were not enough there is another Catholic Mary between the Catholic altar and the Orthodox altar, a baroque statue of Our Lady of Sorrows. Her gold and begemmed halo was stolen, along with her platinum earrings and her tiara, by irreverent and daring burglars who ventured into the church while the Muslim custodian of the shrine was sleeping at his post, a few weeks after the Israelis conquered the city in 1967. Fortunately most of their loot was quickly recovered.

Downstairs is the Sepulcher of Christ, sheltered in a little temple that stands in the middle of the church, beneath a dome in whose vast space motes of dust float in the sunlight. Here too the rock that marks the sacred site, the rock that was rolled to close Jesus' tomb ("the Rolling Stone," as the guides call it), is protected by a marble slab. Here too there are numerous ineffective lamps (five Roman Catholic, five Greek Orthodox, five Armenian, one Coptic). Here too there are crowds of kneeling pilgrims. But the crowds are outside the tomb, lined up to get in. For the little temple that marks the tomb is so small, only four or five worshippers can gain access at one time. They share the space with an elderly clergyman who guards the shrine's ornaments and its collection plate, in which can be seen bills from many lands and of all denominations, a day's work for one of Jerusalem's numerous money-changers. The irony of seeing the money at Christ's tomb is lost on few visitors. Nevertheless, the money is needed, for the church is always in dire need of repair. All its walls are hidden by wooden scaffolds. Looking down on the worshippers as they deposit their mites are three Christs—not Father, Son and Holy Ghost, but Orthodox, Catholic and Armenian—ascending to heaven in three icons, done in three mediums (silver, gilt-bronze, and paint) and three styles (Byzantine, neo-classic and late Victorian). It is again a routine reaction for visitors to be distressed by the presence of three Christs at the tomb, but perhaps their presence there is as normal and sensible as is that of the collection box.

To the stone of the tomb, as to the other sacred stones of the city, the supersitious are accustomed to bring objects or even people to be prayed over. A child comes in with his parents. He is four or five years old and he looks like a little friar, for he wears the clothes of a Franciscan, in which his parents vowed to clothe him for a year if he recovered from some illness or misfortune. In his little habit, he comes before the risen Christ—in this case the Roman Catholic one—to show that he is indeed fulfilling their vow. Or a middle-aged lady walks in with a package in a paper bag to be blessed. She rubs it over the marble covering of the tomb and prays and then takes it upstairs to Golgotha and then out to the church vestibule to repeat the process at the stone where Christ's body was anointed. What is inside—a picture of someone? clothing? a gift? a cookbook? money? And where else does she take it? The rock of agony in the Garden of Gethsemane? The Virgin's tomb? The place of the flagellation? There are dozens of other Christian shrines scattered throughout the city; they are all almost as sacred and they all have their power.

All of them are in a different style, depending on who controls them. There is a monastery that looks as though it had been transported from a Greek island; an imitation English Gothic cathedral, with an English cathedral garden; an authentic French Gothic church; a barn-like midwestern American Evangelical church with stained oak pews and a Christmas tree at Christmas. And because the Franciscans are the custodians of Roman Catholic holy places there are numerous Italian churches, most of them done in bad Italian style. One of the worst is at the first station of the cross, the site of the flagellation and the imposition of the crown of thorns; here the Romans, attempting to compensate for their ancestors' cruelty to Jesus, betrayed him again. The church was built, an inscription says, in the seventh year of the Fascist era, 1929, and it is done in an ugly Fascist monumental style. But there is a splendid Italian touch: over the altar is a gold ceiling mosaic depicting a great crown of thorns; every worshipper who approaches the altar and every priest who celebrates mass there must feel it pressing down on him almost as Jesus must have felt it pressing on his head. In the mosaic dozens of drops of blood are seen falling from the crown; only Italians or Spaniards would think of showing them there.

When Italian churches are bad they are horrid, but when they are good, they are very, very good. One of the best, and it is by the same architect responsible for the chapel with the crown of thorns, is the Church of Dominus Flevit, "the Lord wept," located on the site of an old Byzantine church half way down the Mount of Olives at the place where Jesus overlooked Jerusalem and wept over the destruction he foresaw for the city. The church is small, but its ceiling is extraordinarily high, and cunningly designed so that it catches every whisper, magnifies it and echoes it again and again. In that space the sound of weeping would resonate so it would seem the entire city could hear it. In the side of the church a great window is cut, a picture window we would call it; and through it one can see a view of the doomed city as within a picture frame.

One of the finest churches in Jerusalem is the ancient Armenian Shrine of Saint James in the southwest corner of the city, set within the vast and peaceful Armenian compound that is sheltered from the rest of Jerusalem by fortress-like walls. A visit to the church is a marvelous theatrical experience. On a major holy day the place is filled with worshippers who sit on the floor on fine Oriental rugs and watch while from behind the altar a splendid procession emerges. Priests beautifully costumed in stiff embroidered robes walk into the center of the church singing ancient hymns. One bears candles, a second swings a golden censer. They march across the church and out a door and then in another as the mass is celebrated. The Armenians have one of Jerusalem's richest collections of church treasures. Only a small part of it is displayed but it is a splendid sight. During the service there is almost an hour of marching and singing, amidst the bright dresses of the worshippers, and jewel-like rugs, beneath glittering chandeliers and brilliant icons, angels with rainbow wings, dragons, golden-crowned saints, and everywhere on the walls, shining blue tiles. Then suddenly into the resplendent church comes a preacher, tall and ancient, and dressed from head to toe in black. Slowly, almost balletically, he takes his staff and plants it before him; and when he begins to speak, he starts to sway from side to side slowly in rhythm with his words, looking like some desert saint come down off his pillar to instruct the world. Armenian is a soft and melodious language; it seems especially so after the harshness of the Hebrew and Arabic one hears in Jerusalem, and without understanding a word of it one can listen to the sermon for an hour, and enjoy it.

The only other place in the city that is comparable to the Armenian compound in both beauty and tranquility is the Haram, the sacred enclosure of the Muslims. The very name *haram* literally means taboo, and taboo it is to pious Jews who are forbidden entry by a sign placed above one of the gates by the rabbinical authorities: "Notice and warning," it says in Hebrew, English and French, "Entrance to the area of the Temple Mount is forbidden to everyone by Jewish law . . ." Nevertheless Israelis now flock into the enclosure all agog at the architectural wonders that confront them. Today there seem to be more Jews there than Muslims; but even Jews and Muslims together hardly crowd the vast pavement. The tourists cluster about the Dome of the Rock and the worshippers devote their attention to al-Aqsa Mosque and the fountain where they wash their hands and feet before prayer— leaving most of the Haram's 35-odd acres for the casual visitor, white-hatted strolling Muslim religious dignitaries, and playing Arab children who are not above asking visitors for *baksheesh.* The north end of the Haram is a large garden with scrubby grass and dozens of trees, fenced off but still green and welcome after the emptiness of the hills and the crowds of the streets. Along the sides are arcades where scholars who lived in the adjoining monastic establishments used to sit and study. For decades, perhaps centuries, most have been abandoned, although some are inhabited by private families or minor functionaries of the mosque. One can push open a massive door to climb crumbling stairways for two or three flights to discover another massive door that this time does not push open. Or look in through a grating to see a ruined and filthy room. At intervals there are gates, most of them closed, and one of them, labeled on maps the Gate of the Latrines, now civilized by a sign on it that says WC. There is a dusty and chaotic museum of Islamic art; usually it has closed or is just closing. There are numerous little fountains and domes, high Turkish domes, low Arabic domes, a dome resting on massive blocks of Jerusalem stone, a dome floating over delicate arches that are raised on narrow pillars. And at the center is the great Dome of the Rock, golden and higher than all the rest, seeming to hover between earth and heaven.

It has been called the most beautiful building in the world. It is surely one of the most beautiful—in a class with the Parthenon and the Taj Mahal. Unlike both those masterpieces, it is brightly colored (as the Parthenon itself once was). Beneath the golden dome the building is mostly blue, an ancient-Egyptian blue, tempered by lots of green. It is faced with thousands of tiles: at the top a band of blue tiles with swirls and flowers; below that a band of nighttime blue with the white letters of a Koranic chapter sweeping across, "Has not man regarded how We created him out of a sperm drop," it says, "Then . . . forgotten his creation; he says 'who shall quicken the bones when they are decayed?'" The answer is there for all to see: "He shall quicken them who created them the first time. . . ." Below the inscription is a carpet of blue, green and white tiles, repeated over and over again around the building's eight sides. Next is a Persian garden of stylized trees or flowers, rich green, dark blue and red, and then a band of lace, bright yellow, intricately knit together. And so on and so on. Finally one reaches marble—rose, blue, green, every color but white—which covers the walls of the bottom half of the building.

Inside the shrine is, of course, a disappointment. After such an exterior almost anything would be. It is certainly ornate enough—all gold and gilt-carved wood, stained glass and marble. Recently it was restored and now boasts thick new Persian carpets, like a Waldorf-Astoria, a plate-glass door at the entrance that would be suitable for a bank, and on the wall inside that door, a dial telephone, for what telephone calls it is hard to imagine. The sacred rock is at the center behind the iron railing that was placed there by the crusaders; it and the plate glass are the only unadorned things in the shrine. The rock is very big, Jerusalem-colored, and pitted with dozens of holes, cracks and indentations, each of which has some significance. Twelve are Mohammed's footsteps, one is the imprint of his head, twelve more are footprints of the prophet Enoch—Methusaleh's father—and others were made by the fingers of the Angel Gabriel.

From almost every eminence in Jerusalem the dome can be seen. It appears as a symbol of the city in the art of Christians and Jews as well as of Muslims: in medieval Christian maps, it is labeled Templum Domini or Templum Salomonis; in Jewish representations, the Holy Temple. Jerusalem's souvenir shops feature reproductions of it manufactured for sale to Muslim pilgrims, in three-dimensional pictures and garish paintings and prints and on shining and rather sleazy carpets. It is available too in large mother-of-pearl constructions three or four feet long for rich and nostalgic visitors. Over the doorways of many Muslim houses in the old city, its picture appears painted in bright colors by a folk artist, surrounded by flowers and birds, and an inscription that commemorates the householder's pilgrimage to Mecca, "in the name of Allah the Merciful and the Compassionate."

Beside the shrines of the Christians and Muslims, the Wailing Wall of the Jews seems insignificant. It is nothing but a wall, absolutely unadorned, except for clumps of grass growing in crevices among the stones, bits of paper placed in its chinks by the superstitious and containing petitions to heaven, and a few ancient prayers and inscriptions chiseled on its face. Before it now is a vast, dusty space containing only a table or two in which prayer books are stored, and a railing that separates male and female worshippers. At all hours there is someone there—Chassidim in long black coats and side curls, bobbing back and forth as they pray, Jewish tourists from America disappointed by the simplicity of it all and annoyed at being separated from their wives, armed Israeli soldiers who are called upon to fill the quorum for prayer. The Israelis have ambitious plans for beautifying the shrine. A new avenue will lead up to it from the Dung Gate—which in Hebrew has a slightly more refined name, the Trash Gate. A plaza is to be built before the wall, leading from it to the new Churva Synagogue, designed by the architect Louis Kahn and incorporating the ruins of the old Churva, which before 1948 was one of the Jewish quarter's major synagogues.

In its heyday the Jewish quarter boasted scores of synagogues. Now they are mostly in ruins, though plans have been made for the restoration of many. Among the most famous ones in the old city were, along with the Churva, the Sephardic Synagogue of Jochanan ben Zakkai—built on a site where that worthy supposedly prayed, and the Synagogue of the sect of Karaites built below ground level in fulfillment of the biblical verse: "Out of the depths I have cried unto thee, O Lord." Despite the ruin of the old Jewish quarter, there are still hundreds of synagogues in Jerusalem. One, built in the new part of town in the nineteenth century, is well above ground level to show the world that Jerusalem's Jews were rising out of the depths. It is called the Tent of Moses—not Moses the prophet, but Moses the benefactor, Moses Montefiore, who founded the synagogue. There is as well a Tent of Joseph, and another of Jacob, and others of Rebecca and of Peace. There is a synagogue of the Lovers of Peace, another of the Sons of the Covenant, a Persian synagogue, a Bokharian synagogue, a Yemenite synagogue, all run down and tiny, an American-style Reform synagogue (one of two in the city) very new and very shiny and very embattled, its congregants scorned as virtual heretics by those who attend Jerusalem's other synagogues.

There is the prayer-house of this or that town in Poland or Hungary or of the followers of this or that Chassidic *rebbe*. There is a large, rather official synagogue, Jeshurun, which became Jerusalem's main synagogue when the city was divided. Next to it is a rundown garden. Plans were made for landscaping the place with trees, but then someone cited a biblical verse that said, "Thou shalt not plant thee a grove of any tree near unto the altar of the Lord," and the landscaping plans fell through.

Most of the city's synagogues are simple—almost unadorned on the outside as they had to be for centuries in Jerusalem and in the lands of the Diaspora. But particularly in the synagogues of the eastern Jews there are attempts at decoration within; often they are naive, but sometimes the interiors are of great beauty. One synagogue will have old Kilim rugs on the floor, another will have walls innocently painted to simulate marble, and a Persian carpet over the Ark that contains the sacred scrolls, instead of the traditional cover of velvet. Another will have a red and blue neon crown above the Ark and, to the amusement of Western visitors and the delight of the congregants and presumably of God, the four letters of the divine name outlined in blue neon above the worshippers where it glows with an unearthly light.

Many of the synagogues cluster in the area around Mea Shearim, a stronghold of Jewish Orthodoxy of a particularly narrow kind and thus one of the big tourist attractions of Jerusalem. To it come Jews from America or Argentina seeking to see once again the grandfathers who disappeared into Buchenwald or Auschwitz or into Seventh Avenue. On the night before the Sabbath or a holiday, the life of the quarter is most visible. Bearded men go between the houses carrying great pots of food, prepared for the following day when cooking is forbidden. Boys with shaved heads and sidecurls walk by with a towel and good clothing under their arms, headed for the bath house. Little girls still too young to have to wear the heavy stockings their mothers must wear wash off the pavement in front of the houses and sweep the Jerusalem dust aside with an archaic broom, not the long handled broom witches fly on and modern housewives use, but the short broom of the Arabian Nights street sweeper who must always bow low as he works.

From one of the houses comes the sound of two little boys learning to sing. They must be the cantor's sons, learning his trade the way the shoemaker's sons learn his. They are eight or nine years old with little piping voices that fly and dip over and around his formidable sonorities. He calls on God for mercy, justice, and life. They do the same. He thanks God for prosperity; they echo and accompany. He rejoices in the giving of the law. They call for the rebuilding of the temple speedily, speedily, in our time. Higher he calls to them in Yiddish, and in Hebrew they respond. In this quarter of town, not only in Mea Shearim itself but in nearby streets, the people's language is Yiddish not Hebrew, which is still considered too sacred for daily use. God can be exhorted in the holy tongue, but not man. "Samuel come here," "Esther finish the sweeping," in Yiddish. "Heal us and we shall be healed, comfort us and we shall be comforted," in Hebrew. One prominent Jerusalem lady recalls that in the early years of the century, her mother was driven in fear from the neighborhood by a crowd of Chassidim who put on their Sabbath hats and gathered in front of her house to stone her and call her a whore for the crime of studying Hebrew. Stoning malefactors is still the practice in this neighborhood. When automobiles drive through the streets on the Sabbath they are welcomed with a shower of stones.

As a result of these and other attempts by the Orthodox to control the behavior of their fellow citizens, tension between religious and non-religious Jews is high. The non-religious Jews have a nostalgic affection for Judaism which, after all, kept their nation alive for millenniums. Nevertheless it would not be surprising if one day there were riots in the Jerusalem streets between the religious and the secular Jews, similar to those the school children read about when they study the history of the city in the days of the Maccabees. Every time the pressure from the Arabs diminishes, angry murmurings are heard in the parliament about the need to lessen the power of religion in the country. This rift between the religious and the secular Jews is characteristic of social life in the city's Jewish community—and, indeed, characteristic of life in the city as a whole.

Most of the Jews in the city look down on their fellows. The old settlers, whose families have been in Jerusalem for centuries, are snobbish about newcomers. Among the old settlers, the Sephardic or Spanish Jews, as the senior group, tend to patronize the Ashkenazim. The Ashkenazim on their part also look down on the Sephardim since, in Israel, Ashkenazim control the country's political and intellectual life. Of course, this makes the Sephardim even more hostile. The European Jews look down on Jews from Arab lands, and the Jews from Arab lands resent the European Jews. The German Jews despise all the other Jews, considering them crude, and all the other Jews detest the German Jews for their Teutonic arrogance. Indeed the slang term for German Jew, *Yecke*, has acquired a secondary meaning that makes it unfit for use in polite society. Outside the Jewish community, the situation is similar. Muslim Arabs mistrust Christian Arabs and Christian Arabs fear the Muslims. The Greek-speaking Orthodox scorn the Arab-speaking Orthodox. Since 1948, the Franciscan and the Dominican Orders in Jerusalem have been very hard put to keep peace between those brothers who favor the Jews and those who favor the Arabs. Among the Muslims, separation is usually along communal lines; among Christians it tends to be sectarian.

Jerusalem itself seems like an island riding on a sea of empty hills, and within the city each group seems to live on an island of its own. There is an Armenian island, the compound inhabited only by Armenians—some 2000 of them who live behind walls built high to guard against Arab attacks. Only one gate gives access to the area which is in effect a small independent town covering about an eighth of the old city—and containing its own school, printing plant, monastery, clubs, library, and churches. Now that Jerusalem is relatively law-abiding, the Armenian island has become something of an archipelago, for a few streets nearby shelter Armenians too, among them a hilly lane called "Ararat."

North of the Armenians there is another island, of Syrian Christians who dwell near the store-front Syriac Orthodox club, with its two billiard tables, and the Syriac Orthodox Church that contains an authentic portrait of the Virgin Mary painted by Saint Luke himself—far more authentic, the Church's priests claim, than all the other authentic portraits of Mary in the world. There are Muslim islands, composed of refugees from Jaffa or Haifa, or of immigrants from the towns of Nablus or Hebron, who make up a large part of the Muslim population of the town. Each group tends to stick together and to shun intermarriage. The Hebronites are resented by the other Muslims, for they have acquired a reputation similar to the one Jews have had in Europe and America; they're very industrious and enterprising and they are said to be stingy too. There are dozens of Jewish islands, often big stone barracks standing isolated from each other and from the landscape in touch only with heaven. There are the Hungarian houses and, the Bokharian houses. There is a western suburb inhabited primarily by Oriental Jews and it is Oriental in appearance, with helter-skelter alleys and malodorous and colorful markets. If the streets were cobbled and the buildings higher it would look just like the old city. There is a pleasant and leafy quarter inhabited by German refugees, and, out in the hills—in the suburbs, naturally—a building called the Anglo-Saxon hostel where Jewish immigrants from Canada, England, and the United States live together ghettoized again, but this time as Anglo-Saxons instead of as Jews.

On its little island, each variety of Jew struggles to maintain its own Jewish way of life. For the German Jew this tends to mean lots of music and the opportunity to visit Baden-Baden occasionally; to the Americans it means endless soul-searching; to the Hungarian and Ukrainian Jews it means often a type of superstition that has much in common with the icon-kissing piety of the eastern European peasant; and to the Jews from North Africa— the Jewish men at least—it means having lots of sons and sexual freedom and keeping women in their place. The biggest group of

Jews in the city are the modernists—who include among their number delegates from most of the other Jewish islands in Jerusalem. They think of themselves first as Israelis, not as German refugees or Chassidim or Sephardim or Jews. To them belong the city's library, art galleries, theater company and hospitals, the department store and the supermarket.

They have placed their stamp everywhere in the city. Jerusalem may be full of biblical evocations, with streets named after Solomon, Samuel, Amos, Ezekiel and, of course, King David, and signs on the buses and in the public buildings that proclaim, "Thou shalt not smoke," but still, the twentieth century is everywhere in evidence. Even in Mea Shearim the residents have all the modern conveniences: vinyl tablecloths, plastic flowers, plastic washtubs— who knows, perhaps even Orlon prayer shawls. In washrooms, toilet tanks above the client's head announce themselves as "The Best Niagara," promising and usually delivering an abundant waterfall. In the dining room of the best hotel, the King David, that traditional Jewish favorite, gefüllte fish, appears on the menu as "Carpe farcie à la juive." Almost everyone goes to the movies (Israelis see more films per capita than citizens of most other nations), and the sites where Paul Newman performed his miracle of illusion in *Exodus* are pointed out with as much enthusiasm as those where biblical worthies performed theirs. There are art films at the museums, recitals of the classical guitar, weightwatcher clubs and nightclubs.

And there are modern buildings—State of Israel Modern— uninspired but rather harmless architecture, with a few Middle Eastern touches, a low dome here and there, and blank walls. The buildings built under the British in the twenties and early thirties were constructed in a style that might be called King David. It features rough stone walls, flat roofs and battlements, along which one would not be surprised to see strolling a bearded warrior in a long tunic, looking worried. State of Israel Modern might well be called King Solomon style; it seems to have been influenced equally by the Bauhaus and by MGM. It features long vistas, sugar cube buildings, cascades of steps and stone terraces crying out for Gina or Sophia to sweep along them, dressed in a flowing white robe and carrying a basin on her head. Both the center of Reform Judaism in Jerusalem and the headquarters of the Orthodox rabbinate, which many inhabitants call the Vatican, are in King Solomon style.

Each island community in Jerusalem has its own fortress—a church, a synagogue, a compound or neighborhood—and the handsome new university campus, spread across a stony valley west of the city and built in King Solomon style, is the fortress of the modern Jews. Aside from the government, the university is almost the only force in the city seeking to break down the venomous barriers that exist between the communities. Clergymen of various faiths study there together. Efforts are made to enroll Arab students, although that involves the risk of nurturing terrorists. Jews and Arabs are enrolled in classes to learn each others' language. Some of these classes take place, not at the university, but in the heart of Jerusalem on the Via Dolorosa at the Convent of the Sisters of Sion—the order that was founded to convert Jews to Catholicism. Some of the Sisters are themselves studying Hebrew, for there has been considerable success in enlisting members of the Roman Catholic clergy to the cause of bringing concord to Jerusalem. "The power of heaven has broken down the walls," said one Dominican monk after Jerusalem was reunited in 1967. "It is up to us to follow its lead." With the optimism or perhaps the naiveté symptomatic of Jerusalem, the university has set its sights far beyond the city and is constructing an institution called the Truman Center for the Advancement of Peace, the aim being no less than the abolition of war throughout the world.

Aside from the university, almost the only place where the residents of each island mix is in the streets of Jerusalem, particularly in the old walled city. There black-robed, bearded Chassidic Jews, dark, archaic and numerous like Hebrew letters, walk past Greek priests wearing long black robes and past Arab peasant

women wearing long black robes too, but robes of velvet, beautifully embroidered with panels of rich decoration above the heels
and around the bodice. (Supposedly these are modeled after the
gowns worn by the crusader ladies.) There are black Muslims—
the real thing—descendants of Nubian slaves whose families have
served for centuries in the Haram esh Sharif, and black Ethiopian
monks who live on the roof of the Church of the Holy Sepulcher,
and black secularist students from Africa studying at the Hebrew
University. Lounging Arab men, wearing the *keffiyeh*, or Arab
headkerchief, sit in the streets on little stools out in front of the
cafés, waiting sometimes for years for work that never comes. As
they wait they suck on a rented water pipe and ogle the women
walking by, emancipated Arab women in tight but modestly cut
dresses, and even more emancipated Jewish girls in shorts or mini-
skirts. They scarcely glance at refined Muslim ladies, whose heads
are covered with veils of black or white. Young men stroll by;
Syrian Arab or Greek Orthodox, Armenians, Muslims or Jews, all
sporting mustaches; and old porters—Muslims or Armenians—
carry enormous loads on their backs through streets too narrow
for donkeys to negotiate. There are always donkeys in the streets,
too, usually black or gray but occasionally a larger white one such
as Jesus rode into Jerusalem on the first Palm Sunday; and little
black kids being driven through the streets along which their ancestors were driven to be sacrificed; and even an occasional camel,
which the Arab children always run alongside cheering because the
Arabs know they are supposed to love camels, and because today,
with Muslims out of power, any man riding through Jerusalem on
a camel will evoke the memory of the Caliph Omar, who first conquered the city for Islam. There are children everywhere running
through the crowded markets, often calling out "Shalom," if they
are Arab, and wearing Arab headdresses if they are Jews. In the old
city they unceasingly pester the tourist who has just come from the
Church of the Holy Sepulcher with offers to conduct him to the
Church of the Holy Sepulcher, or to the Dome of the Rock, or to

one of the many stores in the old city where they sell, cheap, absolutely authentic relics of antiquity.

That shop might be the "Pilgrim Souvenir Shop" on the Via Dolorosa, or the "Ninth Station Bazaar" at the ninth station of the cross or the "Eighth Station Souvenir Bazaar" at the eighth. The tourist shops of the city tend to be named with due reverence for the environment, with the possible exception of one called the "Land of Peace Souvenir Shop." At the site of the house of Saint Anne, mother of the Virgin, is the "Saint Anne Souvenirs Store." Nearby, on the Via Dolorosa, is the "Saint Veronica Silver and Gold Workshop," and close to that, at the place where Jesus' image was miraculously imprinted on a handkerchief with which Veronica wiped his brow, is, nicest of all, the "Veronica Photography Shop."

"Wholesale and Retail," proclaim the signs. "If you don't buy just smile," they say. Or "Walk in please, walk out pleased," humbly reminding the traveler that this is the Orient, he is the master, and the shopkeeper is there to serve his whim. "How much does this one cost?" the customer asks after having the stock spread out before him. "You are my friend," the shopkeeper replies, and the bargaining begins. If the customer breaks off without a purchase, the shopkeeper will attempt to cajole him back with servile smiles and even more effectively with dramatic price cuts. Then, if that doesn't work, the shopkeeper will surrender. "It is up to you," he will say with a set smile and a shrug of the shoulders, and then he will retreat to his own island. The friendship is over.

Beside the fake antiquities one can buy some real ones, Roman and Byzantine coins or vials of Roman glass. But the chief stock in trade is religious souvenirs: mother-of-pearl crucifixes manufactured in Bethlehem; rosaries, made of olive wood or mother-of-pearl or silver or plastic or even of olive seeds purportedly from the Mount of Olives; glass bottles containing holy water from the River Jordan; pressed wildflowers, mounted on cards that say "Flowers from the Holy Land"; "nativity sets" made of olive

wood; one can purchase the complete set or, as with a charm bracelet, buy one piece at a time—St. Joseph, or the Virgin and Jesus, or
a wise man, an ox or an ass. Also available are crowns of thorns,
quite cheap, in varying sizes. They are made of the thorn tree that
was used to make Jesus' crown of thorns, *spina christi*, which still
grows wild in the vicinity. They hang on hooks, high on the wall,
outside the stores. To get one down the shopkeeper will take a long
stick with pincers at the end, exactly like the stick the grocer uses
to get down a big box of Wheaties from the top of the pile. "Large
or small?" the proprietor will ask and whichever the tourist says
the storekeeper will answer, "I'll pick out a nice one for you." The
most popular souvenirs are crosses, like the ones crusaders wore on
their return from Jerusalem. Each of the arms is itself a cross so
that the owner seems to be wearing five crosses. The crusader
crosses can be quite fancy, with precious stones at their centers, or
made of mother-of-pearl, or plain silver. Or they can be cheaply
made in painted metal, like charms in a gum-ball machine. Whichever kind one chooses is overpriced. Women wear them pinned to
their dresses or on chains around their necks; men wear them in
their lapels. Every shop sells icons too—some old and painted, most
modern, imprinted on cheap metal like political buttons. The most
popular subject is St. George who is shown wearing the breastplate
and the tunic of a Roman soldier and spearing a fiery dragon with
his lance. His cult is widespread in Palestine among both Christians
and Muslims. In Jerusalem he is honored at four Muslim shrines,
two Greek Orthodox, one Coptic and one shared by Christians and
Muslims.

The shops also display icons of that other and later martyr,
John F. Kennedy, who is shown with his attributes, not a lance and
a dragon, but a striped flag and an eagle. He appears depicted on
plush Arab rugs such as one can buy in New York for a few dollars, the kind that in the West show the "Bedouin on the Camel,"
the "Pyramids and the Sphinx," the "Two Playful Kittens," and
"The Last Supper." In the Jerusalem next to Kennedy on a rug, are

Jesus on a cross and Nefertiti on a pocketbook and, now that Jerusalem has been reunited, Moshe Dayan on a keychain. In this hall of fame the mighty meet and travel together just as they did on earth and doubtless do in the heavenly Jerusalem too.

The souvenir shops cluster near the Church of the Holy Sepulcher in the Christian Quarter, and along the Via Dolorosa. In them pilgrims unwilling to confine their purchases to religious goods can acquire rugs, trays and pitchers of hammered brass, sheepskin jackets and fine Arab embroidery. For bolts of cloth, shining damask tablecloths, shining silk shawls, one goes to the souks at the center of town where the cloth markets have been located for centuries. For twine or rope, wood, hammer or nails, one goes to the market in back of the streets where fancy goods are sold. (Near here the nails for Christ's cross must have been purchased.) There is a street of furniture makers and of shoemakers, a street where empty wheat sacks are sold, old U.S. army uniforms, and discarded finely worked brass pitchers and trays, which the more up-to-date Arab ladies are throwing out in favor of the bright plastic jugs and basins in lollipop colors that can be seen for sale in the markets on the other side of town. There is a street for the sale of grain and spices and there is a market for the sale of vegetables, for in Jerusalem everything has its place.

That is difficult to believe for the old city seems like a maze. How can one find one's way through its narrow alleys that show the passerby only shops and a few forbidding doors. Past the doorways are courtyards leading into other courtyards. In them narrow stone stairways lead up to still other courtyards—located on rooftops. All the courtyards give access to the small and hideously decorated apartments in which most of the inhabitants live. Often, instead of a residential court, there is a religious one containing a church, synagogue or mosque; and often both species of building mingle in the same court. It is as deceptive, as disorderly, as hard to fathom, as Jerusalem's history or as Jerusalem's social fabric. Nevertheless, everything in it has its place. True, there are constant encroachments. A house, a shrine, a shop may be Jewish or Arab, Catholic or Greek Orthodox one year and something entirely different the next. But the encroachments balance out. If the balance goes one way for a decade, or a century or two, the system eventually rights itself—as in a lake where a balance is always maintained although an over-aggressive plant or animal may dominate for a time. All three faiths have managed, through incredible adversities, to maintain their place in the city. History has managed to smooth them all out.

And for proof of that, there are the tombs. They are on all sides of the city for Jerusalem is more thickly populated with the dead than with the living. They are everywhere, underfoot. Although in ancient times there was a law that no corpses remain in the sacred city, it was not always enforced; and even before the fall of the Jewish state, the dead crept in. Like the living they are of all races, all faiths. They are found in the crypts and walls of the churches, in the museums, on the once-forbidden Temple Mount. Like the living they lie each in their place, yet all mixed together— old English clergymen who fell asleep in Christ at Jerusalem, peacefully as they would have at Bournemouth; a Russian Grand Duchess who was murdered by the Bolsheviks and later transported to the Mount of Olives; a mummified Egyptian who imagined himself sailing endlessly through the skies with the sun god, not lying through centuries exposed to the curious gaze of slave Hebrews; the rabbis of the ancient Sanhedrin, the Romans of the Tenth Legion, Persians who slaughtered Christians and Christians slaughtered by Persians, and beneath the Church of the Holy Sepulcher, Adam—the father of them all. The museums are filled with their coffins, huge archaic pottery jars for the reception of entire corpses, neat little classical ossuaries, sarcophagi adorned with garlands and posies carved in stone. North of the city is the garden tomb, where General Gordon imagined that Christ was laid. If he was not laid there, someone else was. Around it are Muslim cemeteries, with their twin-posted gravestones, and a little way beyond, past villas and hotels, the Tombs of the Kings—actually a tomb cut out of solid rock to accommodate the remains of a first-century Mesopotamian queen who converted to Judaism. Beyond the Tombs of the Kings are the Tombs of the Judges—a village of tombs on the very outskirts of town, where the leaders of Jerusalem's Jews were laid to rest around the time of Jesus. Here there is a street of tombs, little shelters and some not so little, into which one can walk and where in ancient times mourners sat together visiting with the dead; some of the tombs are like temples with broad façades or classical pediments.

To the west of the city are tombs of the Israelis, in a military cemetery set in a beautiful garden and filled with soldiers who died in battle for Jerusalem. And beside it, on a height with nothing in view but Jerusalem and the Jerusalem hills is the tomb of Herzl, the second Moses, who led the Jews back to Jerusalem. And nearby, on a hill named Mount of Remembrance, a tomb of another sort called *Yad va Shem*, literally "hand and name," figuratively, a "monument and a memorial." (In ancient Semitic the word "hand" sometimes meant "tomb monument," for hands were carved on gravestones.) This is an institute dedicated to the six million Jews who were murdered during World War II, during what in Israel is called "the holocaust." It contains a building with memorials of Europe's dead Jewish life and a list of names of the six million who now, as it were, rest at Jerusalem in accordance with Isaiah's prophecy "I will give them an everlasting name that shall not be cut off." South of the city beside the tomb of King David is another equally awesome memorial of the holocaust. Here not people but places are commemorated, thousands of them, each by a stone fixed to a wall; there is room after room with walls covered with stones each with the name of one of Europe's murdered Jewish communities engraved upon it in square black Hebrew letters, and here and there a picture of a memorial candle, a burned wooden synagogue, or a naive representation of the stones of the Wailing Wall.

Bones are found at almost every building site. Cries of desecration and pleas to stop the building arise from religious leaders and archeologists, but the building usually goes on. And then there are the cemeteries. Ostensibly they are segregated according to the faith of the corpse, but actually there is little room to allow the luxury of segregation. Crusaders and Saracens lie together downtown, in the field beyond the furniture store. Opposite the eastern wall of the city, beneath the Intercontinental Hotel, lie Muslims and Christians and Jews, on top of each other, beside each other. Each war creates new graves and destroys old ones. The 1948 Arab-Israeli war was especially bad in this respect. After it, the Arabs cleared a way through much of the Jewish cemetery on the Mount of Olives to build a new hotel where American-style hamburgers and ice cream sodas are sold. The gravestones were re-used for building military bunkers, pathways, house walls and steps.

It is east of the city where the graves are thickest. Just outside the walls of the Haram is a hillside of Muslims who lie beneath the place where Mohammed ascended to heaven and facing the hill from which they hope they too will some day rise. In the valley between Jerusalem and the Mount of Olives there are large ancient tombs. One is attributed to Absalom who, the Bible says, built a monument there (actually it dates from the first century), and another is attributed to the prophet Zechariah. They are big cubic structures, one topped with a pyramid, the other with a pointed roof like a pagoda. Above them, acre on acre, are the glinting stones of graves. There were in 1948 some 50,000 Jewish gravestones alone on the Mount, and although a great many have disappeared along with the bones beneath them, they are still a formidable sight; they ascend in haphazard rows, thousands and thousands of stones holding down skeletons that some day will rise on that spot and dance. Dry bones and stones—looking at the gravestones on the mountain there seems little to distinguish one from the other. Both are ruined and dusty; both are the same color.

It is here, among these gravestones, on the mountain outside the shrines where the people have merged into the hill, that Jerusalem seems most earthly. Here where the dead inhabitants of Jerusalem are, it is said, waiting for heaven, the heavenly Jerusalem seems most distant. But for this the dead of Jerusalem have an answer. It is the text by which they lived, and because of it they have commanded that their corpses be brought here. "Out of my flesh I shall see the Lord," they said. And now they are out of it, and perhaps they do.

Index

Aachen, 159
Aaron, descendants of, 23, 74
Abdu-Heba (King), 21-22, 25
Abel, 5
Abraham, 5, 57, 65, 145, 161, 164, 197
  comes to Canaan, 17
  descendants of, 23
Absalom, 222
Abyssinia and Abyssinians, 37, 136, 227, 237, 242
Acre, 21, 185, 198, 201-2, 233
Adam, 5, 292
Adonizedek (King), 20
Aelia Capitolina, 122-23, 125, 147, 208, 264
Agriculture
  fertility cult in, 19, 24, 53, 62
  Jerusalem and, 18, 24
Ahaz (King), 57
Akhnaten (ruler of Egypt), 4, 22-23
Aleppo, 209
Alexander the Great, 4, 78
Alexandria, 78, 83, 112, 139, 178, 212, 214
Alexandria, Patriarch of, 155
Algeria, 200
Allenby, Gen. Edmund, 259
Alliance Israélite, 255
Alphabet, 18-19

Amalekites, 27
Amalfi, 184
Amarna, 21
Ammon, 65, 70
Ammonites, 27, 33-34, 51, 62, 157
Amos, 53
Anastasis, see Church of the Resurrection
Anath, 51
Anatoth, 64
Animals, sacrifice of, 4
Anne, Saint, 129
  church of, 196, 244
Anthropology, 248-49
Antichrist, 8
Antioch, 81, 117, 140
Antioch, Patriarch of, 126, 155
Antiochus III, 80-81
Antiochus IV "Epiphanes," 81, 83
Antipater, 92-93
Anti-Semitism, 173, 224, 253
Antonia fortress (Jerusalem), 94, 105-6, 111, 113, 115
Antoninus Martyr, 133
Antony, Mark, 93, 94, 95
Aphrodite, 128
Aqaba, Gulf of, 37, 190
Aqsa Mosque, al-, 162-65, 182-83, 193, 195, 208

Arabia, 11, 37, 65, 122, 144-45, 150, 160
Arabs, 44-68
  conversion of, 240
  nationalism of, 261-68
  See also Crusades; Muslims
Aramaeans, 28, 52
Archeology of Palestine, 249-51
Ariel (as name for Jerusalem), 44, 60-61
Ark of the Covenant
  Philistines take, 28, 34
  Solomon crowned in front of, 36
  in Solomon's temple, 41-49
Arles, 134
Armenian Quarter (Jerusalem), 184, 235, 277-78, 284
Armenians, 136, 184, 200-201, 208, 218-19, 227, 229-31, 235-38
Asa (King), 53-54
Ascalon, 185
Ascensions, 11
Ashkenazic Jews, 284
Ashur, 54, 56
Asia, Jerusalem and, 7, 36
Asia Minor, 21, 34, 37, 68, 134, 140, 170, 198
Assassin clan, 181
Assyria 14, 51, 62
  conquers Palestine, 52-56
Aten, 22-23
Athena, 71
Athens, 9-10, 68
Atonement, Day of, 42
Attica, 61
Austria, 238

Baal, 19, 51, 57, 62
Baalbek, 181
Babylon, 3, 98, 137, 140, 142, 144, 199
  conquers Jerusalem, 61-67
  conquers Palestine, 53, 61

Persia conquers, 67
Bagdad, 153, 159, 177, 181
Bal al-Amud, 123
Baldwin I (King), 188
Baldwin IV (King), 181, 191
Balfour Declaration, 258
Balkans, 170, 238
Banu Zayd, 207
Baqa, El, 197
Barbarossa, Frederick, 4, 198
Bar Kochba, Simon, 122
Basilica of the Resurrection, 141
Basilica of Saint Mark, 182
Battle of the Yarmuk (636), 145
Bedouins, 188, 207, 210, 214
Beersheba, 40
Beirut, 117, 212, 240
Ben Hur, Rephaiah, 70
Benjamin, tribe of, 25, 27, 29
Ben Nachman, Moses, 205-6
Bernard, Saint, 197
Bertinoro, Obadiah de, 224
Bethany, 105, 130, 185
Bethel, 25-26
Bethlehem, 18, 22, 25, 126-27, 134, 136-38, 141, 144, 178, 217, 230, 237-38
Bethshean, 28
Bible, 73
  Jerome's translation of, 136-37
Black Rock of Mecca, *see* Kaaba
Bohemia, 198
Bonaparte, Napoleon, 232-33
Boniface VIII, Pope, 211
Bordeaux pilgrim, 134-35
Brahmins, 79
Brutus, Marcus Junius, 93
Buraq, 163, 194
Byron, Lord, 56
Byzantines, 139-40, 142, 144-45, 152, 155, 167, 210, 236

Caesar, Augustus, 93, 95

Caesar, Julius, 92-93
Caesarea, 110, 117, 125, 140, 151
Caiaphas, house of, 129-30
Cain, 5
Cairo, 153, 166, 177, 178, 181, 191, 199, 204, 207, 209, 229
Caligula, 108
Canterbury, 182, 211
Cappadocia, 136
Carcassonne, 134
Cassia, 47
Chaldees, 64
Champagne, France, 154
Chanukah, 85-86
Chapel of Derision, 219
Charlemagne, 159-60
Chartres, 160, 177
Chaucer, Geoffrey, 74, 211
Chemosh, 51, 53
Child sacrifice, 24, 255
Children of Israel, 23
Children's Crusade, 199-200
China, 12, 201
Chosroes (Emperor), 140
Church of Dominus Flevit, 277
Church of the Holy Sepulcher, see Church of the Resurrection
Church of the Nativity, 134, 141, 144, 178, 230, 237-38
Church of the Resurrection (Church of the Holy Sepulcher), 5, 128-29, 131, 146, 149, 156-57, 159, 165, 167, 174, 178-79, 182, 184, 189, 197, 200-201, 210, 216, 218-19, 228-30, 232-33, 235-37, 246, 251-52, 288
Church of Saint Anne, 196, 244
Church of Saint James, 228, 230
Churva Synagogue, 281
Cicero, Marcus Tullius, 92
Circumcision, 84
Citadel of Jerusalem, 94

Cities, holy, 3-4, 9, 11
Clermont, Cathedral of, 169, 171
Coelesyria, 136
Coinage, 71
Cologne, 173
Congo, 188, 239
Constantine the Great, 4, 117, 128-30, 141, 182, 236
Constantinople, 118, 134, 139, 147, 172, 182, 199, 221, 226, 240, 257
Constantinople, Patriarch of, 155, 170
Conversion, religious, 148, 240, 242-43
Copper, 37-38
Coptic Church, 143
Copts, 184, 230, 237-38, 242
Cordoba, 204
Corfu, 213
Council of Jerusalem, 124
Court of the Gentiles, 96-98
Court of Israel, 97
Court of the Priests, 97
Covenant, 58-60
    See also Ark of the Covenant
Crassus, Marcus Licinius, 92
Creation of the earth, 4-5, 42
Crete, 15, 34, 213-14
Crimean War, 238-39, 244-45
Crusades, 12, 14, 153, 155, 160, 164, 170-80, 186-94, 197-205
Cyprus, 213-14
Cyrus of Persia, 67

Dacia, 134
Damascus, 25, 33-34, 51-52, 150-51, 153, 178, 181, 191, 199, 204, 209, 215, 225, 234, 261
Damascus Gate, 146
Dan, 29
Dan, tribe of, 25
Darwin, Charles (*On the Origin of Species*), 249

David (King), 4, 8, 11, 145, 161-
  62, 208
  death of, 36
  dynasty of, 87
  Jerusalem and, 12, 51, 63
  as king of Israel, 32-35, 38-40
  Saul and, 30-32, 34
Dead Sea, 14-15, 18, 26, 89, 135,
  217
Death, in Jerusalem, 6-8, 19, 292-
  95
Delphi, 92
Dervishes, 203
Deuteronomy, Book of, 58-59
Diaspora, 97-98
Dome of the Ascension, 161
Dome of the Rock, 6, 64, 149-51,
  158, 160-61, 162, 165-68, 183-
  84, 189, 193, 195, 203, 222, 239,
  255, 261, 268, 280
Durham, 182

Earth, sanctification of, 3
Eastern Orthodox Church, 170-80,
  227, 236
Economy of Jerusalem, 18, 36-37,
  63, 132, 153-54, 209, 211
Edom, 33, 51, 157
Education, 78-79, 80-81
Egypt, 14, 62, 65, 68, 84, 117, 135,
  139, 142, 158, 177, 200-201,
  204-6, 208, 210, 224-25, 227-
  29, 232-33
  economy of, 36-37, 150
  "execration bowls" used by, 17
  Exodus from, 25-26
  Pharaoh's daughter in Solomon's
    harem, 39-40, 50
  religion of, 22-23
  rules Palestine, 18-22, 25, 52, 80,
    173-74, 235, 239
Elijah, 161

England, 154, 170, 172, 198, 205,
  211, 232-33, 240, 242
  Zionism and, 257-63
Essenes, 89, 102-3, 124, 135
Etham, 50
Ethiopia, *see* Abyssinia and Abys-
  sinians
Etruria, 3
Euphrates river, 17, 34, 65
Eusebius of Caesarea, 125, 128
"Execration bowl," 17
Exodus, Book of, 103
Exodus from Egypt, 25-26
Ezekiel, 66
Ezion Geber, 37-38
Ezra the Scribe, 71-72

Falastin, 151-53
Farming, 14
Fasting in Jerusalem, 6
Feast of Booths, *see* Sukkoth
Feast of the Invention of the Cross,
  128
Feast of Weeks, *see* Shavuoth
Fertile Crescent, 15
Fertility cult, 19
  Jews and, 24, 53, 62
Flanders, 172
Florus, 110
Foucher of Chartres, 177, 180
Founding of Jerusalem, 15-20, 23-
  34
France, 170, 198, 205, 230, 232-33,
  238-39, 244, 258
Francis, Saint (Francis of Assisi),
  200
Franks, 183-84, 186-87, 191-93, 199-
  200
Frederick Barbarossa, 4, 198

Gabriel, Angel, 56, 161, 163
Gad, tribe of, 225

INDEX

Galilee, 28, 101-2, 108, 112, 122
Gate of Mercy, 162, 222
Gath, 31
Gaza, 20-21, 177, 189, 199, 202
Gefüllte fish, 286
Genoese, the, 181, 184
George, Saint, 290
Georgians, 229-30
Germany, 170, 198, 233
    Jerusalem and, 246-48, 257
Gethsemane, 106
Ghazzali, al-, 202-3
Gibeah, 27-30
Gibeon, 18, 26, 69
Gihon, spring of, 15, 20, 34, 36, 43
Gilgal, 25
Gilgamesh, 183
Godfrey de Bouillon, 172, 178, 219, 236
Gods, 3, 11, 16, 22-23
Golden Gate, 162, 222
Golgotha, 5-7, 101, 123, 130, 134, 165, 182, 229, 250-51, 273
Gomorrah, 56
Gordon, Charles George "Chinese," 250-51, 292
Gordon's Calvary, 250-51
Grain, 16
Greece, 170, 184, 200, 236
Greek culture, 79-82, 140
Greek Orthodox Church, 170-80, 227, 236
Greek War of Independence, 236
Gymnasium, 81-82

Habiru, 21
Habsburgs of Austria, 4
Hadrian (Emperor), 122-23, 125, 146
Hag, 76
Hagarites, 157

Haggai, 67-68
Haifa, 177
Haile Selassie (Emperor), 37
Hakim, al- (caliph of Egypt), 166-68
Halukkah, 254
Haram esh Sharif, 97, 149, 161-64, 195, 200, 202-4, 208, 218, 222, 249-50, 278-80
Haran, 17
Harit, 207
Hasmoneans, 87, 90, 92, 111
Heaven, 6, 104
Hebrew University, 260, 265, 287
Hebron, 17-18, 21, 32, 164, 261, 285
Helena, Saint (Helena Augusta), 126, 128-29, 132
Hell, 6, 8, 10
Hellenism, 79-87
Henry II (King of England), 191, 193
Heraclius (Emperor), 142-43
Heraclius (patriarch), 197
Hercules (Herakles), 81-82, 183
Herod (King), 93-102, 104, 107, 149, 222
Herzl, Theodore, 247, 256-57
Hezekiah, 54, 55-57
Hierosolyma, 79
Hierosolyma est perdita, 121
Hierosyla, 79
Hinnom, valley of, 25, 57
Hippicus, 94
Hiram of Tyre, 38
Hittites, 27
Hodierna, 181
Holy Sepulcher, Church of, see Church of the Resurrection
Hospitallers, 189-91, 193
Huldah, 222
Hungary, 173
Hunt, Holman, 248-49

301

Hyksos, 17
Hyrcanus, Aristobulus, 87-88, 90-91
Hyrcanus, John, 87, 90-91

Idumeans, 87
Immaculate Conception, 239
Immortality, 104
India, 38, 79, 136, 154, 188, 209-10
Indus river, 150
Innocent III, Pope, 197
Iraq, 162
Iron Crown of Lombardy, 127
Isaac, 5, 145
Isaiah, 54, 67
Ishbosheth, 32
Ishmael, 164
Ishmaelites, 157
Islam, 13, 148, 153-54, 156
    See also Muslims
Israel, Kingdom of, 50, 52-59
Issachar, tribe of, 25
Italy, 170, 172, 184, 209, 225, 257

Jabiya, 145
Jacob, descendants of, 23
Jacobites, 184, 197, 218
Jaffa, 39, 86, 185, 212, 214, 253
Jaffa Gate, 68, 94
James, Saint, 211
Jannaeus, Alexander, 87-89
Jason, 82
Jebusites, 16
Jefferson, Thomas, 41
Jehoiachin (King), 63
Jehoiakim (King), 54, 62-63
Jeremiah, 57, 59, 63-65
Jericho, 14, 18, 56, 69, 185
Jerome, Saint, 126, 134, 136-38
Jeshoshaphat, valley of, 164
Jeshurun synagogue, 281
Jesse the Bethlehemite, 30

Jesus Christ, 4-5, 8, 11, 14, 23, 75, 98, 100-101, 103-8, 119, 123, 127, 131, 138, 145, 146, 153, 156, 160, 163-64, 174, 182
    See also Crusades
Jewish Agency, 260
Jezreel, plain of, 28, 30
Joash, 53, 54
John the Baptist, 102-3, 135, 145, 162
Jonah, 145
Jonathan, 30, 32
Jordan River, 10, 14, 87, 108
Jordan Valley, 14
Joseph of Arimathea, 100
Josephus Flavius, 91, 94-95, 100, 107, 112, 115-16
Joshua (Jason), 82
Joshua (prophet), 59
Josiah (King), 54, 56-58, 60-62
Judah (Judea)
    kingdom of, 50-59, 65, 67, 79, 164
    Romans come to, 89-118, 122
    tribe of, 23, 25, 26, 31-32, 61
Judas Iscariot, 131, 156, 176
Judea, *see* Judah
Julian the Apostate, 130-31
Juno, 123
Jupiter, 93, 123
    temple of, 146, 150
Justice in Jerusalem, 20

Kaaba, rock of, 7, 145, 149, 165
Kabbalah, 223
Kahn, Louis, 281
Karates, 281
Kempe, Margery, 211
Khapiru, 21-22
Kidron, 53, 54, 56, 69-70, 106, 153, 162
Kings, Book of, 53

Knesset, 86

Knights, 170-81, 183, 186-87, 211, 219

See also Crusades

Koran, 103, 147, 149-50, 161, 164, 180, 196, 202, 204, 223, 240

Kotel Maaravi, see Wailing Wall

Kublai Khan, 201, 211

Kwakiutl Indians, 7

Lachish, 21

Lamentations, Book of, 123, 239

Last Supper, 75, 106, 125, 131, 182

Lazarus, 130, 134

League of Nations, 258

Lear, Edward, 248

Lebanon, 15, 28, 39, 67, 87, 234, 258

LeBruyn, Charles, 249

Leopold (Prince of Belgium), 239

Levites, 23, 48, 56, 60, 64, 69-71, 110

Life, Jewish concern with, 44-45, 47, 103-4

Lithuania, 12

Luke, Saint, 132, 285

Lydia, 71

Macarius (Bishop of Jerusalem), 128

Maccabee, Judah, 85

Maccabee, Simon, 86-88

Maccabees, 84-87

Maccabees, First Book of, 83

Maccabees, Second Book of, 82-83

Maccabeus, 85

Magi, 132

Maimonides, 103

Mainz, 173

Malik, Abd el- (caliph), 149-51

Man, creation of, 5

Manasseh (King), 53-54, 57

Manasseh, tribe of, 225

Mandelbaum Gate, 263-64

Maronites, 179, 184, 240

Marseilles, 184

Matzoh, 75

Maundrell, Henry, 219-20

Mea Shearim (Jerusalem), 282-83, 286

Mecca, 4, 7, 145, 149-51, 160-63, 165, 190, 204, 214, 261

Medina, 145, 151, 160

Meggido, 62

Melchizedek (King), 20

Melisende (Princess of Jerusalem), 181

Men, laws concerning, 10

Menelaus, 82

Merchants, 61, 289-91

Meshod, 252

Mesopotamia, 15, 17, 21, 34, 68, 136

Messiah, 87, 89, 102-4, 121, 140, 225-26

Midianites, 27

Milan, 134

Min, 51

Ming dynasty, 209

Missionaries, 239-49

Mizpah, 69

Moabites, 27, 33, 62, 157

Mod'in, 84

Moesia, 134

Mohammed, 4, 6, 10-11

  Jerusalem and, 12

  See also Islam; Muslims, Night Journey

Moloch, 57

Mongols, 201

Monotheism, 13, 145, 156, 192, 197

Montefiore, Sir Moses, 254-55, 281

Moody, Dwight, 251

Morocco, 225

Morphia, Lady, of Melilene, 181

Moscow, 4, 221

Moses, 7, 40, 59

Mosque of David, 147
Mount Carmel, 7
Mount of Joy, 215
Mount Moriah, 49
Mount of Offense, 49-50, 53
Mount of Olives, 7, 15, 105-6, 109, 113, 135, 141, 146, 150, 153, 155, 157, 161, 163, 174, 182, 197, 222, 237, 244, 294
Mount Scopus, 28, 113, 260
Mount Sinai, 7
Mount Tabor, 7
Mount Zion, 49, 106, 125, 130, 141, 211, 214, 247
Muslims, 4, 6-9, 103, 144-68, 195-231
   See also Crusades; Islam
Myrrh, 47
Mystics, 154, 202-3

Nablus, 185, 285
Nachmanides, 205-6
Napoleon, Louis (Napoleon III), 238
Napoleon Bonaparte, 232-33
Narbonne, 134
Nasser, Gamal Abdel, 8
Nathan, 36
Nationalism, 233
   Arab, 261-68
   Jewish, 251-67
Nazareth, 233
Nebuchadnezzar (King), 4, 8, 63-65
Negev, 31, 37, 87
Nehemiah, 68-72, 77, 141-42
Newman, Henry Cardinal, 240
Newman, Paul, 286
New York City, 9
Night Journey, 4, 147, 149, 202
Nile River, 190
Noah, 5
Norwich, 182

Novgorod, 182
Nubia, 22

Oil, Jerusalem and, 12
Omar ibn al-Khattabi (caliph), 145-55
On the Origin of Species (Darwin), 249
Ophel, 69-70
Ophir, 38
Orthodox Church, 170-80, 227, 236
Ottoman Turks, *see* Turks
Oultrejourdain, 181
Our Lady of France convent, 245
Outremer, 189

Paganism, 130
Palestina (name), 122
Palestine Exploration Fund, 249
Palladio, 41
Parthians, 92, 121
Passover, 60, 74-75, 104-6
Paul, Saint, 47, 98-99, 104, 124, 134
Pax (goddess), 117
Peking, 4, 211
Pella, 113
Persia, 67-68, 70-71, 74, 78, 136, 140, 142, 144, 155, 158, 161, 164, 177, 182
Persian Gulf, 233
Pesach, *see* Passover
Petakh Tikvah, 256
Peter, Saint, 211, 214
Peter the Hermit, 172
Petra, 97, 149
Pharisees, 88-89, 101-2
Phasael, 94
Philistines, 27, 51, 54
   King David and, 30-35
   King Saul and, 29-30
Phoenicia, 28, 51
Pilgrims to Jerusalem, 6, 9, 12, 46, 74, 97-98, 132-39, 159-60, 163-

64, 185-86, 201-2, 211-23, 245-46, 260, 270-95
Pisa, 184
Pisans, 181
Pogroms, 173, 224, 253
Pola, 213
Poland, 198
Polo, Marco, 211
Pompey, 90-91, 116
Pontius Pilate, 106-8, 125, 131, 211
Pontus, 136
Portugal, 209, 225
Priests, 44, 49, 74, 78, 80, 82, 85-86, 93, 120
Procopius, 139
Prophets, 23, 43, 53, 89
  destruction of Jerusalem and, 61-62, 64
Protestant Reformation, 220-21
Proverbs, 73
Prussia, 241
Prussia, King of, 240
Psalms, 73
Ptolemy, 78, 83

Qumran, 89

Rachel, tomb of, 164
Ramleh, 151-52, 202, 214
Rashid, Harun al-, 4, 159
Raymond (Count of Toulouse), 172
Raynald of Châtillon (Lord of Kerak and Moab), 190-91
Red Sea, 10, 34, 37, 233
Religion, 13
  of Egypt, 22-23
  See also Crusades; specific religions
Rephaim, plain of, 33
Resheph, 51
Restoring the Science of Religion (al-Ghazzali), 202-3

Reuben, tribe of, 23, 225
Reubeni, David, 225-26
Revelations, Book of, 9, 172, 244
Rhineland, 172-73
Rhodes, 213
Richard the Lion-Hearted 183, 198-99
Romans, 89
  Jerusalem and, 90-118, 199
Romanticism, Jerusalem and, 12
Rome, 3-4, 14, 86, 197, 209, 211, 230
Rothschild, Baron Edmond de, 255
Rovigno, 213
"Rum, King of," 160
Russia, 170, 230, 233, 239-40, 242, 245-46
Ruth, 33

Sabbath, 10, 72, 119, 129
Sacrifices, 4, 44-49, 58, 67, 142
  for Passover, 60-61
Sa'd, 207
Sadducees, 88, 101-2, 105, 120
Safed, 6, 233, 261
Saladin, 4, 190-92, 194-98, 200-201, 205
Samaria, 56, 70, 108, 174
Samaritans, 52, 87, 108, 121, 139
Samarkand, 204
Samson, 82, 183
Samuel, 29, 30
Santiago da Compostella, 211
Saracens, 186, 189-91
Sardinia, 238
Saul (King)
  David and, 30-32, 34, 36
  Philistines and, 29-30
Scandinavia, 154
Scribes, 19
Second Crusade, 198-99

"Second Golgotha," 230
Seljuk Turks, 167-68, 173
Sennacherib (King), 8, 55-56
Sephardic Jews, 284
Serbs, 221
Setj-'anu (ruler of Jerusalem), 17
Shabbatai Zevi, 225
Shavouth, 75-76, 105
Sheba, Queen of, Solomon and, 37, 162
Shechem, 18, 21-22, 40, 59
Sheep Gate, 69, 185
Sheshbazzar (prince), 67
Shethiyah, 64
Shiloh, 25, 28-30
Shrine of Saint James, 277
Sicarii, 69
Sidon, 181
Siloam, 163
Simeon, tribe of, 50
Sinai Desert, 25-26, 58-59
Six-day War, 11, 266-67
Smyrna, 225
Socrates, 82
Sodom, 56
Solomon (King), 4, 16, 51, 73, 161, 163, 208
  death of, 50-51
  dynasty of, 63
  as King, 36-49
  Queen of Sheba and, 37, 162
  temple of, 8-9, 11, 14, 35, 38, 40-50, 52, 56-58, 67-73, 80, 85, 96-102, 119-20, 130-31, 146, 149, 183, 218, 222, 250
Somaliland, 38
Sophronius Patriarch, 144-47
Spain, 90, 205, 211, 224, 230, 238
Speyer, 173
Spices, Solomon's trade in, 37
Stephen, Saint, 124
Stone Age tools, 15

Stones, 11
  holiness of, 10, 16
  of Jerusalem, 269
  worship of, 148-49
Sudan, 174
Sufi mystics, 197, 207
Sukkoth, 76-77, 88, 105, 108
Sumer, 3
Sumerians, 15
Synagogue, 73, 79, 205, 281
Syria, 17, 21, 28, 33-34, 37, 50, 62, 65, 80-81, 85-86, 90, 139-40, 142, 144-45, 149, 152, 155, 158, 162, 173, 205, 207, 242, 258
Syriac Orthodox Church, 285

Talmud, 164-65, 223
Tarsus, 98, 134
Tekoah, 69
Tel Aviv, 25
Templars, 189-91, 193, 195
Temple
  Canaanite, 19
  Hebrew, 8-9, 11, 14, 35, 38, 40-50, 52, 56-58, 67-73, 80, 85, 96-102, 119-20, 130-31, 146, 149, 183, 218, 222, 250
Theudas, 108
Thomas à Becket, Saint, 193, 211
Thracia, 134
Tiberius, 140, 157, 191
Tigris-Euphrates rivers, 190
Tisha b'Ab, 64, 116, 148
Titus, 8, 112-14, 117, 158
Tophet, 57
Torah, 73, 78, 80, 84, 88, 98
Toulouse, 134
Touro, Judah, 255
Tower of David, 184-85, 122, 227
Trade, Solomon and, 36-37
Transjordan, 207
Trees of Jerusalem, 14-15

Tribes
secession of northern, 50
Solomon acclaimed king by, 36
ten lost, 225
See also specific tribes
Truman Center for the Advancement of Peace, 287
Turkey, 246, 257, 259, 261
Turkoman tribes, 207
Turks, 173, 210, 226-31, 232-40, 253
See also Seljuk Turks
Turner, J. M. W., 248
Tutankhamen, 4
Twain, Mark, 12
Tyre, 38-39, 61, 72, 129, 185
Tyropoeon valley, 99

Uganda, 257
Universe, center of, 6-7
Urban II, Pope, 169-70, 182
Usury, 61, 72
Uzziah (King), 53

Vandals, 118
Venice, 181-82, 184, 209, 212, 218, 230
Venus, 123
Vespasian, 112
Via Dolorosa, 12, 177, 217
See also Jesus Christ
Victoria (Queen), 240, 247, 249
Virgin Mary, 8-9, 10, 127, 129, 132, 141, 164, 196, 247
Vulgate, 136

Wailing Wall (Kotel Maaravi), 6, 97, 157-58, 163, 205, 222, 252, 261, 266, 268, 280
Waqfs, 196
Warawa Shalem, 16
Wilhelm II, 246-48
Wilson, Woodrow, 258
Winchester, 182
Women
laws concerning, 10
sacred prostitutes, 19, 57
Wool, religious laws concerning, 10
Worms, 173

Yad va Shem, 293
Yaqar'ammu (ruler of Jerusalem), 17
Yarmuk, Battle of the (636), 145
Yavneh, 120
Yemen, 152-53, 158, 224

Zachariah, 162
Zacharias, 141
Zadok (priest), 36, 56
Zakkai, Jochanan ben, 281
Zamzam, 163
Zealots, 109, 112, 115, 117, 121
Zechariah, 53-54, 162, 222, 294
Zedek, 20
Zedekiah (King), 63
Zeus, 71, 83-84
Ziggurat, 3
Zion, 4-5, 10, 15
Zionism, 251-67
Zoroastrian religion, 141
Zubair, al- (caliph), 151

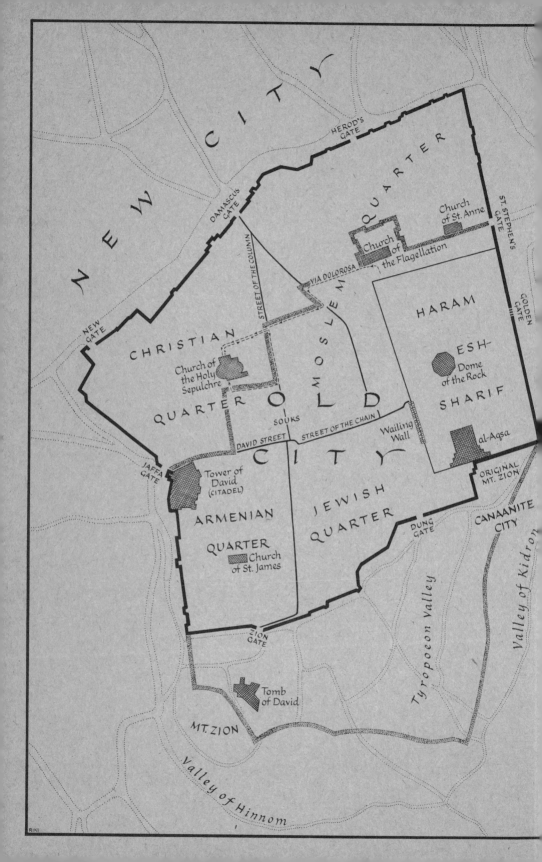

NEW CITY

HEROD'S GATE

QUARTER

DAMASCUS GATE

Church of St. Anne

ST. STEPHEN'S GATE

STREET OF THE COLUMN

Church of the Flagellation

VIA DOLOROSA

HARAM

GOLDEN GATE

NEW GATE

CHRISTIAN

M O S L E M

ESH-

Church of the Holy Sepulchre

O L D

Dome of the Rock

QUARTER

SHARIF

SOUKS

C I T Y

DAVID STREET

STREET OF THE CHAIN

Wailing Wall

al-Aqsa

JAFFA GATE

Tower of David (CITADEL)

JEWISH

ORIGINAL MT. ZION

ARMENIAN

QUARTER

QUARTER

Church of St. James

DUNG GATE

CANAANITE CITY

Tyropoeon Valley

Valley of Kidron

ZION GATE

Tomb of David

MT. ZION

Valley of Hinnom

RIKI